Praise for

TRIUMPH & HOPE
GOLDEN YEARS WITH THE PEACE CORPS IN HONDURAS

The author, a veteran human rights advocate, took her humanitarian vision to Honduras with the Peace Corps, providing inspiration to others, especially to retirees considering their next life passage. This compelling true story will stay with you long after you close the book.

—T. Kumar, Asia Advocacy Director
Amnesty International USA

Barbara Joe lucidly details the experiences of an "Older And Knowing Soul," referring to the support group for over-50 volunteers that she spearheaded. The unique perspective of this tale incorporates lessons derived from a lifetime of humanitarian endeavors and frankly informs future volunteers, allowing us former volunteers to nostalgically relive our own service.

—Mitchell Harrison
Peace Corps volunteer
Honduras 2003-2005

The author writes with passion and love, following a trail charted by her parents when she was just a little girl. *Triumph & Hope* takes readers on a journey of discovery to mysterious and remote places that have remained close to her heart. This compelling autobiographical narrative is a remarkable expression of the human spirit, inspiring readers to engage in similar journeys of triumph and hope that will surely enrich their lives.

—Humberto Rodríguez-Camilloni, PhD
Professor of Architecture and Director Henry H. Wiss Center
for Theory and History of Art and Architecture, Virginia Tech

Going back in time, Barbara Joe's childhood memories provide a jumping-off point six decades later for her return to Honduras as a Peace Corps volunteer. She brings to Honduras, and to her book as well, a lifetime of professional and personal experiences (including personal tragedy), which shaped her deep commitment and passion to her volunteer work, recounted in this touching and straight-talking account from the eyes and heart of a woman devoting boundless energy to the cause of assisting others.

—Abigail Terrones
Peace Corps volunteer
Honduras 2003-2005

TRIUMPH & HOPE
GOLDEN YEARS WITH THE PEACE CORPS IN HONDURAS

BARBARA E. JOE

To Bridget,
World traveler,
Story teller,
and international
citizen,
Barbara

For my children Melanie, Stephanie, and Jonathan; grandchildren Natasha and Andrew, great-grandson De'Andre, also in loving memory of dearly departed son Andrew, foster son Alex, mother Virginia, father Leonard.

And for the residents of El Triunfo (The Triumph) and La Esperanza (The Hope), Honduras, who took me into their hearts and homes and reflected a true spirit of triumph and hope.

All individuals and incidents described are real, not composites, using true names, except in the few cases indicated. No need for invention since real life is amazing enough! Last names are included only for public figures. Photos courtesy of the author.

*   *   *   *   *   *   *   *   *   *   *   *   *   *

Beyond those mentioned above, I'd like to acknowledge my brother Bob and sister Betty, avid fellow explorers of this astonishingly wide and diverse world. Also, Connie and T.J., who provided valuable technical assistance, and those who so painstakingly reviewed each word of my manuscript: Amy, Brenda, and Sarah (Sarah, who is blind, proofread by listening).

ABOUT THIS BOOK

You've bought a T-shirt labeled "Made in Honduras" and wonder about a nation unfamiliar to most North Americans. Or you'd like to know more about Latinos living in the U.S., or to better understand the idiosyncrasies of Spanish, fast becoming our second language. If so, you'll meet some special people and find much useful information here.

Or you may have considered joining the Peace Corps yourself. Whether you're a recent college graduate or a retiree still young at heart, your age is no barrier. If a grandmother in her sixties like me can do it, so can you. President Carter's mother, Miss Lillian, joined the Corps at age 66 and her great-grandson also became a volunteer. Just as Miss Lillian's example inspired me, I hope to inspire you. With only one life to live, why not live it to the fullest? It's never too late for a new beginning.

Peace Corps is now actively reaching out to volunteers of all ages, including seasoned folks with valuable professional skills. Among 78 million boomers, many are healthy, idealistic, and ready to give back to the world. As Peace Corps director Ron Tschetter, himself a former volunteer, observes, "Older volunteers can bring a higher level and breadth and depth of experience and expertise." Seven percent of today's volunteers are over 50 and Tschetter hopes to increase that figure.

After a certain age, your ability to face challenges will stand you in good stead. And if you've also had your share of sorrows, you may find, as I did, that Peace Corps service offers a healing experience. My neighbors in the towns of El Triunfo (The Triumph) and La Esperanza (The Hope) expressed those same qualities in their daily lives, as is gratefully acknowledged in this book's title. *Triumph* and *Hope* are real places that evoked such feelings in me as well.

Whatever your age, Peace Corps service allows you to make a personal contribution while finding real-life adventure in the process. Instead of becoming an armchair traveler or tourist looking in, why not become a hands-on player looking out at the world from a fresh perspective? And beyond offering personal fulfillment, Peace Corps also helps counteract negative impressions of our country abroad.

So, what is service really like, beyond the glossy photos adorning recruitment brochures? Not glamorous, but enriching in unexpected ways, with its inevitable share of successes and failures, joys and sorrows. Service can pull at your heartstrings, but can also simply be fun. You need to be receptive and open to what comes along. And while each volunteer's experience is special and unique, certain aspects are standard: the painstaking application process, routine training components, and 27-month tour. I tell it like it is, no sugar-coating, letting you know just what to expect at each step along the way.

Despite descriptions here of accommodations made for certain disabilities and medical conditions, and of tactics used to assuage homesickness and loneliness, this frank recital may end up convincing you that the Peace Corps is simply not for you. You then may want to explore shorter service with a religious group, medical brigade, or sister city mission.

So, here is my story, part memoir, part guide. At age 62, I obviously joined with a different perspective and different life experience than a more typical 20-something recruit. Therefore, this is not a conventional Peace Corps narrative or travelogue-type book. It necessarily confronts the central tragedy of my life, my older son's death, recounting how my service helped soften my grief.

Just as no two lives are the same, no two Peace Corps experiences are alike. So if you choose to become a volunteer, your own story will be different but no less meaningful. In any case, be prepared to gain much more than you give.

CONTENTS

Author, age 3, on left, with mother and brother
Honduras, 1941

Author's father assembling maize god statue
Copán, Honduras, 1941

Author with maize god statue more than 60 years later
Copán municipal museum

PROLOGUE:
THE LONG ROAD

Copán, Honduras, 1941

It's early 1941 and I'm almost three years old. With chubby legs splayed out, I'm clutching onto a saddle horn for dear life, bouncing along in front of my dad, trying not to fall off our very tall horse. Mama follows along with baby brother on a smaller mare. I need to pee, but am afraid to dismount, leery of this empty, scary place. It's pitch-black, with moon and stars veiled as cold rain pelts down, stinging my exposed skin and leaking inside my poncho. Muffled bird and animal cries echo through the darkness. I shiver, whimpering softly, hoping Daddy won't hear. Everything is hazy, but now looking back, I'm not sure if that's just the haze of memory or honest-to-goodness mist in the air.

Though the muddy trail ahead is obscured, Daddy, peering out under his broad-brimmed hat, urges our mount forward. "Almost there, *allí no más,*" he reassures Mama, using a favorite Honduran phrase. Mama is skeptical. She's heard that before from local folks. It turns out four more hours still lie ahead to our destination—the archeological site of Copán. With no vehicular road into the ruins, we've left our Model-A Ford behind with a trusty guard. My parents are solid mid-westerners; Daddy is originally from Stavely, Alberta, Mama from Duluth, Minnesota. Yet they've dared bring their two small children along on this bold exploration of the vast unknown.

On that long-ago night, when our bedraggled family finally clip-clops into the town bordering the ruins, we find a hilly place with cobblestone streets, adobe houses, and welcoming kerosene lamps. Sixty years later, after a life filled with challenges and tragedies, I will retrace my family's footsteps to this very place, this time, as a Peace Corps volunteer. I will gaze again on the maize god statue on display in the Copán municipal museum, a statue that my father unearthed and so painstakingly pieced together back when I was just a toddler.

The image of my father leading us through that misty, murky night so many years ago forms one of my earliest memories. That unforgettable journey planted the seed of adventure forever in my soul—a seed that would eventually lead me back to Honduras once again.

A Dream Lost and Found

Fast forward to 1998, Washington, DC, to my 60th birthday, a watershed for resolutions. Blowing out the candles, I make a wish.

"Hey guys, I'm going to join the Peace Corps," I announce proudly to Melanie, Stephanie, and Jonathan, my three grown kids.

"Yah sure, Mom," older daughter Melanie murmurs, winking at her brother and sister, "You've been *saying* that, but when are you actually going to *do* it?"

Like many Americans, I had long harbored a dream of joining "some day." Back in 1961, President Kennedy's inspiring announcement of the Corps' formation captivated my imagination: "To those peoples in the huts and villages across the globe struggling to break the bonds of mass misery, we pledge our best efforts to help them help themselves." I was further inspired by Martin Luther King Jr.'s "I have a dream" speech, which I heard live at the Lincoln Memorial two years later. But the time for dedicating myself fully to humanitarian service wasn't quite right. I was newly married, finishing up a master's degree at UC, Berkeley, and launching my own career while supporting my husband in his. Then came job changes, a cross-country move, the arrival of children. The Peace Corps seemed to have passed me by. But the secret longing remained, even through hard times, including a bitter divorce and working extra jobs to support my kids as a single parent. Fretting about bills and starved for sleep, I indulged in daydreams of future Peace Corps service when my benevolent instincts would burst into full flower.

Then, in 1994, all my dreams came to a paralyzing halt with the sudden death of my 27-year-old son, Andrew. At the heart-stopping moment when I learned of his death, my immediate reaction was: "NO! Let's backtrack just a tiny fraction of a second and freeze-frame right there." It's hard even now to write about, but it's central to my life's story.

Andrew died in his prime, a star that blazed brightly, but too briefly. It happened on his sister Melanie's birthday—forever after, a bittersweet occasion. A serious work injury to his back requiring surgery, along with other complications, converged at that fatal instant when my Andrew —never Andy—stopped breathing forever in his sleep. Mentally, I turned back the clock, giving me time to fly down to his Florida home to check on his nighttime breathing, just as when he was small. Or I pictured him still living right now in one of Stephen Hawking's parallel universes. I kept replaying Andrew's last voicemail message, "Hi Mom," pretending he was still alive. My other kids appropriated his clothes, including an oversized work shirt with his name stitched on the pocket still worn by his sister Stephanie.

I later derived some minuscule comfort from his last words on the phone only days earlier, "I love you Mom." After his death, this routine farewell suddenly loomed large and significant. I clung to it, silently repeating it over and over.

I recalled when Andrew was in preschool looking over his classmates and idly thinking that by the law of averages, one or more might not make it to age 30. That one turned out to be my own son.

When Andrew died, the hurt went too deep for any sort of comfort. If not for my other kids and small granddaughter, I might have gladly followed him to the grave. Why go on living anyway if I couldn't even keep my son *alive*? Isn't that a mother's first duty? As a child, he'd had all his immunizations, ate right, got an education. So what?

Andrew seemed to be pulling me after him with such magnetism that I had to physically resist with all my strength, struggling simply to move my leaden feet forward, feeling so fragile that if I actually stumbled and fell, I might shatter into a million pieces. Heartache proved more than mere metaphor, such a crushing sorrow that it hurt even to breathe. No anesthetic existed to dull the pain. Like other bereaved parents, I'd gladly have exchanged my life for my son's.

Death gives no second chances, no opportunities for course correction, no refunds or reprieves. The broken egg cannot be made whole, the cream separated from the coffee, the burnt log resurrected from the ashes. Some overlap exists between male and female, young and old, rich and poor, gay and straight, but the most absolute opposites are *dead* and *alive*. As a character in Kenzaburō Ōe's novel *A Personal Matter* observes, "You can't make the absoluteness of death relative, no matter what psychological tricks you use."

In one instant, the loved one is breathing, skin warm, full of future possibilities; in the next, all that has stopped forever, never to revive. Time stands still and, at that final instant, my son remains frozen in memory as he was: tall, strong, brash, energetic, restless, friendly, irreverent, mischievous. I hold fiercely onto that image.

Since Andrew died in Florida, my kids, granddaughter, and I held his funeral there, returning with his ashes for a memorial service in Washington. We were stopped by a highway patrolman on our drive back because my granddaughter wasn't belted in. "The child's age?" he inquired. "Twenty-seven," I replied, automatically referring to my son.

Back in Washington, my parents arrived promptly at noon for our memorial service there. "What's for lunch?" Dad asked, glancing impatiently at his watch. I almost smiled through my tears at his ordinary presumption, mindful of that reassuring cliché, "life goes on."

What now were my options? Only to die or simply go on living. By sheer inertia, I did the latter. Constant tears left me thirsty, with salty lips, my food tasting like dry sawdust. I lost 20 pounds in a week and woke daily to the stark realization that my Andrew was dead. All my diplomas and awards became stupid pieces of paper stuck on a naked wall. I felt like smashing my once-precious collection of Victorian china dolls, their life-like but lifeless eyes slyly mocking. Resenting the very existence of beetles scurrying across the sidewalk, I crushed them angrily underfoot —how dare they live when my son was dead?

A man I was dating was shunted aside. He acted as though everything was normal, infuriating me. I lacked the strength to confront him, preferring a clean break. However, I did feel comforted by a series of mystical experiences (coincidences?) related to my son that I still cannot fully explain.

On Andrew's gravestone, we placed a phrase from Whitman, "I stop some where waiting for you." Even now, just repeating that line causes my eyes to well up with tears, "Andrew, child of my heart, you shouldn't have to *wait;* we belong together right here and now." It's still hard to say goodbye.

Sometimes I would tell myself that if Andrew had never been born, if I had never known and loved him, I would not be suffering now. But I quickly banished that fearsome thought. At least we had him for 27 years. Every life is finite, and even though my son's was cut short, I'm thankful for his time with us. Do I ever yearn for amnesia? Not really.

Later, when a young woman was killed in an auto accident, her grieving mother apologized, "So sorry for not supporting you more when Andrew died. I never knew." Before losing her own child, how could she possibly have understood? Another friend observed, "You've survived other traumas, like divorce." "Yes," I admitted, "But that was just a pinprick compared to this."

On the first anniversary of Andrew's death, another cruel blow fell; a Cuban foster son, Alex, placed in my home as an unaccompanied minor by a refugee agency, was also cut down in his prime. The youngest of 12 children, he was just 16 and imprisoned in eastern Cuba back in 1980 when Fidel Castro opened the jailhouse doors and forced inmates onto boats waiting at Mariel. Alex never divulged the reason for his jailing, but it probably was for being gay, an identity that emerged full-force in this country.

Ten years later, Alex discovered he was HIV-positive. At the time, we both accepted this as a death sentence. I secretly speculated that if he'd never left Cuba, he might have avoided this fate since Cuban AIDS patients then were strictly quarantined, reducing the population's infection risk. As if reading my thoughts, Alex took my hand after revealing his illness, "Don't worry, *mamacita,* I have no regrets. Better a short life and free."

And so Alex also died prematurely. I'd like to forget he suffered, but he did. Antiretrovirals soon became available, but too late. Years later, I made a pilgrimage to Alex's hometown in rural, impoverished Holguín province and tracked down his tough-as-nails elderly mother who still rolled her own cigars and drew her water from a well. A physician sister asked, "How could he have gotten AIDS?" "Well, he was gay," I said. "Oh no, not here," she insisted, "Gringos must have taught him that." I said no more.

After this second untimely death right on the heels of the first, a dark mourning veil enshrouded my entire existence. Nothing was dependable. Nothing mattered. Friends were ignored. Time was no longer linear; recent and distant events merged; despair, anger, and sadness flowed together in a molten stream. Until Andrew died, I'd always managed to bounce back, like an inflated bottom-weighted doll that springs upright when repeatedly punched. But now, after losing both boys, I was down for the count. "Dear God," I asked, "does anyone deserve all this?" I neglected my other kids, young adults basically on their own, but still needing maternal guidance. They were hurting, too, especially Jonathan, who worshiped his older brother.

Now, with the passage of time, am I reconciled? Absolutely not. Divorce, a job layoff after years of faithful service, my parents' demise, all are losses

I can accept. I know Andrew and alex are dead and we won't ever see each other again in this life, but I've neveraccepted the rightness of that loss. It's very hard to bury our children. But as long as we still have breath, we must learn to live and to contribute in a different way, just as someone losing vision or a limb must forge a new path forward.

Do I envy parents whose children are marrying, having babies, advancing in careers? Who are *alive* and breathing? Yes, and I envy their innocence and naïveté, their blithe belief that their kids will always be there.

On scales of major life stressors listed in self-help books—a parent's death, divorce, being robbed, job loss, surgery (all of which I experienced in short order)—a child's death doesn't even appear. Death of a spouse is usually given the highest stress rating, but that's a normative event. A child's passing is simply ignored, which used to make me angry when seeking solace in such books. I especially gritted my teeth when well-meaning folks passed along copies of *Don't Sweat the Small Stuff* and *Chicken Soup for the Soul.* Children's deaths are definitely *not* "small stuff" nor do the saccharine stories repeated in Chicken Soup books (one by a pre-trial O.J. Simpson) offer any relief.

Some attribute others' misfortunes to personal failings, expecting their own virtue to be rewarded. But, as former president Jimmy Carter famously remarked, "Life is unfair." (President Carter sent me a thoughtful condolence note when Andrew died.)

After a son or daughter's death, even close friends and relatives tend to avoid both the bereaved parent and any mention of the deceased, who remains the unacknowledged elephant in the room. Yet most of us would rather have our loved ones remembered. I'm particularly grateful to a friend who regularly recalls my son's birthday. Some fear that mentioning our kids will remind us that they have died—as if we could forget! Or they wishfully pretend we've "gotten over" our loss, or may worry that our bad luck may become contagious. I get little reaction if I remark that my parents are deceased, but my son's death is a real conversation stopper.

"So, Barbara, how many kids do you have?"

"Three on earth and one in heaven." No, best to just say *three.*

If I attended a support group for every difficulty my family has faced (no time for details here), there wouldn't be enough hours in the day. But one that *has* proved helpful is The Compassionate Friends, simply bereaved parents getting together for mutual support. Daughter Melanie took me to my first meeting.

I would never recommend losing a child to gain appreciation of his or her intrinsic value and the worth of life itself. Yet, for all the pain involved, as per a Spanish saying: "There is nothing bad from which good doesn't flow." For one thing, I cherish my surviving children even more. And lesser losses barely register.

I've also acquired a more cosmic outlook, experiencing love, tolerance, and empathy for every human being who's ever walked on God's green earth. I've intuited the space-time continuum of philosophers and scientists, with space and time blending seamlessly into a single warp. My senses and emotions have become more acute, arousing feelings never before experienced. Might this merely reflect changes in brain chemistry caused by a psychic shock, like those reported for dying persons? Who knows?

I've also lost the lingering shyness dogging me since early childhood. If I've remained upright after surviving my worst fears, what more can touch me? Well, yes, of course, losing another child or a grandchild *would* hurt. I'm certainly still vulnerable there.

*   *   *   *   *   *   *   *   *   *   *   *   *   *   *   *

Even before these untimely deaths, my life had been moving toward Peace Corps service. Starting out from my Boston birthplace, our family traveled widely and moved often. Spanish fluency acquired as a teenager in Colombia, where my father worked for the Organization of American States, served me later in volunteer activities. I joined Amnesty International, prepared Spanish-language materials on health topics for the Pan American Health Organization, and wrote a free weekly column for a local Spanish-language newspaper.

For more than 16 years, I worked for the American Occupational Therapy Association, just outside Washington, DC. As a former social worker, I found occupational therapy, combining psychosocial intervention with physical rehabilitation, compatible with my professional experience. At first, I was involved in a pioneering effort to evaluate the efficacy and efficiency of treatment, an approach now integral to all health-care monitoring. Later on, I became a writer and editor for a weekly association magazine.

After my divorce, despite all my logistical challenges as a single working mother, I served as an election monitor in Chile, Nicaragua, Haiti, and the Dominican Republic, reconnecting with Jimmy Carter, whom I'd met during his presidency. I volunteered briefly in Guatemalan, Salvadoran, and Nicaraguan refugee camps in the 1980s and added my grain of sand to Central America's peace process (and met Costa Rican President Oscar Arias and Mother Teresa there).

In Colombia, I aided occupational therapists treating disabled children. In Cuba, I visited orphanages for abandoned youngsters, as well as psychiatric and rehabilitation hospitals and nuns serving the terminally ill and prisoners' families. I had brief sojourns at an Argentine ranch for wayward teens and an Uruguayan family shelter. All this, during vacations from my regular job. In each far-flung locale, I threw my energies into the tasks at hand, but never stayed long enough to make a lasting impact. It was frustrating, say, while teaching adult literacy, to have to leave abruptly for home. I felt I was just dabbling. "Some day," I told myself, "I'll join the Peace Corps and really follow through."

My son's death, followed by that of my foster son, then of a former lover, put such plans on indefinite hold. My father's subsequent demise further rocked my emotional equilibrium. Then I underwent emergency surgery for a flare-up of a gall bladder condition too long ignored. Soon after, my ex-husband passed away, extinguishing forever the chance to get on speaking terms with him again. While these continuing blows sapped my strength, they also heightened my awareness of my own mortality. Pummeled repeatedly by the angel of death, I wondered if I might be next and never get to fulfill my Peace Corps dream.

That dream resurfaced with renewed intensity. I realized that while losses such as divorce, illness, and death do leave their mark, they aren't the whole story. Our achievements, over which we have more control, also define our personal legacy. In that spirit, I finally decided that my "some day" to join the Peace Corps was *now*.

***Author & family with President Jimmy Carter,
late son Andrew at far left***

Washington DC, 1979

Son Andrew days before his injury and death in 1994

Cuban foster son Alex who died of AIDS in 1995

CHAPTER 1:
NOW OR NEVER

Many Are Called, Few Are Chosen

So I had decided, but joining the Peace Corps involves more than that. Much more: filling out a lengthy application, undergoing a rigorous physical exam, providing detailed references, sending fingerprints to the FBI, and having an in-depth interview with a regional recruiter. Applicants often fall by the wayside during this process, which can take over a year.

Peace Corps now has 8,000 volunteers in more than 70 countries (with Mexico just added in 2004), any of which could open up entirely new vistas. There was much of the world I'd never seen, despite having visited more than 45 countries, but I narrowed down my choice to Latin America, since I already spoke Spanish, and to health work, my area of greatest expertise.

My recruiter was a former volunteer, a pre-requisite for his job. "Do you have a significant other?" he asked first, pen poised.

"Hey, are you allowed to ask that?" I retorted. Yes, he insisted, because longing for a lover back home was the number one reason why volunteers quit early. I denied any current romantic encumbrances.

"How would you feel," he continued, "living in an isolated village without any phones, running water, or electricity?" No problem, I assured him, been there, done that, albeit for limited periods.

"I realize that Peace Corps is not for sissies," I added somewhat defensively, "I know it takes a certain amount of intestinal fortitude. But out there in the boondocks, I get the same sort of rush that inspires wilderness campers and mountaineers. Besides, millions of human beings already live that way."

The most crucial question was simply: "*Why* do you want to join?"

That answer required considerable self-examination. Not to improve my Spanish or to travel, since I already was fluent and had traveled widely. I hesitated before replying: "Trite and naïve as it may sound, I just want to make a difference—do something practical above and beyond my service during short-term vacation trips." After years of abstract policy-analysis, I longed to accomplish something tangible, to actually "walk the talk."

Searching again for the right words, I said, "I'm not out to save the world, but, still, you never know, my small contribution might end up like that butterfly's wing that triggers a chain reaction." We both laughed, but I wasn't joking.

Since reportedly only one in ten applicants actually makes it through, I kept my fingers crossed, hoping to be among the lucky ones. What if, after all my decades of waiting and dreaming, I was ultimately rejected?

The call when it finally came was unexpected, an unfamiliar female voice on the phone, "How about going to Honduras as a health volunteer?" Silly question, the answer, of course, was *yes*.

After hanging up the phone, I realized the enormity of my commitment. I'd be leaving behind my widowed mother, adult children, and preteen granddaughter, as well as my cherished century-old house, embarking on a journey whose outcome was uncertain. But now the die was cast. I couldn't quite believe it, my Peace Corps dream was finally coming true! In the millennial year of 2000, that seemed quite fitting.

Moving all my furniture suddenly felt too daunting, so I decided to rent my house furnished, something the rental agent warned against (he turned out to be right). Meanwhile, I rushed around acquiring items for my expected 27-month stay, including a Spanish-language edition of the hands-on medical text *Where There Is No Doctor.* Only two suitcases were allowed. What to take? Should I pack only hot-weather clothes? Our final destination within the country was not specified.

Not everyone I exuberantly informed of my acceptance was enthusiastic or even knew where Honduras was located: "In South America? What do they speak there? Isn't the Peace Corps just for youngsters? Aren't you kind of old to be living under such primitive conditions?"

Women friends were perhaps a tad envious, but not really anxious to follow my example. Surprisingly, men, at least my contemporaries, were dismissive, pegging me as a hopeless romantic plunging in way over my head. Their doubts fueled my own. Monotony, boredom, frustration, loneliness are well-known scourges of Peace Corps service. Did I have the inner resources to withstand them, or would my personal losses make me especially vulnerable? Rather than distancing past tragedies, might the isolation of service actually make them worse?

One middle-aged guy dubbed me "a bleeding-heart liberal," another pronounced my plan "pretty wacky," a third urged me to satisfy my do-gooder instincts by donating to charity, "Why get your hands dirty when you can just write a check?"

But I *wanted* to get my hands dirty! Money is fine, but someone actually has to roll up their sleeves and do the work. I'd also bought into the Peace Corps motto of empowering people to help *themselves,* which necessarily requires establishing a personal relationship with them. Technical skill is not a volunteer's most important attribute. Gaining trust is. I would come to see highly competent professionals fail as volunteers for lack of "people" skills. Flexibility, imagination, initiative, commitment, those would turn out to be the essential qualifications. I assured my friends, "To me, starting over with a completely clean slate actually sounds pretty exciting."

My arguments fell largely on deaf ears. A particularly vociferous male critic, perhaps with ulterior romantic motives, declared, "Have you completely lost your mind? Out there all by yourself, your son's ghost will rise up to haunt you. Your life might even be at risk. Mark my words, you'll be home by Christmas at the very latest."

"Yes, and I could be hit by car tomorrow," I countered, "Remember Howard Hughes and all his meticulous precautions? He still died. Is that any way to *live?*"

But his words still stung and I had to force them aside. I was well aware that fate can thwart our best intentions. Yet barring catastrophe, I was determined to stick it out. I've never been a quitter. My kids, thankfully, were supportive, "Mom, you can do it." And I felt the spirit of my late son Andrew encouraging me as well.

People in other countries are acutely attuned to the United States, expressing an insatiable curiosity about our way of life—often freely embellished by fantasy. But few Americans have fully explored the myriad self-contained worlds existing beyond our own borders, worlds not only fascinating in their own right, but offering fresh perspectives on ourselves as well. Peace Corps affords volunteers the rare privilege of immersion in one of those other worlds and, by extension, helps them feel at home almost anywhere on earth. It's one thing to experience foreign adventures as virtual reality through books, movies, and video games, quite another to actually *live* them in real life, with all the ups, downs, and surprises that real life affords.

Fair warning: if your idea of a good time is to hop into your climate controlled car, call ahead on your cellphone for Chinese take-out, and pick up your meal steaming hot after paying by credit card, Peace Corps service is *not* for you. No, no, no. Instead, you might climb up a tree to pluck off an orange, grow vegetables in your own backyard, or harvest wild herbs. You're likely to be barehanded, just face-to-face with Mother Nature, igniting a wood fire to cook with, while fanning the flames under the pot. And your personal life will be an open book. No one can expect privacy in a rural area of a developing country, especially not as a foreigner and an American to boot. You will always stand out.

You can drive yourself crazy realizing that restaurant dishes are washed by hand in cold water, ice cubes contain tap water, and drinking straws are recycled. So, the Peace Corps is certainly not for everyone. But it's an experience that can prove life changing. Diplomatic service and Congress are top-heavy with former volunteers.

But neither is it only for young people, though the average age is 27. Service can also enrich life for more seasoned folks lacking further career ambitions who may actually have more to offer. It's never too late to test out your strengths and forge a new path. In rural areas of developing nations, age is highly respected. Older volunteers, despite the popular association of rigidity with advancing years, have often, in my observation, been more adaptable and less anxious than younger ones. By a certain age, while you may not have survived losses as severe as mine, nonetheless, your strengths have been honed in the crucible of experience. Peace Corps, recognizing this, recently installed 50+ recruiters aiming for a 15% total. Over-50 volunteers have already grown from 1% in 1966 to 7% today, assigned mostly to agriculture, IT, business, teaching, and the environment. Where else can they combine adventure with self-fulfillment and helping others?

Admittedly, it's harder (though quite do-able) to learn a new language later in life or to manage chronic health conditions in a remote area offering only rudimentary medical services. Still, I would appeal to my age-mates to seriously consider joining the Peace Corps, where you will find a warm welcome despite your years. It may be your last chance before retiring to the golf links or bridge table to make a meaningful contribution. If you end up having an experience like mine, you won't regret it.

Buen Viaje, Good Journey

Our training group, some 50 strong—nervous, curious, giddy with excitement —gathered in Miami in the spring of 2000 for the send-off to Honduras. Well, actually only 49 showed up, since one got cold feet just before boarding the plane. Our group was designated as Honduras South 5, referring to our final destination within the country. Some recruits had never been outside the U.S. or even, in one case, outside his home state. Two had volunteered previously, both in Africa. Together we represented a wide range of experience.

We were pretty evenly divided gender-wise, with three married couples, all in their twenties, and ethnically diverse, including folks of Caucasian, African American, Asian, and Southeast Asian origins. One member of a couple may also join alone, provided the spouse consents. I would later meet a volunteer my own age whose husband had stayed behind, visiting her periodically. Soon that arrangement proved untenable and she returned home.

In Miami, as a warm-up exercise, we were each asked to identify our favorite band. Limp Bizkit, Spinal Tap, and Pearl Jam were mentioned, also Metallica, Motley Crue, and Hootie and the Blowfish. What!? Almost apologetically, I named folk singers and classical composers, even opera, which pretty much placed me back in the Dark Ages. I even heard a few smothered titters and gasps, though my advanced years were no secret. At 62, I was far and away the oldest recruit present, the only grandparent, and for most of my time in Honduras, the oldest volunteer in the whole country. Most recruits were younger than my own children.

There were also three men in their fifties, all destined to marry younger Honduran women, one a bride of 21. Since most volunteers are single when they join, it's hardly surprising that many will tie the knot during their service. Romance is not usually touted as a Peace Corps perk, but it happens.

If a volunteer should impregnate a local woman, we were advised that Peace Corps will cover her medical costs, an outcome still best avoided. With disquiet, I would later notice a few male volunteers gravitating toward underage Honduran schoolgirls dazzled by their attentions. While older female volunteers rarely got hitched, a never-married volunteer in her forties, met later on, became pregnant by a young Honduran and married him, though not always enjoying smooth sailing thereafter. Peace Corps assumed her pregnancy-related costs.

During our orientation in Miami, concerns were more immediate: "Stay in regular touch with your parents so they won't be calling their congressman asking about you."

Furthermore, no beards allowed; no tongue, eyebrow, nose, or lip jewelry; and a single pair of earrings for women only, leading to loud protests that precious piercings would close up. Also, tattoos had to remain covered to avoid gang connotations. More rumblings, why wasn't all this mentioned during recruitment?

Several recruits identified themselves as vegetarians. One, a vegan (consuming no animal products, not even milk or eggs), astounded us by cheerfully munching down corn flakes mixed with orange juice. Vegetarians were assured that the typical Honduran diet of beans, rice, and tortillas was pretty well balanced, especially when supplemented with seasonal fruits and vegetables. Out in the hinterland, where we would all be living, meat was a rare delicacy reserved for honored guests, so vegetarians would need to inform hosts before a poor chicken was sacrificed on their behalf.

After two days in Miami, with passports and paperwork duly stamped, we were ready for final departure, having been officially designated as PCTs, Peace Corps trainees, the first step toward becoming PCVs, full-fledged volunteers. We had also been initiated into a vast lexicon of acronyms, including ET for early termination, AS for administrative separation (equivalent to a dishonorable discharge), and COS for close of service. In Spanish, we learned, trainees are called *aspirantes,* candidates *aspiring* to become full-fledged volunteers.

After a two-hour flight from Miami, we shared a magic moment as our plane dove down over the green mountains ringing Tegucigalpa, the Honduran capital. Excitedly, we clustered around the oval windows, abandoning our seatbelts. Already familiar with third-world tropics, I felt a pang of recognition as lush vegetation, ramshackle buildings, and horse-drawn carts came into view. When the plane slammed to a halt on the too-short runway, we all sent up a spontaneous cheer.

Paradise Lost

Our first few days are spent on retreat in a small hotel in the wooded mountain town of Valle de Ángeles, Valley of Angels, an hour's bus ride from Tegucigalpa.

The first admonition: "Never, ever drink tap water."

Next: "Never flush away used toilet tissue," as plumbing systems will clog, especially since newspaper or cornhusks frequently replace paper.

A fellow trainee surveys each of us, asking: "Whom do you most admire?" Without hesitation, I name my mother, whose cheerful outlook fortified her through numerous household moves and sudden widowhood after 59 years of marriage. Now in her late 80s, she's mastered e-mail just to be able to communicate with me here.

Gathered on that first idyllic sunny afternoon around a swimming pool, simply getting acquainted, our group discovers we are not an elite chosen few after all, as has been intimated, but simply a cross-section of ordinary folks with various talents and foibles typical of any motley human assemblage. This proves reassuring. We launch into feel-good songs: "Lean on Me," "We are the World," "Kumbayah," triggering sniffles of homesickness.

But, mostly, we feel pretty upbeat—almost euphoric—pinching ourselves to make sure all this is real. Here we are, lounging together in a lovely tropical setting, as if on an exotic vacation. Indeed, some are already frankly looking forward not so much to *Cuerpo de Paz* (Peace Corps), as to *Cuerpo de Paseo* (Vacation Corps).

Invited by a local priest to attend a baptismal ceremony for 25 babies all dressed in white and an older gentleman in a dark suit and flipflops, we clap enthusiastically. That same evening, we venture out together for pizza, really more like cheese and tomato sauce spread over ordinary bread dough. But never mind. This is fun! We've fallen head-over-heels in love with Honduras during this brief honeymoon.

But reality soon comes crashing down. One by one, some twenty folks begin vomiting and spiking fevers before being diagnosed with severe dehydration and E-coli at the nearby Adventist hospital. Whether because of previous exposure or just plain luck, I escape. I visit several hospitalized patients hooked up to IVs, all feeling understandably glum. Then a trainee is called home because his brother has died. A somber mood extinguishes our initial high spirits. This isn't going to be just one long vacation after all.

After everyone recovers, we move in with our assigned host families, some in Valle, others in neighboring Santa Lucía, 14 kilometers away, where our training center is located. At the center, we are scheduled to undergo three months of language, cultural, and technical training in preparation for two years of actual service.

CHAPTER 2:
BOOT CAMP

En Familia

During training, we were each assigned to live with a local family, in my case in Valle de Ángeles with Luis and Irma, a thirtyish couple with two sons, Luis Ariel, age 6, and Diego, 3.

"Goodness," Irma exclaimed when I first appeared, "I didn't expect such a *mature* person." Recovering herself, she hastened to explain, "We requested someone who wouldn't come home late or drunk, so that must be *you*." Most other trainees called their hosts *Mamá* and *Papá*, hardly appropriate for me.

Irma and Luis insisted on calling me *Doña Bárbara* until I insisted they drop the Doña, a rather formal title. Their small house boasted the luxuries of a phone, a flush toilet, and electricity. Apparently, we were being introduced gradually to a more primitive lifestyle.

Husband Luis, a rotund, perpetually frowning fellow, born and raised in Valle, worked at the local office of Hondutel, the national phone company. He often bellowed loudly, demanding peace and quiet. His mother lived nearby in a crowded, busy household with three adult offspring and their families. A short, plump gray-haired widow, she boasted 10 children, 46 grandchildren, and six great-grandchildren, all together comprising, in her opinion, a living legacy superior to that of high-ranking national leaders. I introduced myself to other neighbors, including a barefoot, smudged-faced urchin delivering tortillas made daily by his mother and the next-door family operating a plant nursery whom my hosts suspected of stealing underwear off their clothesline.

Few Hondurans enjoyed the luxury of a home phone because of cost and limited availability. Often someone had to die to liberate a number and the entire national directory was only an inch thick. So most callers relied on Hondutel, waiting patiently in line at a local office, first to pay, then to call, a process involving complicated paperwork at each step, thereby providing coveted civil service jobs. Hence the growing popularity of cellular phones, although Hondutel refused to put through calls to cellphone numbers.

Due to his privileged position as a Hondutel employee, Luis had commandeered a precious home phone, its dial kept locked to prevent his wife from making outgoing calls, though she could still answer when it rang. Irma, pert and pretty with a bleached forelock, had a daughter by a previous marriage living in San Pedro Sula to the north, and Luis certainly didn't want her making any long-distance calls up there.

Irma's mother, also named Irma, shuttled back and forth between Valle and a son's home in another city. Days after my arrival, she showed up unannounced, causing Luis to grumble, "Heaven help us, not her again."

Doña Irma, a shaky, nervous, emaciated lady, barely ate anything, so Luis couldn't complain about the grocery bills. She lived on cigarettes chain-smoked through a racking cough and rum delivered by the tortilla boy on the sly. She had once attended Tulane University and still spoke quite passable English.

The house had only two bedrooms. Since Peace Corps (PC) mandated private bedrooms for trainees, parents and kids had to double up, while Irma's mother occupied a maid's cot in a kitchen alcove. I got the second bedroom all to myself, furnished with a hard bed, a harder pillow, and one very threadbare towel. What were that pillow and mattress stuffed with anyway, sawdust? I bought a softer pillow in Tegucigalpa.

A giant TV on a decorative metal stand, flanked on either side by vases of artificial flowers and smiling family photos, dominated the living room. The TV blasted away from dawn to midnight, while the rusty, rumbling refrigerator was unplugged nightly to save on electricity. I soon became weary of nonstop soap operas. In one, a guy raped a beautiful young woman who ended up falling in love with him to save her honor! I did enjoy *Betty La Fea* (Ugly Betty), a Colombian soap spoof about a bespectacled, dowdy secretary who blossomed and eventually married her clueless boss. (An English-language version subsequently débuted in the U.S.)

Weekday evenings, Luis rode the bus into the city to attend business administration classes at the national university, paying tuition of only $7 per semester. When not in class, he was often out drinking at a local bar, infuriating Irma, especially when her spies reported seeing him consorting with another woman, referred to only as "that slut." Irma didn't appreciate being left home with the children, always underfoot because she never allowed them to play outside with the trash-talking neighbor kids.

The bored older son would tease the younger one until he cried, prompting Irma to whack a belt repeatedly on the floor, though she seldom actually walloped him. With my own kids, I rarely raised a hand, much less a belt, so was horrified, but hesitated to intervene. I tried to set an example by talking softly to the boys, praising their drawings, and playing games with them. Was this belt rattling just a cultural difference or did it verge on child abuse? Many Americans also believe,"Spare the rod, spoil the child." When Luis Ariel, the 6-year-old, got really wound up, I'd take him out for a time-out walk, even after dark. "No fair," he'd blubber, "Diego grabs my things; but mama only punishes *me*."

I was concerned that Diego, at age three, wasn't talking yet, but when I gingerly suggested a pediatric evaluation, Irma just laughed. The older boy drank only black coffee, rejecting milk, meat, eggs, and any other visible source of protein, subsisting mainly on plain tortillas. His brother still drank a bottle of reconstituted powdered milk. Thank goodness for that!

Irma cooked supper over kindling fired up in an oil drum in the back yard, where chickens and ducks roamed freely and orange trees hung heavy with a seedy, acidic fruit used only in cooking. I often joined her out there, warming my hands over the fire in the evening chill. Occasionally, she lit a kitchen stove hooked up to a tank of compressed gas, later storing leftover food in the oven instead of the refrigerator. Despite the cool climate, I was uneasy about eating cooked food left out unrefrigerated.

I asked Irma to please not salt my food, because of my mild high blood pressure, but she ignored me, arguing that otherwise it wouldn't taste right. Sugar was also used copiously.

As for drinking water, "Don't worry, I always boil our water," Irma assured me, keeping it in recycled plastic soda bottles that the boys imbibed from freely instead of using a glass. Here I was, in Honduras as a health educator, reluctant to bring up questions of balanced nutrition, sanitation, and proper food storage with my own host family.

Before leaving Valle, I ordered a cake for Luis Ariel's 7th birthday from a woman living 2 kilometers uphill. I had to hike back down a precipitous grade, gingerly balancing the large, colorfully decorated sheet cake while barking dogs nipped constantly at my heels. Somehow, cake and I arrived intact and Luis Ariel reveled proudly in his special day.

School Days

Away from the classroom for 40 years except to teach or give a lecture, I found it humbling to return to the student role. Our training curriculum seemed a combination of kindergarten and boot camp, with classes held daily except Sundays.

Our days began far too early. My hosts had listed hot water as a perk of their home, but their *electroducha,* an electric heater inside the showerhead, was broken. To reach the training center by 7:30 am, I had to get up at 6, take my turn under the ice-cold shower (invigorating at that early hour), and, by 6:45, be standing outside on the highway waiting for the bus to Santa Lucía. Because of the elevation and start of the rainy season, although the sun usually broke through by mid-afternoon, early mornings were foggy, drizzly, and just plain chilly. Remembering Honduras as the balmy tropics, I'd brought nothing heavier than a sweater. And, with no indoor heat, we actually felt colder inside than out.

We took our lunch to "school," as in my childhood. The bus brought us back at 6 pm, in time for supper. Hardier trainees enjoyed traversing the 14 km. back to Valle on foot. Sometimes I walked 4 km. along with them to a junction and caught a bus from there.

Half of our training schedule was devoted to language instruction, graduated according to proficiency. Some trainees were rank beginners, barely able to say *buenos días,* yet chosen for their technical skills. Each student was required to reach a minimum language level before swearing-in as a volunteer. I was excused from language classes altogether, having scored "superior" on an oral test given to incoming trainees.

Knowing Spanish already and being familiar with the culture proved enormous advantages. I was drafted for interpretation when Spanish speakers addressed us during cultural awareness sessions. Hondurans tried to place my accent, "You can't be *gringa*—gringos don't speak good Spanish. Are you from Colombia, Cuba, Mexico, perhaps?" I'd probably acquired a little of each along the way.

On a field trip to a local elementary school, our training group observed a secret-ballot student vote and the election victory of a sixth-grade girl. In the country-at-large, the affirmative action goal was 33% female candidates for mayoral and legislative offices, though fewer women ended up actually winning.

Honduras's major political parties are *Liberales,* whose color is red, and *Nacionalistas,* represented by blue. Instead of red and blue states, there is a checkerboard of red and blue provinces. No one, from president on down to mayor, can hold administrative office for more than one consecutive four-year term. Carlos Flores, president when we arrived, belonged to the Liberal Party. His American wife often gave radio talks in heavily accented Spanish.

Civics Lesson

We were soon given a crash course about a country unfamiliar to most. Some trainees took copious notes while others quietly dozed or gazed out the window. In land area, we were told, Honduras is about equivalent to Louisiana. On a wall map, we noted that because of the isthmus' twists and turns, Honduras has no east and west coasts, but rather a long northern Caribbean coast and a shorter southern Pacific coast. Guatemala lies to the northwest, with Belize just across a bay. To the south are Nicaragua and the Pacific Bay of Fonseca. Neighboring El Salvador, tucked into a southwest corner, has the same population as Honduras, but one-sixth its landmass. Salvador, lacking room for large-scale farming, but thanks to massive remittances from U.S.-based countrymen, shows more industrial development and has adopted the American dollar as its official currency, along with Ecuador and Panama (small nations with virtually no control over policies affecting the dollar's value). The Honduran currency is the *lempira.* Right after our arrival, the exchange rate was 14 to the dollar, but changing daily.

Founded in 1578, the capital, Tegucigalpa, meaning "silver hill" in an indigenous language, was so named because of its once-rich ore deposits. According to our instructors, *Teguc* (pronounced "TEH-goose") had grown from just 400,000 twenty years before to well over a million inhabitants, our instructor said.

Hondurans, 7 million strong, were a young population, with 40% under 15 and more than half under 19 (compared to a median age of 40 for non-Hispanic whites in the U.S.). Although population density was not yet excessive, the government was intervening aggressively to curb future growth. Our own impact on population would be indirect, consisting mainly of encouraging kids to graduate from high school and set goals for the future, though we *were* allowed to discuss available birth-control methods if specifically asked.

Honduras was described to us as the poorest country in the hemisphere after Haiti, followed closely by Nicaragua, though some experts would actually place them on a par. Honduran per capita income, adjusted for inflation, had remained virtually flat for more than 20 years. The minimum wage, nominally $70 per month, was simply not enforced. Forty percent of Hondurans were living on less than $1 per day, with the same percentage estimated to be malnourished. Few citizens paid taxes, only 5%. Illiteracy was 26%. These were not just dry statistics, but a measure of the challenges we faced.

When we arrived in 2000, Honduras ranked 107th among 162 nations on the UN's Human Development Index (HDI). By comparison, that same year, Mexico ranked 55 on the HDI. The per-person income and productivity difference between Honduras and Mexico was proportionately equivalent to that between Mexico and the U.S. Yet, despite their poverty, surveys showed average Hondurans to be slightly more satisfied with their lives than Americans. This surprising finding sparked considerable discussion. "Maybe we have more to learn from Hondurans than vice versa," I observed.

We were repeatedly warned about violent crime in the region. El Salvador came out on top, followed in order by Honduras, Nicaragua, Guatemala, and Costa Rica. Crime was fueled by leftover civil-war arms, the growing drug traffic, and frequent natural disasters.

Twenty thousand Honduran youngsters lived on the streets while an international agency, Casa Alianza, offered them shelter in major cities. At least 100,000 kids under 13, the legal working age, were estimated to actually be employed. Young people would constitute much of our clientele.

A U.S. embassy official reported that 6,000 immigrant visas per year were granted to Hondurans—a drop-in-the-bucket compared to demand—mostly to spouses of Americans or to those with legal relatives in the States. The country's largest source of hard currency was family remittances from U.S.-based relatives. We learned that more than $150 million was being returned in the form of remittances, a figure that would reach $1 billion by my departure and almost $2.5 billion by 2007, fully 25% of GDP, constituting a backdoor form of foreign aid. The bulk of direct foreign aid came from the U.S., with contributions also from Canada, Germany, Holland, Italy, Japan, Spain, Sweden, and Taiwan.

For Hondurans, applying for a U.S. visitor's visa, we soon learned, was usually an exercise in futility. A visa interview required an embassy appointment months in advance and a $100 fee (yes, in dollars). This entitled visa applicants to a two-minute stand-up interview in front of a small window of bullet-proof glass, with their fate decided up or down, usually down, with no right of appeal and no refund for a denial. Nonetheless, we trainees observed daily lines stretching around the block in front of the embassy, a fortress protected by high guard towers and abundant razor wire.

I would come to marvel at how Hondurans so gracefully accepted the blatant unfairness of Americans coming into their own country with no prior visa while they themselves were usually denied access to our country, despite compliance with burdensome requirements. For them and many others, the virtual impossibility of obtaining *legal* entry undermines the claims of anti-immigrant forces. One woman I met had dutifully "waited her turn" for 17 years to enter legally, but her husband never lived to see the day.

Some 12,000 Americans resided in Honduras, an embassy official reported, and another 10,000 tourists visited on any given day, a fair number, but less than to neighboring countries. Meanwhile, a dozen U.S. citizens were typically being held in Honduran jails where embassy staff visited them periodically.

The U.S. still maintained a Honduran airbase called Palmerola, a Cold War remnant resuscitated by the "war on terror." Later in my tenure, a Blackhawk helicopter would crash near the base, killing five American soldiers engaged in training exercises. GIs transferred from the Far East reportedly had introduced a drug-resistant VD strain known as Rosa Vietnam, this according to reliable sources, not our instructors.

A Rose by Any Other Name

While Spanish *per se* was no problem for me, I needed to brush up my *hondureñismos,* honduranisms.

I was taken aback when host Luis came home demanding, "Give me something to feed my parasite." Say what? This disconcerting phrase turned out to mean, "I'm hungry."

And if you're hungry, what might you eat? Perhaps *tajaditas,* "shreds," popular at bus stops, an unlikely combination of coleslaw and fried plantain chips, topped with hot sauce, served in a plastic bag. Or *mondongo,* a favorite tripe soup. And *mantequilla,* that is, *butter,* readily available in other Spanish-speaking countries, was unknown here, that name being reserved for heavy cream poured over refried beans. Margarine, sold in unrefrigerated blocks, *was* available but looked pretty unappetizing, like the hateful stuff we used to get during World War II.

Labels for kids included *cipotes, cheles, chavalos,* and *chingüines,* terms not found in the dictionary, and a pen was a *lápiz tinta,* quite logically an "ink pencil," a name new to me. Another new word was *jalón* or ride, from the verb *jalar,* to haul, useful for hitchhikers like ourselves. *Chimba* referred to a homemade musket emitting only one shot before reloading. I discovered that the verb *coger,* normally standing for catching or grabbing something, here referred to a sexual coupling. So I no longer was allowed to *catch* a bus, only *take (tomar)* a bus.

Pogamos las pilas, let's install our batteries, simply meant, "let's go." *Macanudo* and *todo chequeleque* referred to something really super-duper. *Vaya pues* (literally, "go then") was equivalent to "so long." *¡Púchica!* meant something like "wow!", with *¡guau!* the anglicized version. *Porfa* was short for *por favor.* Such common sports anglicisms as a *fútbol gol, béisbol jonrón,* and *voleibol* needed no translation, likewise for a boxing *nacáut* (knockout). Another anglicism was *guachemán,* watchman.

Although avoiding such usage myself, I soon found poor adults referred to as "boys" and "girls," as in: "A boy came by, asking for you today," when the "boy" turned out to be a grandfather my own age.

I noticed that when someone couldn't see or hear well, it was said the person doesn't look or doesn't listen *(no mira, no escucha).* Peanuts, which I'd always called *mani* were now *cacahuate. Calcetines,* known to me as underpants, were socks and *medias,* previously socks, became long stockings. Money was *pisto,* not *dinero,* as in: *No ando pisto* (I'm not carrying any money). A drunk was called *bolo,* not *borracho.* To clean was not *limpiar,* as was my habit, but *asear,* and cleaning powder, *ase.* Candies, previously *dulces,* were now *confites.* I soon adapted.

Because English and Spanish share so many Latin roots, I warned fellow trainees about homophones—that is, words that sound alike in both languages, but have different meanings. *Embarazo* looks a lot like "*embarrass*" in English and, though a woman might be embarrassed by an *embarazo,* the latter means a pregnancy. *Compromiso* is a commitment, a betrothal, while our own *compromise* might be rendered as *un término medio,* a middle ground. Unlike what you might imagine, *tributario* usually stands for a tax and *edificación,* for a building. *Grocerías* are swear words, not groceries. *Bigote* is not a bigot, but a mustache. *Propio* refers to something belonging to someone, not something proper, while *proper* is more properly rendered as *conforme. Parientes* are not parents per se, but relatives. *Relaciones,* in turn, has sexual connotations. All these are pitfalls to be avoided.

I winced when hapless newbie trainees announced *"finito"* at the end of a talk, an adjective meaning delicate. Or referred to a door as *"éxito,"* a word signifying success. Their listeners looked puzzled, but were too polite to comment. Trainees, in turn, were puzzled when Hondurans exclaimed, *"¡Cómo no!"* literally "How not," meaning "Of course!" I modeled wrapping my mouth around robust, clear Spanish vowels, using softer consonants, the reverse of English pronunciation.

I learned a few new constructions myself, such as "I almost don't like her," actually meaning "I don't like her at all." Or "the big guava says," standing for "a big fat lie." *Gran poco,* literally "big little bit," turned out to be really a quite lot.

Gender usually presents major challenges to non-native Spanish speakers since nearly all nouns are gendered with matching adjectives. Most nouns ending in "a" are feminine with those in "o" masculine, but exceptions abound and the same word may have both feminine and masculine forms. For example, *la cura* (the cure) is feminine, *el cura* (the priest), masculine. While common across Latin America, here in Honduras I was puzzled anew at hearing parents address a girl child as *mamá* and a boy as *papá,* or by the corresponding diminutives.

We trainees soon discovered street addresses to be non-existent, with locations identified only as "30 meters north of the church" or "the corner where the old oak once stood."

I was often asked to help local teachers and students with English instruction. The idea that English grammar and pronunciation might differ from those of Spanish encountered some resistance. In Honduras, as elsewhere, people grow up regarding their own language, customs, and beliefs as the norm, others as deviant. Three schoolboys asked how I'd ever mastered English, such a difficult language. "Same way you learned Spanish," I replied, "as a baby."

How hilarious! As far back as they could remember, everyone always spoke Spanish, no one actually *learned* it. People were obviously born knowing Spanish and acquired English only through arduous study. I then taught them to say "How are you?" and "See you later," in English, which they chanted over and over in unison.

Health 101

Although language and cultural awareness instruction had little to offer me, I learned a lot in health education classes. Members of each service sector—agriculture, natural resources, municipal development, economic development, health, and water and sanitation—participated in regular breakout sessions in their own specialties. Our primary task as volunteers would be to offer training in new practices and techniques related to our sector and to prepare community leaders to carry on after our departure.

"Your goal," we were advised, "is to promote *sustainable* behavior changes and work yourselves right out of a job. Remember, *empowerment* is your watchword."

But unlike innumerable U.S. government, charitable, and religious organizations, we arrived empty-handed with no funds or other tangible resources at our disposal, just information and expertise to share. In health, our subject matter encompassed maternity care and midwifery, HIV prevention, nutrition, infant care, and child survival—including treatment of the main killers of those under 5, namely, respiratory infections and diarrhea. An infant with diarrhea can die of dehydration within hours, making it important to keep liquid flowing in, both breast milk and a rehydration solution.

We trainees hardly needed more sophisticated medical knowledge; on the contrary, we had to simplify without distorting and learn to communicate effectively with largely uneducated folks. Accordingly, we invented instructional games called *dinámicas,* sang songs, drew pictures, and created papier- mâché models of common foods. I made a green buzzing fly from a toilet paper roll, complete with colored tissue-paper wings and pipe-cleaner antennae. Guided by a dangling string, this creature landed on excrement (brown Play Doh) before hopping gaily onto dishes to spread the germs. We practiced hands-on tasks such as measuring out chlorine powder for water purification, making a re-hydration solution with salt and sugar, and building a latrine.

The Honduran health system looked pretty good on paper: a network of city hospitals, public clinics, and local health volunteers. Yet on a field trip to a large public hospital connected with the Teguc national medical school, a young health trainee burst into tears over the cumulative impact of broken elevators, filthy restrooms, dark crowded wards, dirty floors mopped endlessly by bent old women, and sick crying babies lying two and three per crib.

Each obstetrics ward, with six or eight beds, was a virtual assembly line, with newly delivered mothers still wearing street clothes clutching their newborns on bare narrow pallets, sometimes sharing a bed head-to-toe with another mother and her infant. The natural childbirth debate was moot here; except for C-sections, childbirth anesthesia was unavailable in public facilities. Likewise, male baby circumcision was a non-issue. Unless a new mother was having an IUD inserted or a tubal ligation done immediately after delivery, she left within hours to free up a bed.

Even I, though relatively experienced, was unprepared for the insensitivity of an obstetrician giving us a guided tour of a ward full of mothers with sick babies. He loudly cited each one's intimate characteristics: "A fat mother here, her malnourished baby." "This woman neglected proper hygiene, so no surprise her child got sick." "This next one simply isn't producing enough milk." "This patient is 39 years old, so she gave birth to a mongoloid; all females over 34 should be sterilized." "Here's a girl only 16, already with her second baby by two different fathers." "Note this classic indigenous type—straight black hair, dark skin, high cheek bones," patting her head for emphasis. The mothers looked away sheepishly. Passing by, I whispered words of encouragement: "Your child is beautiful," "Hope your baby recovers soon." "Keep strong."

Not all women gave birth in hospitals. Midwives operated in rural areas, sometimes for free, sometimes paid with a chicken or a little cash. We learned that the main problem in small-town public health centers, some with birthing rooms, was absentee personnel—with physicians most often delinquent—as well as inadequate staff training and insufficient medications and supplies, sometimes pilfered by employees. Nurses, with two years of post-secondary education, earned about $300 per month and public health doctors usually over $1,500, a princely sum in Honduran terms, though most conducted a private practice as well, devoting mornings to the health center and afternoons to their own clinic, usually located in their home.

Back at the training center during Spanish classes, I helped out in the office translating documents, being one of few trainees able to write in Spanish, since language training focused mainly on speaking. I also gave talks at the local health center, where I was asked directly about birth control methods, arousing a flurry of interest among several waiting women and a lone man. Although prohibited from offering birth-control advice to a specific patient, we *were* allowed to discuss methods available locally. So I passed around samples of those offered at this particular center: condoms, birth control pills, and injections (a drawing of a syringe).

Mail Call

A bright spot during training was the weekly mail run from the main office in Teguc. Like soldiers in wartime or jail inmates, we greedily coveted each scrap of mail. Snail-mail letters, since we had no e-mail access at the training center, were savored slowly and re-read repeatedly. I collected a growing stack of letters, stored chronologically in their original envelopes. (Before leaving Honduras, I had accumulated an entire suitcase full, regretfully destroyed in a huge bonfire, sending that part of my PC life up in smoke.)

Among my correspondents were 8th-grade Spanish students attending a public school in Astoria, NY, participating in a program called World Wise Schools. I replied to them in Spanish, mirroring their simple vocabulary.

On Sundays, our only free day, we often bused into Teguc to use the Internet, providing a communication revolution for those with sufficient know-how and wherewithal to participate. During my previous sojourns in Latin America, waiting for snail mail had often proved futile. Now, we trainees eagerly sought out city cybercafés that charged by the hour. If the electricity went out or the system crashed, tough luck, and often there was an interminable wait for a free computer, still a small price to pay for instant and relatively reliable communication.

My host "mother" Irma soon introduced me to a local U.S. missionary couple with four blond, blue-eyed children, home-schooled using computerized lesson plans. Paying them for the time used, I was graciously allowed to check e-mail on their computer.

With local church members' labor, along with financial support from co-religionists back home, this family had supervised the building of a chapel and their own American-style two-story home, towering above its smaller neighbors. Their denomination, Plymouth Brethren, was founded in the early 19th century in Plymouth, England. When their children reached college age, they would attend a Brethren institution in the States.

Occasionally, Irma and I accepted this family's invitation to attend their services where the older daughters played guitars and sang. After one service, a prominent member of the congregation declared, "Kennedy secretly established the Peace Corps to promote Catholicism around the world."

Rather than argue, I assured him that was not our mission today.

Just Say *No*

While we health volunteers were busy boning up on health and welfare, we also became human pincushions for our own health benefit, enduring shots for MMR, diphtheria, polio, tetanus, typhoid, Hepatitis A & B, and rabies. Whew! In vain I protested, "Please, I actually *had* MMR illnesses before immunizations even existed; as a small child, I lay quarantined in a darkened room."

"Too bad, everyone gets stuck," was the terse reply.

I soon found myself acting as mother confessor to young trainees missing their own parents, or perhaps finding it easier to talk with me than with contemporaries (the confession-to-a-stranger syndrome). A few expressed condescending admiration for my "bravery" in joining the Corps in my dotage, though I considered myself better prepared than they for what actually lay ahead.

Since alcohol and, to a lesser extent, drug use present risks for sometimes lonely PCVs, our training included sessions on substance abuse. Hondurans encourage excessive drinking by men, so male trainees were cautioned about accepting invitations whose main objective was rarely mere conviviality but, rather, drinking everyone under the table. Cigarette smoking was frowned upon for women, but smokers among us found it hard to quit, since tobacco grows locally and a pack of cigarettes—harsh and unfiltered—cost only about 75 U.S. cents, with a single cigarette less than a dime.

Marijuana and cocaine were expressly forbidden. Such substances were nominally illegal, but local use had grown since Central America had become a preferred trade route for feeding North America's ravenous drug habit. Any discovery or even accusation of drug use, we were warned, would result in immediate termination. (Occasional marijuana smoking by volunteers proved not uncommon in my experience, but cocaine use fairly rare.)

A habitual pot smoker was referred to as a *mafufo*, an excessive drinker as a *patero*. If we became aware of a volunteer's abuse of alcohol or drugs, we were advised to first confront them, urging immediate cessation. Then, if they appeared to be endangering themselves or others, or casting Peace Corps in a bad light, reporting them to higher-ups was mandatory.

In reality, reporting was simply taboo. If anyone noticed excessive drinking, we might approach an individual privately. But knowing full well that an actual report would end their PC career, we adopted an unspoken code of silence like that protecting errant policemen and doctors. Only, say, after a drunken suicide attempt or a drug overdose, would anyone dare blow the whistle. Our country director once asked me confidentially about marijuana and cocaine use among volunteers. "Even if I knew, you know I wouldn't tell you," I shrugged.

During training, several of us put together an illustrative skit. In our impromptu play, I, a near teetotaler in real life, took on the role of a wanton lush to the great delight of my fellows. With slurred speech and unsteady gait, I made passes at male trainees, drank straight from the bottle, and ended up falling down, evoking loud laughter and catcalls from the audience.

Ironically, the young woman acting as my counselor had a real-life reputation for getting soused, yet on-stage she earnestly urged me to stop drinking and to seek help through the PC medical office for my "own good."

In her best school-marmish tone, she scolded: "Barbara, you know you have a serious drinking problem. Unless you can go cold turkey, you need to get help right away."

I called her "a big fat killjoy" who simply didn't know how to have fun, adding, "You're just trying to get me kicked out of Peace Corps." I hoped the role reversal would help her control her own drinking, but it did not.

Safety First

Safety was another training focus. Many, if not all, third-world countries are inherently dangerous, especially for single women. Police are typically underpaid, poorly equipped, spread too thin, and easily corrupted. Most crimes go unreported because of fear of reprisals and the all-too-realistic expectation that nothing will be done anyway. Frontier justice prevails, with aggrieved parties often taking matters into their own hands. As foreigners, PCVs represent especially visible targets, a risk exacerbated by increased anti-Americanism and a gender shift among volunteers, a majority male in the early years, but now 60% female.

An earnest embassy security officer addressing us compared living as an American volunteer in a poor area of a developing country with living as a white person in an inner-city minority neighborhood, "While most neighbors may love you dearly, you still need to watch your back."

The officer further advised, "Don't ride buses, hitchhike, or travel alone."

Good advice, but impractical. He especially warned us about the notorious MS-13 gang, whose members had learned their trade in East L.A. and, now deported back to Honduras, were armed with American, Soviet, and even Iranian weapons left over from recent civil wars. We were told to avoid nighttime bus travel, leaving clubs during the wee hours (especially while inebriated), and visiting San Pedro Sula, a particularly violent northern city, where we were forbidden to go at all.

We were shown disturbing filmed interviews with PCVs who had been raped or injured in robberies. A volunteer from an unidentified country recounted coming home late to find the gate to her residential compound locked. She rang the bell as her taxi pulled away, but before the gate opened, she was abducted by several men driving by. She barely escaped with her life.

Although Peace Corps goes to great lengths to protect volunteers, injury and death can strike during service, just as anywhere else. Rarely, volunteers simply vanish, like a man in Bolivia whose fate remains unknown. Usually one or more volunteer deaths occur annually worldwide, mostly from motor vehicle accidents, occasionally from violence. Because of frequent motorcycle crashes, motorcycle riding was now forbidden. Soldiers know they risk death, but, for the first time, we realized we also faced that possibility.

We learned that more than 250 volunteers had died in service since 1961, including 16 suicides and at least 20 murders. Among the latter was Deborah Gardner, a PCV in Tonga killed in 1976 by another volunteer, Dennis Priven, who stood trial there, was declared insane, then released to Peace Corps authorities who promised to have him committed to a U.S. mental institution. That never happened and he remains free today.

We were told that an unnamed female volunteer, still in Honduras, was riding a bus one night when three armed men ordered the driver to stop and systematically robbed all passengers. Several women were then serially raped, including the volunteer. Immediately, she was started on a nauseating HIV-prevention drug, administered for 30 days. While most victims had recognized the perpetrators, the volunteer alone was willing to identify them. With the U.S. embassy pressing the case and the volunteer agreeing to testify, the robber-rapists were tried, convicted, and sent to prison, a rare outcome.

This volunteer had been automatically subjected to the emergency HIV-prevention regimen because Honduras has the highest incidence of HIV in Central America. The country's first known case occurred in

1985, in a gay man returning from San Francisco. Soon, the virus spread throughout the population. Since then, several volunteers had contracted HIV in Honduras, all from sexual contact. Worldwide, we were warned, more than 23 PCVs had gotten AIDS and three had died: "Despite the new antiretrovirals, don't take chances."

Free condoms were available from the PC medical office.

Different Drummers

With few exceptions, volunteers are all college graduates, sensitive to cultural differences. Despite our own personal allegiance to particular religious and cultural traditions, we know that others may hold contrary beliefs and practices equally dear. But local folks rarely share such cross-cultural understanding, considering their particular truths and customs absolute and self-evident, regarding any transgressions of their norms as wanton and deliberate violations of natural and divine law.

Volunteers must therefore go more than half-way to bridge this cultural divide, especially since we are guests in another country. In Honduras, it would be unwise and counterproductive for gay volunteers to reveal their sexual orientation, for a female volunteer to admit a past abortion, or for her to openly drink alcohol, wear shorts in public, or play pool—things simply not done. In Honduras, we often found our own values of honesty, individuality, and self-expression challenged by local imperatives to maintain social harmony. For most Hondurans, tradition, family loyalty, and group togetherness trump independence. Personal privacy is not even a recognized value.

The notion of a separate gay identity was especially antithetical to the typical Honduran mindset. Rare rebel types might openly cross-dress or live with same-sex partners, but they were few and far between. In one village, a middle-aged couple was surreptitiously pointed out to me. Both were men, but one wore a dress and did all the cooking and washing. Neighbors shunned this couple, greeting them only at a distance. Another male couple in a different town co-owned a shop and slept together in a back room, but each ate dinner with his own wife and kids living on either side. Folks whispered, but no one boycotted their store. Yet open homosexuality was almost universally condemned. To call a man a "faggot" *(maricón)* was an unforgivable insult. Female homosexuality was simply unimaginable.

Which did not prevent same-sex behavior. The penetrator in male-male encounters never considered himself gay and often shuttled back and forth between male and female partners, sometimes spreading HIV in his wake. A loud public controversy arose when a Caribbean cruise ship catering to American gays and lesbians requested docking rights at Puerto Cortés. Local officials hotly debated whether to allow them ashore, finally bowing to the almighty dollar.

Gays and lesbians, out of the closet at home, suddenly found themselves back inside. Revealing their orientation would have put them at risk for harassment and grave physical harm. Most Hondurans could quote strict biblical admonitions against homosexuality and who dared argue with the Bible? So these volunteers invented opposite-sex sweethearts waiting faithfully back home and avoided telltale or flamboyant outfits. They never joined the small gay-rights parade held annually in Teguc, though some watched quietly from the sidelines. A gay volunteer who counseled troubled high-school students, a few expressing fear of homosexual tendencies, never revealed his own preference.

These folks did have same-sex partners from the States visit them posing as friends, or acquired new secret partners among Hondurans or other volunteers. They let their guard down only at confidential meetings of a gay support group and once during a gathering of all 300 volunteers in Honduras, held on the shores of a lake called Yojoa. There same-sex couples danced openly together and cross-dressed in comic skits, spiking their hair with wires and donning dog collars and heavy chains in playful self-parody. A gay man and woman friend in matching outfits paired up as a "lesbian couple."

Gays were not alone in going undercover. Jewish trainees were also advised to keep their religion under wraps, especially during Holy Week, when anti-Jewish sentiment runs high and children play "kill the Jews who killed Christ." A Jewish man in our group whose wife was Catholic regularly accompanied her to Mass, never revealing his true faith. Weekly services were held at a synagogue in Tegucigalpa, where the rabbi and most congregants were foreigners.

Asian Americans, regardless of ethnicity, endured being called *chinito* or *chinita*, little Chinaman or Chinawoman, by perfect strangers. African Americans steeled themselves against being addressed as *negrito* or *negrita*, little blackie, or as just plain "ugly one" (*feo, fea*), since dark skin is openly devalued. Within families, lighter-skinned children are favored, especially the occasional blond. *Moreno* and *negro* (darky and blackie) are also terms of endearment, but African American volunteers were hardly mollified. For our part, we Caucasians were just plain *yanquis* or *gringos,* or sometimes *gringuitos* (little gringos), all pejorative terms. When people started parroting fake English or addressing me as *gringa,* I ignored them, though if they persisted, I called them *catrachos,* slang for Hondurans.

Puerto Ricans were simply dismissed as imposters trying to pass themselves off as *bona fide* gringos. And pity the heavy-set volunteer, who could expect to be nicknamed *gordo,* fatso, while a thin person would be *flaca,* skinny. Short stature invited a label of shorty or midget, while a tall volunteer was a giraffe and a stooped-over guy, a camel. Though younger volunteers might not object to being called kids, I didn't appreciate being addressed as *viejita* (little old lady), *abuelita* (little grandmother), or *tita* (auntie). Finally, people with physical disabilities (none actually among our own group) were unfeelingly labeled the equivalent of gimp, cripple, or little blindy. Hondurans were hardly sticklers for political correctness.

While Peace Corps maintains high health and fitness standards, these have been relaxed in recent years. A challenge under the Americans with Disabilities Act reportedly led to the acceptance of applicants with a history of mental illness, provided a psychiatrist has confirmed their ability to serve without danger to self or others. Nonetheless, adapting to a foreign culture and language in an isolated location often places extra strain on someone with a psychiatric history.

Physical disabilities present another sort of challenge. Housing, transportation, communication—all are infinitely harder than in the U.S., even for the able-bodied. For someone with a disability, rough roads, crowded buses, and outdoor latrines pose special difficulties. Nonetheless, Peace Corps has shown a willingness in recent years to work with certain disabilities. For example, a volunteer with insulin-dependent diabetes had her medication supplied and delivered, and was authorized to buy a small refrigerator to keep it cold.

Volunteer support groups helped counteract the effects of negative stereotyping and other stresses. I joined one called Colors, primarily for ethnic minorities, believing that we white-bread volunteers needed to show solidarity with the full color spectrum. My own family is a virtual rainbow coalition: My ex-husband's parents were Korean, my youngest child was adopted from Colombia, one son-in-law is of Ukrainian heritage, the other is African American, my former daughter-in-law was born in the Philippines, and my grandchildren are delightful mixtures representing the wave of the future.

I also became a peer counselor with SAG (Support Advocacy Group), offering confidential advice to other volunteers, only breaking silence if a life appeared to be in danger. Throughout my PC career, I was drafted to give talks on diversity, cultural adjustment, and other topics to incoming trainees.

Finding no support group for older volunteers, I spearheaded the formation of OAKS, symbolized by a mighty oak tree. We founding members chose the acronym first, then torturously converted it into Older And Knowing Souls. Our members were both pretty savvy and less vulnerable than many younger volunteers to loneliness and depression. Tempered by experience, our expectations were more realistic. However, one OAKS member did quit midway through for health reasons. And a middle-aged couple, who had sold their home and possessions before realizing their life-long Peace Corps dream, quit after a failed robbery attempt.

Eventually, I would be dethroned as the oldest volunteer in Honduras by another Barbara, age 71, a former model and dancer, a slender white-haired grandmother and an advocate of voluntary simplicity. We agreed that having few possessions and a small living space freed up time to do things that really mattered. Barbara visited me soon after arriving, knowing little Spanish and planning to work in the male-dominated field of agriculture. "I wanted something completely different," she explained.

The oldest PCV ever was 86. The most senior volunteer in the Americas during my own tenure was an 80-year-old woman working with disabled children in Bolivia.

Nevertheless, despite such standouts, a few holes showed up in the rigorous screening process. A handful of bad apples surfaced, including one who turned out to have learned Spanish serving a drug sentence in a Mexican prison, his incarceration having slipped through the cracks of the customary FBI review.

San Antonio de Flores

A month into our training, we each were invited to visit a volunteer already working in our sector, in my case, health. I looked forward to getting away from the training center and into the warmer south, the region where we would eventually be placed. Our four-day visit required traveling alone by bus. Those with shaky Spanish wrote down their destination to show the driver. One married woman objected to going alone. Each husband-wife pair would eventually be assigned to the same town, but because they were required to work in different sectors, each visited a different volunteer during training.

Helen, my own host, lived in San Antonio de Flores, St. Anthony of the Flowers. But when I got off the bus at a hot, dusty crossroads, I saw no flowers, just a swarm of black flies circling a pile of rotting garbage. Several giggling women, naked to the waist, were bathing outdoors in buckets of hand-pumped water.

Helen's prior note had said, "Just ask for *la gringuita*."

At the local health center, I found Helen helping three women put finishing touches on a model village to display at the entrance. From matchsticks, they'd created tiny pens to keep Play Doh livestock away from little cardboard houses, with latrines placed at a safe distance. Water barrels were fitted with round tops to keep out debris, while drinking straws served as vents for clay stoves. The women stuck in branches for trees, grinning like schoolgirls with a class project. They'd probably had little actual schooling when young.

At age 26, attractive, red-haired, blue-eyed Helen must have created quite a sensation when she first arrived in Flores. She told me she had once contracted dengue, a serious mosquito-borne illness. Then all Honduras volunteers were evacuated temporarily to Panama because of Hurricane Mitch, so her service had been quite eventful. Now Helen shared a three-room dwelling with a single mother and her three children. The whole family occupied one room, renting out the other two to Helen.

I accompanied Helen on her rounds. First stop was at a three-room elementary school, located up a steep mountain. Like most towns, Flores offered education only through sixth grade. After that, students had to travel by foot or bus to the district high school in a larger town. Most quit school by sixth grade or before.

A teacher at the school, under Helen's gentle guidance, outlined a sixth-grade curriculum for sex and AIDS education. Each teacher, two women and a man, presided over a two-grade classroom. Sporting rumpled blue and white uniforms, most students went barefoot, with some wearing flip-flops and, a few, actual shoes without socks. Some carried shoes to wear only in class.

Further up the mountain, we visited a local health volunteer, a *guardiana*, who distributed aspirin and antibiotics and was supposed to exemplify good hygiene, yet her own home and yard were littered with trash, and animals had free run inside her house. Another community volunteer, with a neater abode, was designated as a *corvol*, someone who tested for malaria and dispensed anti-malaria medication.

I'd been priding myself on being the only member of our group who hadn't gotten sick. But on my second night in Flores, after eating at a *comedor,* a private home serving hot meals, and settling down with Helen under the mosquito net over her double bed, I suddenly sat bolt upright, then rushed outside to throw up. All night long, I was either vomiting or scrambling up a steep rocky hill to the privy, struggling to hold back diarrhea and flinging stones at barking dogs, glad for my rabies shots. Poor Helen didn't get much sleep either. I felt absolutely wretched, sure that if I'd had a mirror, my face would appear a sickly green. In my misery, I wryly recalled Carlos Fuentes' character in *Gringo Viejo,* "If you eat only things like I saw in El Paso, food wrapped in sealed paper so that even flies can't touch it, then the worm will attack you because you neither know him nor does he know you."

Now, as the worm attacked with a vengeance, I thought of my DC friend's grim warning, "You'll be home by Christmas." But, no, I couldn't quit yet; I'd barely gotten started.

Next morning, we were scheduled to travel by horseback to another village to set up a community pharmacy. Since I couldn't even sit up, Helen went on alone, as she'd already notified folks there. I spent all day lying in her hammock, slowly sipping *manzanilla,* a local herb tea, feeling sorry for myself and for having inconvenienced Helen. Townspeople streamed by to wish me well as word spread about my illness. Later, I munched on a ripe banana and managed to keep it down. That afternoon, I stumbled to the outdoor shower stall to pour water over my body and wash my hair. I also washed and hung up my grubby nightgown.

Flores residents begged me, "Promise to come back here after Helen leaves."

"I'd really like to," I said, "as you have all been so very kind, but Peace Corps decides where to send us."

Several young people whispered in my ear, "Take me with you to the States," a refrain to be repeated throughout my service.

Oak tree logo for our senior support group

CHAPTER 3:
FIELD-BASED TRAINING

Nueva Armenia

Our next reality-immersion experience was five weeks of field-based training, FBT in official jargon. We split up into sector groups, each assigned to a different locale. Our eight health trainees—two men, six women—were sent to Nueva (New) Armenia, a small town off the beaten track. Misinformed about bus schedules, we missed the 7 am bus leaving from the main Teguc market. So, now what? To guard against thieves prowling the market, my companions encircled our luggage, while I inquired about buses to our destination. Finding none, we decided to take a bus to a town along the way, Sabanagrande, and hitchhike from there.

We sat in seats overlooking the undercarriage storage area to monitor our luggage. Once out on the open road, our bus passed slow moving oxcarts, women carrying firewood on their heads, and boys holding out dead iguanas and armadillos for sale as meat.

After arriving in Sabanagrande at midday, we headed toward the dirt-road turnoff to Armenia toting our luggage. A flock of *zopilotes* (vultures) circled ominously overhead as we joined a group of hitchhiking Hondurans. Whenever a pickup drove by, we all shouted and waved in unison, but no one stopped. Finally, a panel truck driver offered to take gringos for $1.50 each, Hondurans for free.

We all rode standing up, packed into a dark, enclosed space, a cattle car, one trainee called it. The interior smelled of rotten fish, not to mention of several Hondurans who had not bathed recently. Whenever the vehicle lurched around a bend, we braced ourselves for balance. Some companions felt carsick but valiantly held back. No one complained. Two hours later, when we stumbled out into the light, we found our host families anxiously waiting.

Armenia turned out to be a charming town with cobblestone streets and an ancient, high-ceiling municipal building housing the mayor's office, with the mayor seldom seen, since he actually lived in Teguc. Beneath the building's overhanging porch was a single dungeon-like dirt-floor jail cell where townspeople passed food in to inmates. The lone policeman had arrested some rowdy drunks the night before, but after they'd sobered up, he removed the cell's padlock and they staggered out. The elevation here was a little lower than our training center, but higher than Flores. In fact, Armenia's balmy climate seemed just about perfect.

New Host Family

Taking in an outsider for the first time, my Armenia hosts were warm and hospitable. Americans can be hospitable too, hosting foreign exchange students and scholars, as in my own family. But it's unusual for Americans to integrate outsiders into their private lives as wholeheartedly as Hondurans do. We enjoyed the rare privilege of living in another place—and, arguably, another time—as fully accepted members of a family and a community.

José Antonio, the paterfamilias, a genial, smiling 50-year-old, proved a tireless jokester. He'd answer the family's occasionally functioning phone—open only to incoming calls—with "No, he's not here, I'm out in the john." A wandering pig sniffing at the front gate was sternly warned, "Keep out."

Pudgy, with curly gray hair, José had to watch his diet because of diabetes. He spent free hours pressing an ear up against the scratchy radio listening to soccer matches. When his devout wife switched to an evangelical station, he didn't complain, just sat there, hands folded, smiling like a benign Buddha.

Don José worked, loosely speaking, as a librarian at the local high school, but only three mornings a week, riding there on the family bicycle. Otherwise, he kept himself busy building a cinderblock wall around his property.

Invited to visit the high school library, I found José sitting there, nervously tapping on his desk, his notebook filled with doodles of voluptuous women and muscular young men. He seemed to have lost any lingering enthusiasm for reading or for introducing young people to its myriad pleasures. The book collection looked meager and unorganized. Several students sat at tables laboriously copying from an ancient encyclopedia. José ignored them except to shush their whispers.

One student, asking my help with English homework, surprised me with her antiquated text, circa 1940, with its dog-eared pages and stilted sample letters: "Dear Madam, In reply to yours of October 5..." Starved for reading matter myself, I combed the shelves and found one book in English, *Factors in Modern History,* published in 1907 by the British Historical Society. I donated several of my own English-language books to the library.

Public school staff belonged to a powerful union, making them virtually impossible to fire, allowing retirement at age 60 with most of their $400 to $500 monthly salary intact. José, a library-science graduate with the only college degree in this town of one thousand souls, considered his tenure secure.

In contrast, wife Lilian, also a public servant and union member, did much more than work-to-rule. She was a real dynamo, a workaholic fueled by a holy fire. Sturdy and solid, with thick gray hair and strong gentle hands, she put in overtime as a nurse at the local health center while also running her own busy household. She had studied nursing for only 10 months, so was largely self-taught. A fervent evangelical, she believed God had called her to her vocation. Long after hours, emergency patients knocked on her door, interrupting her supper and even her slumbers.

Lilian attended church services four nights a week, dragging along her resistant children, while her husband stayed home listening to the radio uninterrupted. She prayed aloud morning and night, her sotto-voice chants drifting over the transom between rooms, and she never failed to say grace both before and after meals, "Lord, thank you for this food and for bringing *Doña Barbarita* to our home. Forgive us for accepting payment for her stay." Every morning, she gave a peck on the cheek to each family member, including me.

The house had only two bedrooms, but according to PC rules, I required a private room, so 11-year-old daughter Aarely doubled up with her parents. A teenage son, named for his father, attended school in Teguc, staying with his grandmother there, but coming home on weekends with the grandmother. An older married foster daughter with three children often showed up as well. Was it fair for me to occupy one whole bedroom and make everyone else sleep in the other? I decided not.

Privacy was impossible anyway because the house, built by father José, had only five-foot interior partitions, about his own stature. Windows had no glass, only wooden shutters, with bedroom door openings hung with flowered curtains flapping in the breeze. Snoring and coughing echoed over the transom. So I invited Aarely to share "my" room and the son as well on weekends—it was *their* room, after all. We wouldn't tell Peace Corps.

Three fellow trainees—assigned elsewhere—came down with dengue, so I hung up my mosquito net from a rope looped over the rafters. "There's no dengue here," Lilian protested, "or malaria either. I'm a nurse, so I should know."

On the living-room wall hung a picture identical to one decorating my Valle home, four dogs playing cards. Both places also displayed a print inspired by da Vinci's Last Supper and a portrait of Jack and Bobby Kennedy under an undulating American flag.

Out back were a latrine and wooden shower stall (with chamber pots for use inside), also an outdoor *pila*—an open cement water storage tank filled up periodically via a faucet. Bathing involved taking a pail of water into the shower stall to pour over your body. A fish named Nemo swam around the pila, gobbling up mosquito larvae, also worms that Aarely found. Armenians rejected chlorinated water for fear of killing their pet fish. Again, I insisted on drinking only boiled water.

Chickens wandered around the backyard, eating table scraps and occasional handfuls of corn. Junior, part coyote, part German shepherd, chased off weasels stalking new chicks. But since he was fed mostly on tortilla dough, he often greedily devoured unhatched eggs. Routinely scolded for eating eggs, he never attacked the chickens themselves.

Meals typically consisted of the basics: rice, tortillas, and beans, the latter kept bubbling day and night over a corner woodstove. Yucca was another diet staple. Sometimes we had bananas in one of their many incarnations: *bananos, butucos, guineos, plátanos*—all with appropriately masculine names, some fatter, some sweeter, some tiny, some bright orange inside. Big starchy plantains were fried or boiled and Lilian made also a drink of mashed bananas, piously preventing its fermentation into alcohol.

We varied the menu with a slice of avocado, homemade cheese, or a green watery vine-grown vegetable called *pataste*. Occasionally, we ate eggs and rarely chicken, both from our own backyard. Lilian would deftly chop off a chicken's head with a kitchen knife amid a clucking flurry of protests from the remaining flock. She never picked a pesky rooster shattering the pre-dawn hours, no, always a scrawny hen. I found it hard to swallow meat from a known animal.

For me, the family obtained milk, which they would never drink themselves. Aarely carried a pan of milk every morning, fresh and warm from a neighbor's cow, and boiled it to pour over my corn flakes. I preferred that to the *rosquillas*—crisp homemade corn biscuits—dissolved in coffee and imbibed by the rest of the family. Once, we baked whole-wheat bread in tin cans in the outdoor adobe oven. On Sundays, Lilian would make *dulce de leche,* a carmel-like dessert of boiled, sweetened milk.

Curious neighbors soon streamed by to meet me, including next-door neighbor Julita, her pet hen, Pollita (Chicken Little), tucked under her arm. Julita shared her cup of coffee with Pollita, who would dip her beak into her owner's spoon.

"She loves her morning coffee," Julita chuckled.

At 91, Julita was a rare never-married Honduran. She had kept house for a diplomatic family, who took her to Cuba before the revolution and later to Miami, where she'd picked up a few English words, proudly recited for my approval: "toast, flower, hat, shoes."

Julita had retired to the wood-frame house her parents had built over a century before, still without running water, but with electric wiring now haphazardly installed. At night, we heard her TV turned up full blast. Julita rented out rooms to teachers who left for Teguc on weekends, providing her with her only income. On a makeshift altar in her bedroom, she often lit votive candles, a worrisome fire risk in her very combustible dwelling.

Life Spring

Reluctantly, I succumbed to Lilian's entreaties to attend her church, Manantial de Vida (Life Spring): "Doña Barbarita, please, your immortal soul is at stake." Her children, always obliged to attend, shot me sympathetic looks.

In the pastor's small living room, thirty congregants raised up their hands with eyes tightly shut, and began swaying and chanting together, their voices rising to a crescendo amplified by the massive sound system. Was it impolite to cover my ears?

During the three-hour service, I cringed at the pastor's description of "the haughty Pope sitting on his golden throne in distant Rome, surrounded by incense and graven images" (murmurs of disapproval here from the audience), while "right here in humble Nueva Armenia, wily Satan with his sharp horns tempts us daily."

Certainly no idols were visible in this austere living room, nothing but a bare lectern and a keyboard and an amplifier set in front of folding chairs, though amplification was hardly necessary. Lilian prayed aloud that her husband and I would eventually see the light. All arms reached heavenward as dark heads nodded in unison.

The sermon touted the Bible as the literal word of God. Those doubting the world's creation in seven days, or daring to question the existence of the perpetual fires of Hell, would soon find out otherwise "amid great writhing and gnashing of teeth." The preacher punctuated each sentence with *Bendito sea el Señor* (Praised be the Lord), to which the congregants replied either *aleluya* or *amén.*

I dared not mention my Catholic allegiance, though Lilian knew I attended Sunday Mass at the cathedral, where parishioners crowded into old movie theater seats instead of pews. There, young people played guitars and everyone sang without benefit of amplification, thank goodness! I often helped two young nuns with recreational activities for a youth group. These nuns belonged to an exclusively Honduran social service order, Messengers of the Immaculate. Both were from poor villages, with their religious vocations offering a rare avenue of upward mobility. The nuns promoted long-term breastfeeding and the rhythm method for family planning, arguing that while these tactics might fail in individual cases, they still reduced the birthrate overall.

On another evening, Lilian again persuaded me to accompany her to services. This time, she became especially ecstatic, almost levitating, with eyes closed, arms outstretched, tears streaming down both cheeks. Everyone seemed to be chanting a different prayer, getting louder and louder. Then a hush fell as the pastor approached the lectern. Short and pudgy, wearing a white shirt and tight-fitting black suit, he looked like an overstuffed penguin. He cleared his throat. Adopting a confidential tone, he recounted his personal history of heart attacks and consultations with a city specialist. He reported praying daily for a cure, casting out the anti-Christ, and surrendering himself totally to God's will. Paraphrasing Isaiah, he asked himself, "Why should I be stricken any more?"

"And then, my brothers and sisters," he intoned softly, fixing a piercing gaze on his rapt audience, "because I had faith, because I *believed,* I was *cured.*" His voice rose, "Glory to God, a miracle! Yes! Yes!"

"Christ Jesus be praised," his followers replied.

"Oh, yes, dear ones, I WAS CURED!!" he shouted.

He clutched at his chest for dramatic effect. Or was it only for effect? Then he crumpled to the floor.

After a moment's stunned silence, the pastor's children rushed to his side. Lilian pulled out her stethoscope and placed it over his heart, her practiced hand grasping the stricken man's wrist. She motioned to have him lifted him onto a couch. There she pronounced that he had suffered another heart attack. I urged hospitalization, but he protested weakly that no transport was available to the hospital, located several hours away. Besides, he preferred complete surrender to God's will.

Knowing that aspirin can help heart conditions, I dashed outside, looking for a shop still open. At a convenience store lit by kerosene lamps, I bought a dozen aspirins wrapped in plastic and rushed back to the house, where the pastor swallowed two with a glass of water. Lilian stayed with him throughout the night, praying, giving him aspirins, and checking his heart rate and blood pressure. At dawn, the pastor sat up, still shaky, announcing, "The good Lord has once more saved my life."

Be Prepared

I was blown away by my fellow health trainees, all in their twenties, who made up for lack of experience with touching sincerity and boundless energy. Ordered to speak Spanish, even among ourselves, some wrote down and laboriously rehearsed each sentence. But to become effective health educators, they would need to learn to speak spontaneously. I held back deliberately during group sessions, letting others take the lead, but found the training increasingly elementary, making me impatient to be out on my own.

I joined the others in recreational activities such as dancing (frowned on by Lilian), hiking, and swimming in the nearby river, where reckless boys swung from overhead tree limbs and dove off towering rocks. Townspeople brought soap down to the river to bathe fully clothed, washing body and clothing together. My colleagues invited me along on excursions, treating me as a peer. But out on the soccer field, I remained strictly on the sidelines, cheering them on. And I began easing out of the mother role.

Fellow trainees expressed shock at the blatant infidelity of Honduran husbands (Americans, perhaps no more faithful, are more circumspect). They also gagged at seeing a nose-blowing hand being wiped off on a shirt.

Or a woman sucking snot out of her kid's nose (you expected Kleenex?) or swiping a finger across food oozing out of a toddler's mouth to slurp it up herself. When mothers chewed meat first before passing it on to their toddlers, even I got a little queasy.

Mother and child formed a symbiotic unit, eating and sleeping together. Our idea of separate beds, much less bedrooms, for small children would have been considered cruel and unnatural. Until babies could walk, they were tied onto their mothers by a cloth sling—in front for a small, frequently nursing infant, in back for a bigger one.

We practiced giving community health presentations to always receptive audiences. I drafted four pre-teen girls to help me prepare a talk on nutrition. Using my scissors and markers, they eagerly created color cutouts of healthful fruits and vegetables. Shy at first, they even helped me give the talk: "Oranges have vitamin C, carrots, vitamin A."

We also assisted a family constructing a latrine, creating a cement base on the advice of a neighbor who warned that his latrine's wooden floor had given way, landing his brother in the muck. Another neighbor advised putting a lid on the seat after a child fell through the open hole down to a murky death.

For the same family, we built an "improved woodstove" *(fogón mejorado)* vented outside, with a compact burning chamber using less wood than old-style stoves. This stove was made of local clay, plant fiber, tree sap, and horse manure (ick)—the same sturdy mixture used to build the family's house. Hadn't I said I wanted to get my hands dirty?

One morning, we caught a bus going south to visit the public hospital in San Lorenzo, a bigger town. Electric fans barely stirred the oppressive heat inside the maternity ward, where we offered encouragement to women in labor. No nurses were around, so I told a mother lying on her back to turn on her side to avoid compressing the baby's umbilical cord. Several trainees appeared uneasy. I was the only one who had actually given birth and also coached my daughter Melanie when her daughter was born.

Fluent Spanish speakers paired up with novices to hitchhike to outlying villages. Another trainee and I visited a rural midwife, a *partera,* in a town with no electricity and water only from a communal well. This midwife, Verandera, had given birth to 11 children, the first two with a midwife, the last nine without, cutting the cord and bathing each newborn by herself. All her babies had survived. She lamented that midwifery was a dying art, since many women now preferred going to hospitals.

"I absolutely forbid my daughters and daughters-in-law to set foot inside a hospital and I've personally delivered all my 25 grandchildren," she boasted. "Only lost three babies over the years, one with a big head, the other with a split spine," references to hydrocephaly and spina bifida, conditions attributable to folic acid insufficiency. Folic acid, iron, and vitamin supplements were available to pregnant women at the local health center, but those particular babies' fathers had forbidden their wives to go there. The third infant victim was born prematurely to a woman nursing another child at the time.

We also met Calixto, a rare male midwife. Verandera confided later that he'd never been asked to deliver a baby because of his reputation for having prurient interests: "He just wants to see women's privates." Oh dear. Unfortunately, his own wife stopped having babies before he took up midwifery. Another villager, a father of ten, Verandera solemnly declared, became both effeminate and impotent after undergoing a vasectomy.

We health trainees decided to offer a two-day workshop for midwives, announced by radio and through notes sent out on buses. Dozens of village women arrived after walking hours with small children in tow, arranging to stay overnight with friends in town. We provided a free daily lunch, a major enticement, and folks helped themselves to extra portions to take home. Even Calixto, the shunned male midwife, showed up, demonstrating good theoretical knowledge that he'd never had a chance to practice. No one sat next to him.

The workshop's climax was an ersatz delivery, with a male trainee playing a pregnant woman with a doll stuffed up under his shirt. In fractured Spanish, he complained vociferously about labor pains as two real-life midwives acted as coaches. After pulling out the doll, they delivered the fake placenta and cut the cord with a clean razor blade as other midwives in the audience tittered and a little girl looked on in puzzled amazement, asking, "Can men have babies?"

A nurse's aide from the health center bragged loudly about how many deliveries she'd performed. "Yes, and she killed my sister through her carelessness," a woman next to me whispered, "although the baby survived."

We passed out official certificates of participation and thanked folks for coming, though if we'd taught them anything new, they were unlikely to change their ways.

Next, we all traveled to the village of Platanal to help out with a baby weigh-in, where the weight of each child under 2 was charted monthly. Mothers whose babies failed to gain were singled out for public scolding by the nurse in charge. I noticed that all underweight children were either bottle-fed or girls. Vitamin drops were poured into empty film canisters for each mother to take home. As we left, we shook the limp hands of the few fathers present, barely touching palms, as is customary. Then we women trainees embraced each mother's forearms in the characteristic female greeting and farewell.

I soon announced a talk for pregnant women about incorporating soy into the diet, emphasizing its protein content, evoking loud protests from men about being excluded, as well as from my nun friends and elderly Julita, who lamented, "You know the baby train has forever passed me by."

So I opened up the invitation. An overflow crowd of 40 showed up. Since soy takes so long to cook, I'd already cooked it beforehand. Helped by audience volunteers, I drained off the cloudy liquid, adding sugar and grated cinnamon bark to flavor a beverage passed around in paper cups. Soymilk spoils without refrigeration, but keeps longer than cow's milk. In a hand grinder, we then mixed the softened soy beans with salt, spices, chopped tomatoes, and onions to make "soy sausage," samples of which were passed around on paper napkins, which, like the cups, were bought in advance—since neither was on hand in local venues.

Everyone enjoyed sampling the snacks, but no one actually grew soy or could afford to buy it. I suggested an alternative, *gandúl,* officially *Cajanus cajan* or pigeon peas, requiring no cultivation and little water. Cooking either soy or gandúl would consume precious firewood, but could be set alongside regular beans always left simmering on the fire.

July 4, 2000

On July 4, along with other expatriate Americans, we trainees were invited to a U.S.-embassy-sponsored celebration being held at Zamorano, an agricultural college located an hour outside of Tegucigalpa. Not only were both national flags prominently displayed and both anthems played over and over, but celebrants were feted with patriotic speeches, a scout color guard, raffles, bake sales, horseback riding, a petting zoo, face-painting, sack races, and costumed cartoon characters. At card tables, chatty American housewives sold cookbooks or took book-group sign-ups. I talked with a few tow-headed kids, all attending English-language schools. It was as though the suburbia of my childhood had been plunked down right here in Honduras. While the embassy endeavored to provide a taste of home, we trainees felt awkwardly out-of-place, viewing our fellow Americans as foreigners, feeling we'd already crossed over.

The college occupied extensive acreage filled with flora from all over the world, including some odd-looking spikey trees originally from Finland. It was founded in 1940 by American Wilson Popenoe, whose traditional New England-style home, converted into a museum, was shown by eager student guides practicing their English. The current director was also an American, but all other staff were from Latin America. Students came from several countries, one-third were women, and most had won scholarships. The curriculum included environmental science, agronomy, food service, and agricultural engineering. A store on the premises sold students' organic produce. Atop a tall tower, like that found on many U.S. campuses, students took turns watching out for forest fires. The college had its own fire-fighting equipment and also worked with community groups on agricultural projects. Since my visit there, I've always had a soft spot for Zamorano's fund-raising appeals.

On our return, our recycled yellow school bus broke down, this one bearing the name Alexandria School District—located just across the river from my hometown of Washington, DC. These buses were all fitted with diesel engines, diesel fuel being cheaper here. Importing even such a used vehicle would be enormously expensive because of duties equal to its cash value. Our driver managed to fix a broken connection between the fuel pedal and engine with wire and twine; then, amid honking Teguc traffic, the bus stopped again. So the driver walked several blocks to the station to get another, as his mother owned the company.

Parting

Two weeks before our scheduled departure from Armenia, while the others were in Spanish class, I noticed a funeral crowd leaving the cathedral. Among the mourners was the lone male midwife, who signaled me to follow to the cemetery. At the gravesite, the family opened the hinged coffin lid, displaying only the deceased's tranquil-looking face. He'd been shot in a robbery of his vegetable cart in Teguc and was just 27, the same age as my son when he died. Several women fell to the ground, emitting loud laments. I expressed condolences and left quickly, tears streaming down my face for both the dead man and my own son.

Before leaving Armenia, we trainees were invited to two school celebrations. One was held on July 14, the Day of Honduranity, at the high school, where a girl wearing high-heeled boots, hotpants, and corn-rowed hair wiggled suggestively in imitation of a well-known singer. Female teachers, all dolled up in frilly low-cut dresses, clapped vigorously. How could they get away with such suggestive outfits when we were admonished to always dress modestly? Then a boy in low-slung baggy pants (alas, that fashion had invaded Honduras), mimicked the exaggerated mannerisms of a certain Latin crooner, kneeling on the floor, eyes closed, both arms flung out dramatically, clutching a mike tightly in one hand.

On July 20, an elementary-school program honored Chief Lempira, the native chieftain whose visage adorns the one-lempira bill. Lempira was said to have been killed in 1516 by Spaniards who tricked him into signing a phony peace treaty. Students with painted faces wearing banana leaves and chicken feathers shot homemade arrows into the air, winning a retaliatory victory against the Spaniards in their lively re-enactment.

At our own farewell get-together, our future site assignments were given out, advising us where we'd be living and working for the next two years. We held our breath as, one-by-one, names and places were matched up. My site, El Triunfo, appeared on a map at the country's southernmost tip, a few kilometers from the Nicaraguan border. Lilian expressed condolences, as she'd done her practicum there years before and had almost expired from the heat. I would be the first health volunteer in El Triunfo, the only one in our group without a volunteer predecessor. Here in Armenia, we had already practiced much of what we'd be doing for the next two years, so we felt prepared.

On our last evening together, we gathered around a wooden cross set on a rocky hillside overlooking the town below. Aarely, my host "sister," accompanied me. One trainee passed out name bracelets she'd made for each of us. Others brought along guitars, but no one played. In perfect silence, we lay on our backs looking up at the stars, enjoying each other's final presence in the cool night air.

Lilian and Aarely sobbed openly when I left. My own eyes welled up with tears

Boy offering dead iguanas for sale

Horses outnumber vehicles in Nueva Armenia

Armenia's open-air jail, allowing food to be passed through to inmates

Doña Julita holding her pet hen Pollita

Bananas for sale in all shapes and sizes

Family with
improved wood
stove

Author assisting
with baby weigh-in

CHAPTER 4:
CLOSING RANKS

Now 45 and Counting

Returning to Santa Lucía to finish training, we compared notes with colleagues in other sectors, feeling more confident now about having something to offer our communities. But two of our original training group had silently dropped out, so only 47 remained. We regarded these defections almost as betrayals. Then two more quit, leaving 45. We closed ranks against further losses.

While the usual tour of duty is 27 months, we learned that extensions are possible. Five consecutive years is the absolute maximum a PCV can stay in any one country, partly to prevent the Kurtz phenomenon, named for the ivory merchant in Conrad's *Heart of Darkness* who went berserk after too many years in Africa. Marines were once reportedly sent in to forcibly remove a volunteer from Guatemala after his five years were up. At this early stage, none of us expected to fall prey to Kurtz. We would count ourselves lucky to survive the full 27 months.

Family Health

In Santa Lucía, I teamed up with another health trainee to discuss prenatal nutrition and breast-feeding with women from surrounding villages, one with twins suckling simultaneously. Not only were some items on our recommended diet unavailable or too costly, but—as our audience soon revealed—folk beliefs interfered as well. Some pregnant women admitted to deliberately restricting food intake to produce a smaller baby for easier delivery. Others avoided avocados for fear of meconium aspiration (a newborn breathing in greenish feces). Others refused prenatal iron, believing it stained their face.

For 40 days after giving birth, following a supposed biblical tradition, a mother didn't bathe, change clothes, or go outside, and consumed only tortillas and cheese. She wrapped her infant's abdomen to keep the navel inverted, a useless practice increasing infection risk. In challenging such beliefs, we sought support from local health center personnel, who needed some convincing themselves. We urged exclusive breastfeeding for the first six months—no bottles for cost and hygienic reasons—and encouraged it up to age 2, since, once weaned, children rarely touched milk again.

Our talk proved so popular that we promised to give another on birth control. This time, to warm up, women pulled written health tips out of a plastic bag, each reading hers aloud or asking for help if she couldn't read. Nuggets of basic health advice were accompanied by instructions to sing, dance, recite a poem, or imitate a cow or rooster, prompting embarrassed giggles all around. We then discussed available contraceptive methods. As for ideal family size, the consensus was four kids, though no one actually wanted any more than the two or three she already had. The lone exception had only one child.

Hurricane Survivors

A field trip to shelters for those displaced by Hurricane Mitch in 1998 revealed that now, two years later, thousands still remained homeless. When disaster strikes, international agencies rush in, but interest quickly wanes, leaving victims to their fate. A few displaced families were building new homes in designated areas with their own labor using donated materials. But these locales were hard to reach, so progress was slow. In one new community I visited, Cuidad España, cinderblock homes were going up, but 22 km. from Tegucigalpa. For car-less folks working in the city, this was quite inconvenient.

Hurricane shelter El Molino 2, a makeshift barracks in Teguc providing one room per family, still had 150 families in residence. Four latrines were located at one end of the building, a communal water pila at the other. For cooking, families set up charcoal braziers outdoors. Mitch survivor Doña Clara grumbled that while shelter residents were labeled freeloaders, it wasn't easy living with her family of seven in just one room with obnoxious neighbors on either side. "We can't put down roots in a temporary shelter," she lamented.

A Crisis Corps volunteer, working at the shelter after service in Ecuador, described the Honduran bureaucracy as maddeningly complex. (Volunteers with Crisis Corps—now called Peace Corps Response—serve several months after completing regular tours.)

Ethnic Diversity

While North Americans often hold a monochromatic view of Latinos, Honduras is a multihued nation. Among visitors to our classroom were a group of Garífunas, Afro-Hondurans whose ancestors escaped from a shipwrecked slave ship two centuries earlier and who still maintained their unique language and customs. More recently, English-speaking blacks had migrated from neighboring Caribbean islands and, like Garífunas, were mostly fishermen.

We also met Lenca Indians from western Honduras, from the same tribe as martyred Chief Lempira. They had lost their original language and religion, but conserved traditional communal farming methods and their own judicial system. The Pech were Mayan descendants living near the Copán ruins of my early childhood, now reviving their language through bilingual education, while the neighboring Tolupanes, still speaking Tol, honored eclipses of the sun and moon and remained hunter-gatherers.

Misquitos living in eastern Honduras and Nicaragua, descendants of South American Chibchas, formed the largest indigenous group, numbering some 200,000, considering themselves one people despite national boundaries. Together, they fiercely resisted the Sandinistas, supported by U.S. Native Americans. Due to early missionary efforts, Misquitos belonged to the Moravian church. Never conquered by Spain, they had maintained their original language and customs, living mostly by hunting and fishing and, increasingly, in their remote jungle habitat, through transporting illegal drugs.

Women washing at communal pila

Garífunas engaging in a traditional dance

CHAPTER 5:
SITE UNSEEN

Honduran Counterpart

S oon we were on the road again, this time to visit our designated future sites. As my bus descended into the central valley, a rush of hot air smacked me full in the face: welcome to southern Honduras.

My local counterpart, Dr. Loni (not her real name) met me at her family home in the provincial seat, Choluteca, a city of 125,000. Just out of medical school, she was now performing a year of community service at the public health center in my assigned town, El Triunfo, located an hour and a half away by bus. Loni was 27, the same age as my younger daughter, looking like a teenager with her pixy smile, dark curly hair, and slender frame. We spent the night with her family before going on to El Triunfo the following day.

Their small three-bedroom dwelling was fully occupied. One bedroom was used exclusively as a storeroom and there was no kitchen because meals were eaten at the family's nearby market shop. In the living room, Loni's father had strung up a hammock, his vantage point for directing household activities and his sleeping place at night. There was a cramped toilet-bathing room with a floor drain, a pila for bathing and scooping up water to flush the toilet, and an adjoining sink for washing clothes and dishes.

Sharing the home were Loni's parents, youngest sister, brother, a female first cousin (whom the brother would later marry, provoking a temporary family rift), and the children of the oldest sister, then living in Teguc with her new husband. Another sister, a university student, came home on weekends. I slept in the girls' windowless bedroom, with its overhead electric fan and bureau drawers bearing generic labels: "blouses," "skirts," "slacks," "underwear." Loni explained that the girls shared clothes since all wore the same size. Loni and her younger sister occupied one of two double beds there, I the other, both with no mattresses or sheets, just woven mesh to let in air from underneath. Not what I'd call comfy, but I did have a pillow. Too hot anyway for sheets.

Loni's mother slept in the adjoining bedroom with her granddaughter in a single bed. The brother shared a bed with his little nephew in the same room, with the cousin sleeping on the floor. I suspected the family of playing musical beds on my account, but they insisted otherwise.

Loni pulled me aside to whisper: "Mamá sleeps apart from Papi ever since discovering his 'other woman' and two daughters living nearby." Loni had met the daughters, now teenagers. When her dad asked me if I knew about his second family, I nodded, quickly changing the subject, not really anxious to hear more.

In the ample back patio, Loni's enterprising father had built a U-shaped cinderblock structure divided into 18 rooms, each rented out to an entire family. Because these families lived so crowded inside, they cooked and hung their washing outside in the patio, letting their kids play together in one giant extended family, reminding me of communal life inside Havana's *solares*—once-opulent mansions now divided into one-room apartments around original courtyards.

The backyard patio was also home to a vegetable garden, numerous chickens including annoying crowing roosters, three talking parrots, two dogs with new puppies, and a calico cat, not to mention a brown monkey with a fierce, toothy grin swinging frantically from branch to branch. Soon, the poor monkey would be electrocuted by an overhead wire.

El Regalón

Several blocks away at the Cholu market, Loni's parents, Doña Lula and Don Agustín, ran a shop called El Regalón. *Regalo* is a gift, *regalón*, a big giveaway. The shop, open from 5 am to 7 pm every day except Christmas, boasted a refrigerator, freezer, and propane stove. For sale were hot coffee, tortillas, honey from the family's own hives, fried chicken, eggs, plastic bags of purified water, sodas (poured into a plastic bag, served with a straw), toilet paper, candy, chips, and soap. At night, metal shutters were pulled down and padlocked to safeguard the premises.

All household members were up, bathed, and dressed by 4:30 am, before the day's intense heat began. Agustín rode the grandchildren to the shop on a bicycle, a parrot clutching onto each handlebar, while the others walked. Everyone ate breakfast there before Grandpa transported the kids to school by bike.

Agustín took up his shop post in a hammock, directing affairs from there, just like at home. His wife, wiping her hands on a smudged apron, did the cooking, standing on her feet all day, helped by her youngest daughter, a high-school student. The parents rarely conversed, but had an effective working relationship, an unspoken understanding about running the household and business. At day's end, Loni's father pocketed the earnings.

I hesitated to eat off a table thick with flies and from dishes rinsed only in cold water. Stray dogs and cats hovered hungrily and a fetid gutter gave off an awful stench. As a physician, how could Loni tolerate such conditions? Growing up there, she probably didn't even notice. I contented myself with a plain tortilla while others scooped up scrambled eggs from a common pan.

Site Visit

Buses didn't travel directly from Choluteca to El Triunfo, only via Guasaule on the Nicaraguan border, where an open market did a bustling business. At the border, in addition to idling buses belching diesel fumes, the road was filled with horseback riders—mostly youngsters mounted bareback—and bicycle transports shaded by colorful umbrellas. For a modest fee, the latter wheeled travelers across the lengthy border bridge, saving them a walk under scorching sun.

On both sides of the frontier, officials laboriously checked the papers of waiting trailer trucks, all bearing faded U.S. logos. Roaming chickens, pigs, and emaciated dogs added to the general hubbub. Duty-free stores on either side accepted only dollars. Nicaraguan stores were larger and cheaper, Loni explained, so it took a wink or bribe for Honduran customs officials to let purchases go through duty-free.

At Guasaule, Loni and I changed buses. As we finally entered El Triunfo, The Triumph, it hardly looked triumphant, actually rather drab and dusty, lacking the characteristic charm of most Honduran towns. I gazed longingly at nearby hills, wondering if it was any cooler up there. Down at a muddy river, women were washing clothes, spreading them out on tree branches to dry. A female trio squatted at water's edge—daughter, mother, grandmother—carefully picking nits out of each other's hair.

Because of the flat terrain, I could ride a bike, which I planned to purchase soon, along with an electric fan and a hammock. I'd already bought a straw hat, so my face was shaded as I explored the town on foot. That first day, my sandals shredded completely on the rocky roads. I got tougher sandals, Tevas, next time.

A prominent local landmark, looking starkly out-of-place, was the brand new Mormon temple, a classic white, sharp-spired structure surrounded by a high, chain-link fence. Standing outside were two young Mormon missionaries wearing short-sleeved white shirts and ties. I introduced myself; one was from Utah but spoke rather good Spanish, the other was Guatemalan. From that day forward, I never saw anyone entering or exiting that temple, but surely the presence of such an imposing structure indicated some Latter Day Saints in town.

El Triunfo proper had about 6,500 residents, with 25,000 in the entire municipality, this, according to Mayor Doña Dilma, a former elementary school teacher, on whom I paid a courtesy call. Her three-year-old granddaughter, wearing a lacy pink dress and shiny patent-leather shoes, was busy opening drawers and playing hide-and-seek under her desk.

When the mayor's four-year term expired, she vowed to quit elective office because, "People around here always expect handouts, never lifting a finger to help themselves."

At the local health center where Loni worked, I met director Doctora Jeanette, a stocky, fortyish mother of three whose husband was a customs agent at the border. Loni later confided that this physician colleague, earning over $1,000 a month (a good salary), was often absent, but had shown up today just to meet me. Jeanette's salary would eventually increase to $1,500. I also met another physician assigned to the center, one of Cuba's excess doctors who had left his family behind for two years of service here.

Dozens of breastfeeding women sat waiting on wooden benches inside, where several nurses and aides were on duty, one mopping the floor whenever kids peed or spilled something. Roaming dogs snapped up most dropped food. When sick children started sharing water bottles, I hastily warned mothers not to spreads germs that way, but they exchanged puzzled looks; who was this bossy stranger anyway?

The health center had no computer, typewriter, or phone, and often lacked electricity and running water. A latrine for patients stood out back, while staff used a bucket-flushed toilet inside. In addition to consultation rooms, there was a small lab with a refrigerator, a pharmacy dispensing free medications as available, and a maternity room with three plastic-covered beds, a scale for weighing newborns, and a nurse on 24-hour duty.

Dr. Jeanette explained that with great effort, she had obtained a diesel generator, needed at night when the center's electricity went out and women were giving birth. "On the very first night," she shrugged, "with the watchman and nurse both on duty, it disappeared. So now we're back to using flashlights once again."

Loni, wearing a white cotton medical coat and stethoscope around her neck, let me sit in on her consults. I asked each patient's permission to observe. Most simply described their symptoms, while Loni scribbled out prescriptions for the pharmacy. With children, she was more thorough, looking into ears and down throats and listening with her stethoscope. Occasionally she took an adult's blood pressure or temperature. Despite the waiting crowd, she carefully explained to patients what their symptoms meant, their medication's name, and what it should accomplish.

Suddenly, Loni was called to attend to a series of emergencies: a young man with two fingers partially blown off by a firecracker, another whose hand got mangled in a sugarcane press, and a third who'd slashed his knee with a machete. She administered numbing injections before suturing, using plastic gloves wherever blood flowed, disposing of needles in a plastic container to be burned later. Donning gloves myself, I handed her necessary items.

AIDS, I soon learned, was no hypothetical threat here, but a full-blown reality. Whole families had perished, husband, wife, and baby in that order. Loni said all pregnant women were tested for HIV, with those turning up positive given AZT to prevent *in utero* transmission and advised not to breastfeed. The center also ran an anonymous support group for HIV-positive patients.

After the center closed its doors in mid-afternoon, Loni introduced me to an evangelical development organization, Corcride, where I filled up my water bottle from a large cooler bearing a company logo. When I asked the secretary where to obtain bottled water locally, she remarked, "Oh, not around here. We just fill this up from the tap." Too late, I'd already drunk my fill.

So, no bottled water. Who ate off the dishes before we did? Did a fly land on my food? Unseen germs everywhere. Honduran kids under five often die of diarrhea, but survivors acquire immunities and rarely become ill in adulthood, certainly not as often as supersensitive, greenhorn PC volunteers.

During my three-day visit to El Triunfo, Loni let me share her bed and camp out in her room, rented from Doña Reina, a native *triunfeña* whose name means "Queen." Loni's private medical shingle hung on the street just outside her room, which also doubled as her after-hours clinic, complete with plastic-covered examination table and glass case of medicines and instruments. She charged patients $2 per visit, plus medication costs.

Her landlady, living in another part of the house, sold used clothing and packaged snacks, rented out rooms, and operated a half-dozen noisy old-style video-game machines featuring Atari, Mario Brothers, and racing cars. But, according to Loni, her main income came from remittances sent by two sons living in the States.

Although Reina was a widow in her late fifties with five adult offspring, she had adopted an infant, now age 6, Reinita (Little Queen), nicknamed Solei. The girl, decades younger than her mother's other children, had not been told she was adopted, although everyone else knew and anyone might spill the beans. Nor did Solei know that a playmate, Carolina, who closely resembled her, was actually her twin being raised by a neighbor. The girls told me proudly that they shared a birthday.

Honduran women past childbearing age often cared for grandkids, fussing over them more than with their own children. There were few empty nests, and pity the poor woman who had never borne a child.

Sleepless in Triunfo

That first night in El Triunfo, probably from the unpurified water, I'm suddenly overcome by severe nausea and cling to the outside of the bed for quicker access to the backyard latrine. Loni gives me an antibiotic to swallow with a plastic bag of purified water. We try settling down.

But whenever we doze off, our slumbers are interrupted by frantic pounding on the front door. With health-center staff away at a workshop, no one is on night duty there. Most patients request medications and injections; Hondurans place great faith in shots.

At midnight, after dozing off once again, we hear a car honking insistently outside. A female voice calls "*¡auxilio!*" (help!). In her nightgown, Loni opens the door just as a car pulls away. Silhouetted alone in the moonlight is a panic-stricken pregnant teenager. "I'm only 16, it's my first baby," she sobs.

Asked whether the car will come back to get her, the girl nods and collapses into Loni's arms. Has she had any prenatal care? "No."

Loni lays the mother-to-be on her examination table and tells her the delivery will cost 1,000 lempiras, about $70. The girl nods again, then shrieks as a contraction hits. Loni instructs her to push, "not from your chest, but from down below, as with a bowel movement." She addresses this unknown girl with the familiar *you*.

Reina, hearing the commotion, appears, also in her nightgown. My stomach is still churning, so I'm in no shape to help. Loni soon notices that the baby's umbilical cord is wrapped around the neck, a potentially fatal development. She needs to birth this infant quickly. To speed things along, she performs an episiotomy without anesthetic and is soon able to unwrap the cord and deliver a healthy 6-pound, squalling baby girl. The cries awaken Reina's little daughter, who calls out, *"Mami, mami."* "I'm coming," Reina shouts, as the child falls back to sleep.

The young mother is exhausted and blood is spattered everywhere. But she manages a smile as the cleaned-up, swaddled infant is placed in her arms and immediately begins to suckle. She asks to take the placenta home to bury in a corner of her house for good luck. Loni places the placenta in a plastic bag and writes out the birth certificate, asking the new mother's name. Soon the car returns and the fee is paid. By now it's 7 am, time to report to work at the health center.

Walking over to the center together, seeking islands of shade, Loni and I run into Seth (a pseudonym), a blond, personable 25-year-old water-and-sanitation trainee, destined to be my sitemate. He and I agree to join forces to look for places to live, while Loni promises to help us after work. She must be tired, I know I am, but she manages to look perky.

Seth seems slightly disoriented and is still shaky in Spanish, so I show him around town. Later, accompanied by Loni, Seth decides to rent a room from Reina, her own landlady, and I agree to rent from Reina's mother, Doña Marina, half a block away. Loni suggests we each pay 500 lempiras a month, about $35, which sounds reasonable enough.

Seth looks forward to having Loni and Reina cook for him over their outdoor fire and, as an only child, to joining a larger family. Raised in a Sikh religion in northern New England, he's a vegetarian who consumes milk and cheese, but no eggs, which he has never tried, nor has he ever tasted meat. Reina agrees that's no problem. The household also includes a cute 14-year-old maid who flirts with an unresponsive Seth. He doesn't mind the other tenants coming and going or the constant clang of video machines. In fact, he rather enjoys all the noise and activity.

Already, Loni and Seth seem taken with each other, though back in Choluteca, I'd met Loni's suitor, an itinerant, guitar-playing textbook salesman. At 27, she's almost over the hill in terms of marriage-ability. She's confessed to being lukewarm about her boyfriend, but still anxious to marry and start a family. Now has she shifted her sights to Seth? I suggest this to Seth, who is younger and pronounces her way out of his league. Vigilant Reina makes sure they're never alone unsupervised. If they go out for a walk together, she always sends little Solei along as chaperone.

The Indomitable *Doña Marina*

My own future landlady, Doña Marina, age 85 and widowed, raised eight children alone. Three, including Reina, still live in town and two have already died, a tragedy we share. She's lost track of the number of her grandchildren, at least 50, along with about 20 great-grandchildren. If that's typical, no wonder the Honduran population is exploding!

Unlike most elderly Hondurans, Marina stubbornly refuses to reside with any of her offspring, preferring to stay in her own home with her maid, a sullen 15-year-old. Unlike the atmosphere at Reina's, Marina's household is wonderfully quiet. Marina also has one of the few working telephones in town, as well as a TV and a refrigerator. Marina warns, "Hondutel [the phone company] listens in on calls," but I really don't care.

I'm enchanted by Doña Marina's ample shaded patio, complete with beckoning hammock, its ambience marred only by a pen full of loudly clucking chickens. At sunset, Marina assures me, they will all roost quietly in bushes inside their enclosure. Banana, coconut, cashew, guava, mango, and lemon trees provide a sheltering canopy from the relentless daytime sun and a flame tree's scarlet blossoms flutter to the ground, creating a glowing carpet.

A tree bearing small, semi-sour yellow fruits called *nances* has attracted a noisy flock of wild parakeets. They chirp and dart, swooping down to attack the highest branches. Marina orders her maid to scare them off, so the barefoot teenager climbs up the tree like a monkey, carrying a can filled with stones. She strings the can over an upper branch, which Marina rattles from below, but to little effect. Marina's three pet parakeets, perched on a low-hanging branch, look skyward, chattering loudly. Their wings are clipped, so they can't join their high-flying fellows.

Meanwhile, a small black dog begins digging furiously, hunting some underground animal, his body soon swallowed up by the hole, only back legs and wagging tail left outside. A single plump black and white duck waddles regally past. Reclining in the hammock, I'm fascinated by these amusing creatures. Then a large green parrot named Veroica begins squawking distinctly overhead, *bueno, bueno, bueno, Doña Bárbara, Doña Bárbara,* followed by fiendish laughter. For heavens sake, did I actually hear my name?! Marina, sitting outside on a plastic chair, nods slyly, admitting that she's taught the bird my name. How can I resist this place? Despite the dirt and noise beyond the gate, this will be my sanctuary.

Marina then invites me to sample a special dish, boiled white flowers (daylilies?) clustered on a stalk, slightly crunchy and bittersweet. Afterward, I join her in the living room to say the rosary with a group of ladies who gather regularly to pray and sing hymns. Next, we all sip tea together. Consulting her tea leaves for omens, Marina predicts, "You and I are destined to get along well." She seems to be trying to cement the deal, but I'm already won over.

Like many older Hondurans, octogenarian Marina has jet-black hair with few strands of gray. Her hearing isn't keen, but her eyesight is still good and her mind remains alert. Tall and big-boned, she sighs often when recounting her life's many travails, which she appears actually to have survived rather well. After dark, I see Marina and her maid standing outside together, stirring iron cooking pots over a brightly burning blaze, their faces illuminated in the firelight. The lines in Marina's face, exaggerated by shadows, give her an eerily wise look.

The room I agree to rent is located across the enclosed patio from the main house, near a locked metal gate. I immediately make a mental note to replace the 10-watt light bulb with a stronger one. While I'll be sharing the household latrine, pila, and outdoor cooking fire, my sleeping quarters will be somewhat private. Adjacent to my room is a storeroom full of old furniture fronting on the street, providing a further buffer.

I notice Marina padlocking her bedroom door in the main house, slipping the key into her apron pocket, a sign her maid is not completely trustworthy. I will need a padlock for my own door. Finding no latrine seat, I plan to buy one.

A big advantage of living at Doña Marina's is her telephone, helping me feel less cut-off. Only 60 phones were allocated to this municipality when the system was installed 10 years earlier, with none added since. Marina was one of the original lucky few. The solar-powered municipal phone system's delicate technology will end up crashing frequently, knocking out service for weeks, especially during the rainy season. Still, a sometimes phone is better than none. While cellphones have become increasingly popular because of scarce fixed phones, El Triunfo has no reception tower and the same will be true in my second Honduran home, La Esperanza.

Loni's family's business, open every day except Christmas

Reina's daughter, left, and her secret twin dressed as Indians

Doña Marina and her young maid cooking together

Rice, a Honduran diet staple

CHAPTER 6:
READY OR NOT!

The Graduates

In August 2000, our formal swearing-in ceremony was held at the U.S. ambassador's residence, a lush seven-acre hillside estate complete with swimming pool, tennis courts, and panoramic city view. Genial Cuban-born Ambassador Frank Almaguer, of course, spoke flawless Spanish. He and his wife had met as PC volunteers in Belize in the 1960s, making him our especially strong advocate.

The ambassador briefed us on the history of U.S.-Honduran relations, including the failed efforts of an infamous American, William Walker, to take over Central America in the 1850s. U.S. banana companies dominated in the 20th century and still remained important economically, although some plantations destroyed by Hurricane Mitch would never be restored. Besides 20 U.S. federal agencies working in Honduras, Almaguer said there were numerous American NGOs (non-governmental organizations) and private firms, including *maquilas* or clothing factories employing 130,000 workers, mostly women. Although maquilas were often accused of offering substandard wages, he argued that American companies actually treated workers better than enterprises from Taiwan and elsewhere, and also paid Honduran taxes, unlike others. Honduran maquila wages averaged $125 per month, half those in Mexico, so Mexican companies were moving in. "Honduras missed out on the 20th century," the ambassador declared, "Now we must make sure it doesn't miss out on the 21st."

Our graduation ceremony was held outdoors. After both national anthems were played, we all solemnly raised our right hand before promising to faithfully complete two years of service—an emotional moment, followed by laughter, tears, and hugs all around.

Right after the ceremony, before moving to El Triunfo, I made a final shopping trip to downtown Teguc. At the cathedral square, I wove among familiar barking dogs, flocking pigeons, child food vendors, curbside preachers, impromptu magicians, sword-swallowers, fire-eaters, and zapped-out glue-sniffing youths crumpled on the sidewalk—all combining in a seething caldron of sensory overload, like in a medieval bazaar. I almost tripped over a legless beggar of indeterminate gender, propelled along on a skateboard, stretching out a claw-like hand in a scene worthy of Graham Greene.

Almaguer, a Clinton appointee, soon would be replaced by Larry Palmer, also a former PCV who had served in Liberia. A dark-complexioned African American with a starkly contrasting white afro, speaking quite credible Spanish, Palmer proved to be warm, funny, and equally devoted to our cause, visiting several volunteers with our country director.

On Duty 24/7

The chaff had been separated from the grain; training was over; it now was survival of the fittest. As PCVs, we would be on duty 24/7, serving as full-time goodwill ambassadors. We were told never to leave our sites without notifying the powers-that-be. Any trips to the northern Caribbean islands for scuba diving, as well as out of the country, would be charged against our few allotted vacation days. We would be required to fill out quarterly reports and program directors in Teguc would visit periodically to monitor our progress.

For living expenses, we'd be granted a monthly lempira allowance equivalent to $200 to cover everything: rent, food, clothing, transportation, postage, phone calls, Internet, and toiletries. While less than a Honduran professional earned, it was more than a laborer's wage. Vacation costs, whether to neighboring countries or back to the States, were not contemplated in this monthly allowance. Our parents would have to cover any such expenses, we were told. Already volunteers were frantically e-mailing home for extra money, yet the whole idea was to approximate the local lifestyle.

I felt relieved to finally be through with training and leaving Luis and Irma's house in Valle, where family relations had become increasingly tense.

Welcome, *Bienvenida*

After swearing-in, we made our separate ways to our designated sites. Dragging along my two heavy suitcases, I met a fellow volunteer in Teguc, where we'd agreed to catch a southbound bus together. Determined to travel in comfort, we bought reserved luxury seats. The fare was triple that of "chicken buses," the converted yellow school buses permitting chickens on board where seats meant for elementary-age kids required adults to sit knees-to-chin, but the extra cost proved well worthwhile: ample seats, air conditioning, refreshments, and even a Sean Connery flick on an overhead screen. Our non-stop trip, Teguc to Cholu, took only 2 hours, half that of an ordinary bus. For my final lap, I had to transfer to a chicken bus, as the luxury bus stopped there.

Each chicken bus had a driver and a faretaker, the latter a preteen or teenage apprentice. Sometimes out on rural roads, the driver let the young faretaker take the wheel to practice driving. Both were employed by the bus owner, who trusted them to hand over the entire fare collection.

I noticed that whenever a bus passed through jurisdictions forbidding standing passengers, they'd all squat down to avoid detection. Sometimes, police would stop a bus, make everyone get out and show ID, pat down the men, and search luggage without explanation. A tattooed volunteer of Puerto Rican descent reported being questioned about gang ties until he flashed his Peace Corps ID. Whenever a bus was stopped, standees had to get off to wait for the next one to come along. This happened to me first on my way to El Triunfo to report for duty.

I eventually arrived with all my gear intact, looking around for Marina's house after being dropped off on Triunfo's main thoroughfare with my suitcases. Although it was August and still officially the rainy season, the ground was dry, the dirt roads deeply rutted. Dust, noxious diesel fumes from passing trucks, and smoke from burning trash, along with oppressive heat, immediately assailed my lungs. Putrid odors filled my nostrils. It was easily 100° F, but townspeople walking along, some shaded by umbrellas, didn't look particularly distressed.

I plopped down briefly on a rock to catch my breath, with my sunglasses steaming up, clothes clinging, perspiration stinging my eyes. I peered up and down, trying to imagine lasting two years in this dismal place, much less accomplishing anything useful. To stay hydrated, I took a swig from my water bottle, now warm as tea. "What am I doing here?" I asked myself. Perhaps I'd be home by Christmas after all.

I soon banished that intrusive thought as folks converged to greet me, appearing genuinely thrilled to see me. "*Bienvenida*, welcome," I heard on every side. Men hoisted up my suitcases to carry to Marina's. Children grabbed my sweaty hands to walk with me, surprisingly trusting. A few begged for dollars, but I couldn't start handing out money. I did give each child a piece of hard candy always carried in my pocket.

Home Sweet Home

I was home at last! My new accommodations were spare, but adequate. Imitating my Armenia family, I had a 5-foot partition installed to separate the living from the sleeping area, but the whole space was no bigger than 12 by 20 feet, smaller than my bedroom back in DC. The single window had wooden shutters and metal mesh, but no glass. A four-inch gap between the exterior walls and tile roof allowed ample air flow, like camping out, but on a year-round basis. I needed furniture, especially a bed. I made a list: oil lamp, padlock, washbasins, chamber pot, woven floor mats.

Seth and I took the bus together to the border, each bringing back a standing electric fan. We ordered beds from a local furniture maker plying his trade in a sawdust-covered back yard where several apprentices wielded diesel-powered saws, while others hand-carved ornate patterns into the wood. I also ordered a desk and chair.

Meanwhile, I slept on a mattress on the floor. Until my bed was finished, I didn't install mosquito netting, enduring frequent bites on wrists and ankles. Geckos slithered across the walls, emitting loud nighttime chatter, but making little dent in the bug population. Bats too swirled around at night, entering through the ceiling opening. Weary of bat droppings, I hung up garlic cloves and a crucifix on the advice of townspeople and, surprisingly, the bat dive-bombing diminished. When it was time to install the mosquito net, the next hurdle was finding nails. I bought several hand-made ones, pounding them in with a rock.

Soon, my little place was organized and furnished, as cozy as possible in a place where bats and other critters enjoyed free range. One night, a scorpion crawled under my net, first pinching, then stinging me. I leapt out of bed, flipping on my flashlight just as it slithered away. I endured a painful abdominal welt for days.

My room was situated several yards away from the main house, which Marina shared with Teresa, her maid, a position that would see several incumbents during my stay. Entrance to the compound was either through a padlocked gate or the main house, with guests screened via a peephole.

Marina rose daily at 5 am. By the time I got up at 6, Teresa had already emptied Marina's chamber pot, lit the outdoor cooking fire, ground corn, and made tortillas. For hygienic reasons, I avoided eating with my housemates, flipping my own tortillas on an iron griddle heated over glowing kindling. Teresa laughed at my oddly shaped tortillas, showing me how to rotate my palms in opposite directions to make them round. Because of my high blood pressure, I took a ladle of beans out of the common pot before salt was added.

Triunfo's open market offered slim pickings: rice, onions, tomatoes, dried fish, and ghastly looking strips of raw beef hung in the open air, swarming with flies swatted away by a girl wielding a palm frond. I rarely eat meat anyway. I bought four eggs and a can of sardines marked in English "Not for sale." Five bananas cost only 10 U.S. cents, but I ended up passing them out to hungry kids before reaching home. Later, I found a giant watermelon, which I carried over to Reina's house to share.

Doña Marina's compound provided me with a welcome status, sense of belonging, and margin of safety. But the loyalty cut both ways, preventing me from ever moving elsewhere lest she suffer a huge loss of face. I also had to live with virtually no privacy.

Marina generously allowed neighbors into her yard to pick lemons, including a bare-foot, gap-toothed wizened lady, who, after peeking curiously into my abode and noticing an empty hammock in one corner, begged me to take her in, "I'll cook for you, wash your clothes, clean house," she vowed. Thanking her kindly for her offer, I said there really wasn't room.

"But I don't take up much room, I'm small; I'll even sleep on the floor," she pleaded. I remained hard-hearted, though I did give her some spare clothing. After months of sharing intimate space with host families, I felt like actress Greta Garbo, "I just *vant* to be alone."

Here, as elsewhere, people often asked me to take them back to the States, promising to become my slave for life. I didn't need a slave and repeatedly confessed to having no special influence with U.S. authorities.

Besides, I'd come to help them improve their lives right here at home.

Not long after I moved in, Marina hired a small boy to chop down a fruit tree impinging on her roof. I dashed outside in protest, fearing the boy might cut his leg, also because the tree provided such lovely shade. Marina said not to worry—she'd stick branches into the ground and water them until they took root, something that actually happened, giving her several small trees instead of one big one.

Water for bathing and washing clothes flowed into the outdoor pila from an overhanging faucet, always left open, since it never overflowed. The municipality turned on its own spigots every few days, supplying pilas all over town. To bathe, you simply poured a basin of water over your body onto the concrete floor. Pila etiquette decreed that your hand should never touch the water, only a basin or bowl. Cool bathing water proved quite refreshing. I got over feeling embarrassed walking outside to the pila wrapped only in a towel. I soon learned that soap and toilet paper left behind would immediately vanish, so I always carried them with me.

The pila had a built-in concrete washboard where clothes were scrubbed back and forth. After being rinsed and wrung out, they were hung up on tree branches or overhead lines to dry. I learned the hard way to scare off flying birds and keep watch over drying clothes to prevent theft.

Pila water was obviously impure, though most residents drank it. Purified water was sold only in small, sealed plastic bags bitten open and sucked from one corner, not an efficient source. I first boiled mine, but it soon clouded over. Then I tried chlorine, but found it hard to calculate the right amount. Finally, Seth and I traveled to Choluteca, each investing in a returnable 3-gallon plastic jug of purified water hauled back by bus.

During brief absences from my room, my perfume, Swiss Army knife, and transistor radio disappeared. I began locking my outside padlock even when going to the latrine. Later, following the antics of a bright-green lizard with gold and orange markings, I spied my radio stashed behind a bush. Upon questioning, Teresa—to whom I'd given clothes, jewelry, and new flipflops—pleaded innocence. Ungrateful girl! Who else could it have been?

Marina's black dog Luchi, her constant companion, was fed, like most dogs, only on raw tortilla dough and table scraps, including discarded chicken and fish bones. One day, Luchi expired from an intestinal obstruction and was buried in a corner of the patio. Marina grieved daily until receiving a little black puppy sired by Luchi, almost his spitting image. Holding the pup protectively on her lap, she murmured, "The Lord took away my Luchi but gave me his little son instead."

Sleepless Again

Three nights running, sleep once more eludes me. The reason: a celebration in honor of the town's patron, Santa Rosa de Lima. The municipal park, half a block from Marina's house, serves as the epicenter of this annual round-the-clock festival. Crowds from surrounding villages arrive by foot, bus, donkey, and bike to drink, gamble, eat cotton candy, shoot darts and pool, ride the diesel-powered merry-go-round, dance to ear-splitting music, and explode firecrackers—all in the open air, like a medieval village fair giving serfs a respite from their daily drudgery.

Teresa gets all dolled up to attend the festivities along with Reina's maid. Though still sore about the theft of my belongings, I give Teresa a pair of sunglasses, which she dons for the occasion. That first night, I try sleeping with a pillow over my ear, but to no avail. About midnight, a downpour begins, which I fervently pray will dampen the revelers' spirits, but no such luck. I soon notice water running down my walls. Marina later promises to have the roof fixed when the rains stop.

On the second night of revelry, La Bomba (The Bomb) is repeated ad nauseum. Bomba dancers wiggle suggestively in a Latin version of the Hokey Pokey. I toss and turn in my bed to the pulsating rhythm. About 4 am, buses begin honking their horns to pick up party-goers.

By night three, I'm exhausted, vowing to be out-of-town this time next year and also for Valentine's Day, reputedly an even bigger and better celebration. At 11 pm on this third night, the electricity mercifully goes out and the music stops abruptly. Blessed quiet! But, alas, a generator is brought in and, if anything, the sound ratchets up a few decibels.

On the final morning, all booths and rides are packed away. Wandering sows trailed by piglets feast on left-over garbage.

My "Son" Seth

From the start, townspeople automatically assumed Seth was my son. Whenever I ventured out alone, they'd rush over, pointing, "He went that way." No need to even say his name. Seth and I did often get together to savor a *chocobanana,* a tasty frozen banana dipped in melted chocolate.

Due to his Sikh upbringing and curiosity about other faiths, Seth soon started reading the Bible in Spanish. He also invited the two young Mormon missionaries, mysteriously called "elders," to give him weekly religion lessons in English, which I joined. They were delighted to learn about my Mormon cousins, but surprised I'd remained unconverted. Seth and I kept an open mind, but were not won over. After a month, because of Catholic landlady Reina's vigorous objections, Seth was forced to stop the lessons.

On my 63rd birthday, Seth joined Marina's family to throw me a surprise party, complete with colorfully frosted cake. As I stood admiring the pink homemade lettering, *Feliz Cumpleaños,* strong hands grabbed me from behind and smashed my face down into the frosting. I came up looking like a Santa Claus gargoyle! Everyone laughed except me. Had I known about this Honduran custom, I'd have kept a safer distance.

I soon became a sounding board for personal problems, something Seth escaped by being young and not yet fluent in Spanish. Women beckoned through open doorways, offering me cups of sweetened coffee before pouring out their woes. "My husband left." "Mamá wets the bed." "My neighbor stole my only bra." "I think my daughter's pregnant."

Who was I, a seer with magical powers? No, just a willing ear, all they really needed. They trusted me to keep their confidences.

Waste Not, Want Not

Always a pack-rat, I was now truly in my element. Folks actually vied for my used bottles and empty cans. I washed out and recycled old plastic bags. No string or rubber band went to waste. Whenever acrid fumes alerted me to burning plastic, I urged reuse of plastic containers.

Since Triunfo had no trash collection, Seth and I debated disposal of our own refuse, which, however minimal, still had to go somewhere. I tried burying mine, which ended up being too much work. Marina just burned hers or threw it out into the street. Vegetable and fruit peels provided good livestock fodder, but non-biodegradables accumulated. Seth asked everyone to pitch in money for garbage collection, an idea that went nowhere.

Whenever departing volunteers discarded clothes on the "free" shelf of the PC headquarters lounge in Teguc, I scooped them up to pass along, trying not to seem like Lady Bountiful. Reina and Marina always argued about who got first pick: "Me first." "No, me first."

"I only give stuff to poor people," Marina piously insisted. "I *am* a poor person," Reina declared, admitting to selling the donated items. I ended up passing clothes out to them just as they came out of my bag, first to Marina, then to Reina, to trade later if they liked. I saw then how giveaways could become problematic and why Peace Corps warned against them.

Out and About

One blistering Sunday morning, Seth and I hitched a pickup ride to a soccer match in neighboring Las Conchas. Seth joined the Triunfo soccer team riding out back in the open rear compartment while I remained in front with the driver, Jesús, a sugar plantation foreman. When he mentioned that his 8-year-old daughter never grew, I recommended that she be checked for parasites.

Jesús, boasting that his new truck had cost the equivalent of $1,500, asked, "Confidentially, what would it sell for in the States?" Noting the non-functioning dashboard, cracked windshield, and missing door handles, I hedged, imagining that he'd actually have to *pay* a junkyard to haul it away: "Circumstances are so different, it's hard to say, but congratulations on your purchase."

After dropping off the soccer players, Jesús eagerly introduced me to his "other woman." Young and pretty, she stood smiling in an open doorway, waiting to hand a naked infant over to Dad.

After polite greetings, I left that little family to look for the local health center, which was closed on a Sunday. Asking around, I met volunteer health guardian Marixa, mother of four children, three with harelip and cleft palate. She confided that she was now getting contraceptive shots to prevent further pregnancies. The town had no electricity, so it was completely dark inside her dirt-floor, windowless abode where we sat drinking coffee.

Marixa invited me to attend Mass with her and her baby, leaving the other children home alone. She instructed her 7-year-old daughter to sweep and straighten up the house in her absence.

The service at the local Catholic chapel—not a full-fledged Mass— was conducted by a lay delegate-of-the-word; all eyes focused on me as we entered. The modest wooden structure was decorated with colored-paper cutouts and congregants sang lustily, accompanied by a toy guitar. A white mongrel dog wandered aimlessly among the pews. In his sermon, the delegate admonished parishioners to "improve our nation and our community so people won't want to leave."

Because I'd run out of drinking water, I returned to see if the soccer game was over yet. But it was a double-header with Seth still in the outfield.

I'm ideologically opposed to the worldwide soft-drink invasion; however, since dehydration threatened, I plunked down coins for a lukewarm coke poured into a plastic bag and bit a hole in one corner to drink.

Next morning, Seth and I traveled to Choluteca to retrieve our monthly allowance from our bank accounts there. On the bus, an oily-voiced patent medicine salesman persuaded several passengers to buy his special lotion—sold in recycled film canisters— reputed to cure dandruff, eczema, acne, wrinkles, and boils.

In Choluteca, with the bank delightfully air-conditioned, we didn't mind standing in line with several fellow volunteers. When the electricity suddenly shut off, a generator was fired up to run the computers, but not the A/C. The enclosed space now became stifling. We ended up spending practically the whole day in the city. Perspiring heavily, we never needed a bathroom—fortunately, since none was available.

At a Cholu clothing store, we fell into conversation with the proprietor, Frank, a short, middle-aged guy self-taught in Arabic, English, French, and German, all without ever having left Honduras. His English was really quite good and, between customers, he read Gide and Goethe in the original. He spoke to his toddler son exclusively in German to teach him the language. Eager to argue fine points of philosophy with us, he added an intellectual dimension sorely lacking in our new life.

Next, we waited our turn at a cybercafe, also generator-powered, as the electricity was still out. E-mail there seemed to come from outer space, unconnected to our local world. I got a message that Doug, a left-leaning activist from Chicago who had once consulted me about a trip to Cuba, had been arrested in Havana for asking too many questions. Two weeks later, I was relieved to learn of his release after pressure from the U.S. Interests Section. Another message reported that Dolores Huerta, a leader of the United Farm Workers, was seriously ill. Back in the 1960s in Sacramento, my then-husband and I were active supporters of Cesar Chavez and the UFW. Dolores, usually pregnant (she had 11 children), slept many a night on our living-room couch while devoting her days to lobbying. Slight, unadorned, wearing an old brown coat, she was the antithesis of the standard lobbyist disbursing cash and making backroom deals. And in her earnest, persistent, and soft-spoken way, she was often more effective.

Back in Triunfo, on Marina's doorstep, I found a sobbing urchin dripping snot and tears into a basin of tortillas. Bigger boys had stolen the 10 lempiras already collected from selling his mother's tortillas, so now Mom would beat him. I handed him 10 lempiras and a piece of candy, but refused any tortillas, which looked rather unappetizing at that point.

Almost Vegetarian

In rural Honduras, meat is a rare luxury, reserved only for guests and special occasions. American carnivores shopping in pristine supermarkets may regard meat as a commodity, neatly packaged and labeled, far removed from animals on the hoof. But here, my latent vegetarian tendencies were reinforced one Saturday afternoon when I heard loud gurgling outside my window, looking out in time to see a cow collapse, felled with apparent gusto by a blood-spattered man wielding an ax. When I protested in horror, Marina hastened to explain that the animal had broken a leg and needed to be put out of her misery. What about the misery of getting her head chopped off?

With evident relish, the man then hacked up the body with a machete. Marina and a toddler great-grandson watched in grim fascination as gobs of black and red blood spurted out and a sickening sweetness filled the air. Family members soon converged, piling bloody chunks of meat into pails. Raw scraps were thrown to Marina's wildly barking tied-up pup. Entrails were tossed into the street where roving dogs soon tore them apart, all except those kept aside for *mondongo,* tripe stew.

Later on, an adorable, frisky goat kid with pert, barely-emerging horns and a pointy beard was summarily butchered, again spattering blood everywhere. Killing chickens was more routine. I never saw a pig being killed, but Seth did. Its pitiful squeals sounded almost human. More reason to give up meat, especially in Honduras.

Author with U.S. Ambassador
Larry Palmer

Girl sweeping under open air meat market

Heads turn at author's entrance to village chapel

Backyard latrine

Village pulpería or convenience store selling snacks and sodas

CHAPTER 7:
CRIME AND PUNISHMENT

Does Crime Pay?

Just when I'd begun feeling really "at home," my resolve was again tested. Most Hondurans were warm and welcoming, but crime statistics proved to be more than abstract numbers. Several victims were personal acquaintances. Twenty-five years earlier, I'd felt quite safe in Honduras, even when traveling alone with my young children. Now, the country had the third highest incidence of violent crime in the hemisphere, right after Colombia and El Salvador. San Pedro Sula's murder rate was even higher than Mexico City's.

Why? Population growth, natural disasters, and the ever-expanding drug trade, as well as regional integration, allowing criminals and stolen goods to move easily across borders. Bank robberies had become commonplace, and armed guards at grocery and appliance stores made shoppers check purses at the door. Robbers sometimes dressed up as women to avoid screenings by hand-held metal detectors applied only to men.

Kidnappings of wealthy persons also surged. After paying a $150,000 ransom, the family of a prominent businessman found his body dumped on their doorstep. Five members of a Teguc family were murdered in their beds. Such crimes remained unsolved. Of the 12,000 Americans residing in Honduras, 17 were murdered the year before we arrived and four just a few weeks after, none of them tourists.

Only two policemen were assigned to El Triunfo, both uniformed and carrying pistols. One sat all day in the office, but with no phone. The second went out on foot patrol, or by bike if he could borrow one, since the police didn't even have a bicycle. A crudely-drawn checklist on the wall documented reported crimes. The rear of the one-room office contained a pair of cots where the two slept.

I once saw the two town cops making an arrest. One pointed a rifle at the teenage subject's chest while the other tied his hands together from behind. The suspect had a nasty bleeding head wound, so they marched him to the health center, where Loni stitched him up.

Houses in El Triunfo, though not out in the villages, had barred windows and heavy metal doors. Mom-and-pop stores passed goods out only through a tiny grate. I once opened Marina's front door to a man claiming to be her nephew. After entering, he demanded cash. She handed him 80 lempiras, shooing him quickly outside and locking the door behind him. Clutching at her chest, she warned me never, ever to let him in—he was a notorious thief. Days later, when the front door was left ajar, he entered once more. Again, Marina paid hush money and pushed him forcibly out, scolding her maid for leaving the door unlocked.

Vast income inequalities among Hondurans, as in the U.S., helped foster crime. Although most people were poor, the middle class was growing and a small wealthy elite resided in major cities. One evening in the upper hills of Teguc, a taxi dropped me off at the wrong address, a high-walled compound with several armed guards on duty. When the gate opened for a car, I glimpsed a hillside mansion with wide curving walkways illuminated by burning torches and heard strains of live music. An elegant lady emerging from a chauffeured limo noticed me standing there. I explained that I was lost. She pulled out her cellphone, dialed the number I gave, and, in perfect English, told my American hosts where to find me.

Several volunteers, though not harmed themselves, were quickly moved to new sites after gangs rampaged through their towns like Genghis Khan, robbing, raping, and killing in their wake.

Purse as Attractive Nuisance

One evening, I'm walking out of Cholu's bus terminal with sitemate Seth and Dr. Loni toward a waiting taxi, heading to a party, when, suddenly, a white T-shirt flashes past, pulling down my shoulder bag, knocking me flat. I black out briefly. Bystanders give chase, but the thief escapes. Opening my eyes, I taste dirt and lie there staring at the ground as sharp pains shoot throughout my body. Even breathing hurts. A lump rises on my forehead and my lips are bleeding. Seth helps me to my feet.

Loni escorts me to her parents' house, while Seth attends the party alone. I spend a painful, sleepless night, then travel by bus to the PC medical office in Teguc. No broken bones are found, but I'm mottled purple from head to toe. A front tooth is cracked, requiring a repair and root canal. Judging a purse to be an attractive nuisance, I don't bother to get another. At the medical office, I learn two other women in our group have also been robbed, one losing her purse, the other her watch. My DC friend's dire warning echoes, "Home by Christmas."

No, no, I can't quit yet, but I'm badly shaken. For once, I'm not sure I will actually stay the course. My kids are never far from my thoughts; what if I should die here without ever seeing them again? Subsequent events hardly prove reassuring.

Weeks later, at a cheap Teguc hotel, I walk in on two men holding pistols on the front-desk clerk. I back out quietly, hastening on to another establishment. There, I leave my room for a bite to eat. Upon my return, several items are missing, including personal documents I'd left behind to avoid being robbed out on the street. Fortunately, our passports are always kept under lock and key at the PC office. This particular story has a somewhat happy ending. Two weeks later, miles away, a woman finds my bankcard, Peace Corps ID, and photo negatives discarded on the sidewalk. She takes a bus all the way to PC headquarters—located in a converted mansion with no identifying signs—and turns everything in.

In Tegucigalpa one early morning, I come upon a naked man lying in the gutter. Is he alive or dead? Were his clothes stolen while he was drunk? Pedestrians step briskly over him. I cannot stop right then but soon return to find him gone.

Back in Choluteca, a guy sneaks up from behind and pulls the gold earrings from my ears, leaving the lobes bleeding slightly. I turn around just in time to see him running away barefoot.

One night in Teguc, Loni recounts being surrounded and relieved of her jewelry by a group of rowdy teens. When two boys seized her and threatened rape, she thought, "Eight years of medical school, now this." Luckily, she carried a bag of fried chicken that she offered, piece by piece, to her tormenters as she backed into a lighted street and haled a cab. Realizing her plight, the driver took off before she could even shut the door.

On another occasion, I'm walking between Loni and Seth when a scruffy-looking couple grabs them both. Fearless Loni, using the full force of her 105 lbs., first punches the boy, then the girl, yelling, "Shame on you! If we had any money, we'd give you some!"

She and Seth then run toward a group of spectators, while the outnumbered attackers flee. What Loni lacks in size, she makes up for in energy and fury.

Later, at a meeting of our South 5 group, a fellow volunteer invites anyone who has *never* been robbed to step forward. Only a handful do so.

Can Lightning Strike Twice?

Human agency is not the only threat to life and limb. Mother Nature can be equally ruthless. Mud sucking at my feet in a flash downpour rips the soles off my hardy Teva sandals. No wonder storms are called *tormentas.*

During the height of the rainy season, I arrive back in Triunfo after dark, on the last of a series of painfully slow buses. It's pitch-black, with the bus's single working headlight reflecting off pelting water. Strong winds batter the vehicle. We pass open doorways where kerosene lamps illuminate families gathered together inside. The electricity is out. The driver indicates my stop. In blinding rain, I step out into a rushing river of swirling branches, mud, and stones, struggling to wade across while shrinking from frequent lightning bursts. After arriving breathless at Marina's, drenched to the skin, I pound frantically over the roar of the wind until her maid finally opens the door, grinning in the candlelight at my soggy appearance.

The patio between the main house and my room is flooded and lightning is still flashing non-stop, so I opt to stay inside with Marina, her maid, and her grandson's wife and toddler daughter. We huddle in a living-room corner where the porous tile roof leaks less copiously, feeling both scared and exhilarated by the fearsome beauty of the howling storm.

I'm just rummaging around in my bag for a drier shirt when lightning strikes only inches away like a giant flashbulb, bathing all our frightened faces in a blinding glare. Then comes an ear-shattering thunderclap that vibrates our whole bodies. Stunned and frozen, scalps tingling, we're like white statues temporarily engraved on each other's retinas. It takes us an instant to even feel scared. We simultaneously burst out in nervous laughter.

"Thanks be to God," Marina murmurs piously, hands folded. "Thanks for what?" I wonder.

I shake my arms and legs to see if they're still attached. The child whimpers. I shine my flashlight on a handful of ash left on the tile floor. I've read that cosmic rays can trigger lightening strikes. It does seem that at that fateful moment, the whole cosmos conspired against us. The closeness of the hit troubles Marina, "Was that God's warning?"

My head is still spinning and my right ear feels stopped up, so I snap my fingers and shake my head as if trying to get water out, but my ear remains strangely silent. I was standing closest to the strike.

When the rain finally stops, bright stars appear above, slightly askew from their North American positions. I slog over to my room, leaving my muddy sandals outside, and climb into bed under the mosquito net, though my heart is still racing and a bright after-image appears whenever I shut my eyes. Is it worth risking life and limb to stay here?

By morning, the sun has dried up much of the water, but the whole town is still without power. When the electricity is finally restored, Marina's house remains dark. A jack-of-all-trades neighbor finds that her makeshift wiring, strung here and there like random clotheslines, is totally fried, while the zapped-out TV needs a replacement part. My battery re-charger is ruined as well, but my laptop, plugged into a circuit breaker, remains unscathed (I end up giving Marina the circuit breaker when I leave).

Hearing in my right ear is still muffled, as though I'm flying high. When phone service is restored, I call the PC medical office in Teguc to have my hearing checked. A Honduran audiologist explains that tiny cilia destroyed by loud noises never regenerate. His prognosis temporarily upsets me. My balance is also affected, always keeping me a bit off-kilter. Although my hearing recovers somewhat, it never returns to normal, especially at higher frequencies. Fortunately, my left ear compensates.

Being robbed and brushed by lightning hardly constitute my Peace Corps dream, but I'm still alive and kicking. Lightning can't strike twice, can it? I feel my late son Andrew urging me on, "Mom, don't give up yet."

Cellphone merchant on guard

CHAPTER 8:
SINK OR SWIM

Diving In

To regain my emotional equilibrium and promote my health agenda, I start going door-to-door, introducing myself. Everyone welcomes me. I cannot imagine arriving cold-turkey in small-town America and being embraced so quickly. Rural Hondurans seem almost too trusting of North Americans, perhaps allowing unscrupulous fellow countrymen to take advantage of them.

Among my new acquaintances is María Elena, a fiftyish mother of eight, who earns $100 a month providing local postal service. Twice a week, she takes a bus into Cholu to pick up our town's mail at the post office there. I'm easily her biggest customer. While others have to stop by her house to collect their mail, she sends one of her sons by bike to hand-deliver mine, a favor always repaid with a piece of fruit or candy. It's a rare week that I get no mail, though thankfully no junk mail for once. Doña Marina expresses astonishment at the volume. During my more than two years in El Triunfo, she receives a single piece of mail, a Mother's Day card from a grandson in the U.S.

Despite our chasm of differences in life experience and formal education, María Elena and I experience immediate rapport. Communication with most Honduran women is a one-way street: I empathize with them but they make little effort to return the favor. With María Elena, it's different; we're on the same wavelength. I'm used to having close women friends back in the States so now I have one here.

Getting There Is Half the Fun

If the medium is the message, so too the journey is integral to the destination. I spend a fair chunk of time just riding buses. How many friends do I first meet on buses; how many child passengers do I recruit for surgical brigades?

An air of anticipation characterizes bus trips. Thank goodness for buses traveling almost anywhere at modest cost, but if time is money, the real price is higher. When a bus breaks down, driver and faretaker slide underneath to make repairs, sometimes flagging down another bus to borrow tools. Flat tires are frequent occurrences, no wonder, with such threadbare treads! Forget about spares; instead, damaged tires are patched on the spot and pumped up manually, a tedious process.

Recycled school buses are often lovingly decorated with fringes and decals of religious figures or naked women, with giant blue eyes painted over the front windshield, not obscuring vision, but giving the bus a human face.

On one bus, the driver's 6-year-old son sits on his lap, gleefully turning the huge steering wheel. Afraid to watch, I start playing hide-and-seek with a cute toddler perched behind me on her father's lap, Ambrosia by name, dressed all in pink from hair bows to socks. It's sweltering, so I gently advise another father to unwrap his tightly bundled newborn, since tiny babies barely perspire and can become dangerously overheated. These fathers are unusual in traveling alone with their kids, a task normally falling to mothers. Ambrosia's dad asks me to take her to a rest-stop bathroom, obliging me to hold her up over the mucky latrine opening. A grimy 4-year-old girl squats on the floor nearby, selling sheets of toilet paper for one lempira each.

Another seatmate is a young lady selling make-up door-to-door. "But, you aren't wearing any make-up," I observe. "No," she replies, "I'm a Christian." Oh.

Other memorable seatmates include one toting three up-side-down live chickens, a boy with a squirming piglet peeking out of a blue baby blanket, and a pert well-dressed young lady with a live squirrel clinging to her shoulder. A few men enter the bus wearing pistols, an unsettling sight.

One rainy evening, a woman yells to the bus driver to stop; it's an emergency. She charges down the aisle, whacking her sobbing four-year-old over the head with her purse. He's soiled his pants. Outside, she cleans him up with wet grass and gets back on again, shoving him ahead roughly toward their seats. I mention how hard it must be for a little child to hold back on a call of nature, earning me her loud rebuke, *"Cochina* [pig], mind your own damn business!"

Once, a seatmate is describing her brother's unjust arrest, when, WOMP! an overhead metal suitcase lands on my arm, leaving a bleeding gash.

"Don't worry," a man across the aisle reassures me, hastening to bandage my arm, "I'm a doctor."

He turns out to be a Cuban doctor and the suitcase's owner. His dream is to open an acupuncture clinic in Teguc. Cuban volunteer physicians sometimes stay on to establish private practices here, abandoning their families left behind. But this guy plans to dutifully return to Cuba, then apply for official permission to emigrate. I'm skeptical. On trips to the island, I've met lifelong loyalists, confident their government will honor a legitimate request, only to be rudely shocked by a denial. One Cuban volunteer doctor, refused permission to return to Honduras, left by open boat, ending up jailed in the Caymans. I fear my earnest fellow passenger will never see Honduras again.

Endless hours of bus travel inevitably provoke hunger pangs. So, at each stop, grubby, shouting, barefoot food vendors, aged six or seven, swarm the aisles. One popular snack is a fluorescent-pink concoction of shredded coconut. Women often sell homemade *pinol*, a corn-based drink, served from a white paint bucket. The cup is dipped into the liquid, handed over to a customer, then rinsed in plain water for the next. As a health educator, should I intervene?

Patent medicine salesmen get on and off, loudly out-shouting each other. Neurovión tablets, touted to cure indigestion, nerves, headaches, and poor blood, sell pretty well. One vendor passes around a laminated sheet of ghastly color photos of suppurating ulcers, including on genitals, curable by his potion. Clowns and musicians entertain, then pass the hat. At one rest stop, I'm unnerved to see a legless beggar wearing a ragged Peace Corps T-shirt.

Buses may leave late, but if they fill up, they simply leave early. I sometimes find myself dashing for a bus while heavily laden, my lungs nearly bursting. Once, running after a pre-dawn bus, I yell frantically and the faretaker jumps off, grabs my bags and lifts me bodily onto the still-moving vehicle. Another time, I forget one of my bundles, then run after the departing bus shouting for it to halt, which it does.

Around El Triunfo, my bike provides my main transportation; "Look out, folks, I'm a fast-peddling granny-on-wheels" wearing my white safety helmet, clanging the handle-bar bell around blind corners. When stopping, I always click my lock into place after seeing Seth's bike stolen from right under our noses.

One sweltering Sunday afternoon, I ride out to cheer on the local soccer team. Leaning my bike up against a wall, I panic when two teenage boys start admiring it too loudly. Looping the metal cord through the frame and front wheel, I quickly snap the lock shut. When I feel around in my pocket for the tiny key, it's gone. Now I'm in a real fix. I have another key at home, a mile away. As the two boys smirk, I tote the bike awkwardly to the house of a known family, asking them to guard it while I go for the spare key. They could easily have cut the cord, but when I get back, the bike is still there.

El Norte

I'm standing out on the open road hitchhiking when a gringo offers me a ride. He once served as a PCV agronomist in Niger, but now works here on Salvation Army housing projects. Unlike us, he can supply needed building materials and deliver them in his pickup.

In our conversation en route, the agronomist and I agree that most Hondurans have conjured up a highly glamorized vision of our country. A minimum wage of more than $5 per *hour* sounds like heaven on earth. Here, they're lucky to earn that in a day. The almost slavish worship of everything gringo makes Hondurans doubt their own talents and achievements, fostering a collective inferiority complex and a hunger to go north instead of trying to improve things here at home. The idealization of North American life is fed by photos, letters, and remittances from migrants who send back highly exaggerated accounts, sometimes boldly posing in front of an employer's house or car, representing it as their own.

The mythology of 19th century America was "go west, young man," with the wild west representing mystery, opportunity, and excitement. For those living south of the border, *el norte* holds the same allure. And just as the pioneers suffered hardship and sometimes death in their westward journey, a similar fate often awaits northbound migrants—getting lost in the desert, being arrested and deported, or expiring inside sealed trailer trucks. Those making a river crossing must shed telltale wet clothes on the other side. But the risks make it all the more thrilling.

I'd met more than one Honduran who had lost a leg while leaping off a Mexican freight train and even helped one, 19-year-old Efraín, obtain a prosthesis. "I jumped off while being chased by police and fell under the wheels," he explained tearfully, "I just wanted to earn money to help my parents."

Young women engaging in prostitution to finance their journey north often returned home pregnant and in disgrace. I encountered one aptly called Ilusión; others were named Lesbia and Fantasía. They told me Mexican police stole all their money and even their shoes. Yet trying to cross the U.S. border is often a rite of passage. Even lone children attempt the trip. Those who manage to escape detection end up working for minimum wages, sleeping on the floor in shifts to save money, and always living in fear of discovery, while sending every spare dollar home via *la Western*, Western Union.

Joint Ventures

One morning, when reporting to the health center, I find Loni and Dr. Jeanette are away at a workshop. Only Cuban physician René and two nurses are on duty. I give René some surplus malaria pills to pass along. He acts quite reserved; is it because I'm American or simply his personality?

Finally we hit on a topic of conversation. The country's violent crime rate shocks Dr. René. Cuba is highly policed; moreover, ordinary Cubans have no access to firearms, while Hondurans can easily buy them or make their own. I help the good doctor suture up the wounds of a young man named Araña (Spider), slashed by a machete for trying to steal a bike. René just shakes his head; in Cuba, both slasher and robber would be arrested. The slasher's neighbors vociferously defend his attempts to kill the bicycle thief, considering the police hopelessly inept and inert.

René is among a bevy of Cuban physicians first sent to Honduras after Hurricane Mitch. Cuba, with its strong educational system, has excess doctors while Honduran doctors, after winning additional government concessions, have practically priced themselves out of the market. Honduran public-health doctors, for working a six-hour day, may earn up to a budget-busting (for Honduras) $2,500 monthly maximum, limiting the number of doctors the government can hire. The gap is filled by Cuban doctors, who receive free room-and-board, plus $300 per month, far above their $20 Cuban salary, a win-win situation. After completing his two years of service, René hopes for a promotion back home. He proves a good sport when Hondurans, with their penchant for name-calling, refer to him as *cubanito,* little Cuban, due to his short stature.

Dr. René warms up to me during our various joint missions: first going house-to-house dumping standing water where malaria and dengue mosquitoes breed, then on vaccination campaigns with a public-health driver. Since PCVs are forbidden to give shots for fear of needle-sticks, I serve only as record-keeper. Infants arrive for vaccinations all bathed, powdered, and dressed in their Sunday best. I always advise a mother to nurse her baby when the needle goes in and often have to steady a tearful teen during her infant's first shot.

I call out the names of women and teenage girls getting shots. Because of scarce vaccines, boys over 10 are immunized only against tetanus after a puncture wound, giving mothers and future mothers priority. Asked for her birth date, one girl shakes her head. "I can't remember that; I was only a baby."

Sometimes we travel up to higher elevations forested with pines not found in Triunfo's intensive heat. Wild flowers of every color spring up after rain—white, yellow, orange, pink, crimson, purple, and blue. Clouds of butterflies and scores of hummingbirds flit among the blossoms. Poinsettias start showing red leaves well before Christmas, often growing into tall trees.

Along the road, we pass pedestrians hauling sacks of corn and loads of firewood, women often carrying both an overhead basket and a baby behind. As a frequent hitchhiker myself, I persuade our driver to offer rides, though he grumbles about the delay of having passengers with bundles and children climbing in and out of the back compartment.

In the village of Perico, barefoot elementary-age kids stand around giggling as younger siblings sob at being injected. The joke then turns on them when most are grabbed to be updated on their own immunizations.

In the remote hamlet of Río Grande #1, I meet Blanca, a volunteer health guardian who, like the postmistress, becomes my good friend. A wiry, energetic widow with 10 children, Blanca cheerfully manages her hardscrabble life without running water or electricity. Intuitively intelligent, a quick study despite little schooling, she's someone I will come to trust unconditionally to promote good health practices.

At my urging, Blanca plants a vegetable garden to supplement the family's corn and bean crops that are harvested twice a year, first in July, again in November. Women attending my talks often promise to faithfully plant a garden, but Blanca actually follows through.

Later, her oldest son rises through army ranks to become an officer directing Honduran troops in Iraq. Blanca is immensely proud. Imagine the son of an impoverished peasant family being chosen for an international mission, although she confesses, "We pray nightly for his safe return."

Another vaccination foray takes Dr. René and me to La Cortesa, where folks gather at a local evangelical church bearing a prominent sign over the door proclaiming, "The doorway is narrow" *(La puerta es estrecha)*. It does look pretty narrow as women come spilling out from the gloomy interior, each accompanied by six, eight, or ten children. A mother of 15 boasts that each child performs regular chores, but I warn her to keep track of her tiniest daughter, seen leaning over dangerously to haul a heavy bucket out of a well. René, father of two, comments that Cubans have fewer kids.

In the village of San Juan, our notice sent ahead by bus apparently never arrived, so we commandeer boys as runners to bring kids in for vaccinations.

On the fourth day of our vaccination campaign, our driver suddenly announces, "No more fuel; time for a break." A nurse with us mutters that he always seems to have enough for driving around on personal errands. Two days later, he shows up again, ready for action. Where did he find fuel? "When I want it, I can get it," he chuckles.

René and I are left holding down the fort together whenever Honduran health workers go out on strike, further cementing our solidarity. In Cuba, strikes are forbidden. Although Honduran public employees enjoy above-average wages, retirement benefits, and job protection, they engage in frequent nationwide work stoppages. Health workers sometimes stay idle for weeks, disrupting the whole system. Teachers are even bolder, once striking for three solid months.

Health center director Dr. Jeanette asks me to start treating patients to lighten her own workload. I explain once again that my role is primarily educational. But I do agree to accompany her the following morning to Guasaule to take Pap smears. So, promptly at 7 am, I wait for her outside the health center, carrying my usual staples: a water bottle, sunscreen, and toilet paper. Soon, a food vendor points to a vehicle whizzing past with Jeanette and her husband inside. Next morning, I ask Jeanette why she left me behind. "Oh," she remarks nonchalantly, "I forgot."

After lightning knocks out the health center's electrical system, we hold a fund-raising raffle with a 500-lempira ($35) prize. Chances cost one lempira each. After enough are sold to cover both the cost of new wiring and the prize money, the lucky number will be drawn. I buy several chances, planning to donate my prize to the center if I win, which doesn't happen.

At monthly health center meetings, local volunteers from surrounding villages gather to offer rather fuzzy vital statistics: Let's see, Beatriz had twins about a week ago (boys? girls? one of each?); the old guy in the hollows died last night (of what?); a teenager in labor came looking for a midwife who returned to find the girl sitting on the latrine, her dead baby dropped below. Jeanette checks appropriate boxes on official reports.

Festive Send-Off

After completing her required year of social service, Loni immediately began searching for a paid public position, landing only a $400-a-month NGO job, supplemented by a private practice in her parents' home. She felt entitled to more after finishing medical school (Honduran medical students enter right out of high school). Eventually, she was hired to head up the public health center in Apacilagua, a remote rural village where I once visited her. With no electricity, its asthma nebulizer was operated with a foot pump; a tiny refrigerator to chill medications was powered by a solar panel.

Before Loni actually left El Triunfo, Reina threw her a farewell party, complete with colored lights, loud music, and spiked refreshments. Dr. Jeanette was a no-show, but the health center nurses came in force, and Loni's sisters arrived by bus from Cholu, bearing an unwieldy pot of *camarones de agua dulce,* fresh-water shrimp, that is, crayfish. Dr. René proved himself a tireless dancer.

A rare balmy evening breeze was blowing. Reina's maid, Alba, age 9, who slept on the kitchen floor with the dog, appeared all freshly washed and combed, wearing a clean, oversized dress that I'd given her. She usually evoked Oliver Twist, but now she looked positively radiant. With Reina's grapefruit trees hanging heavy with fruit, I sent Alba up to pick me a few, tasty as well as good for my blood pressure.

Everyone brought farewell gifts. Mine was practical: a folding umbrella. Others were a ceramic duck, a plastic rosary, and artificial flowers. Seth was especially sad to see Loni leave, as they'd become quite close, even under Reina's watchful eye. Loni's former book-salesman suitor was long gone.

When Dr. René's term ended, we held another big bash. Townspeople were genuinely sorry to see him leave. He took care to dance with every woman present, including me. After thanking us for our kind hospitality, he reported that he was taking his family a six-pack of Coca-cola, which they had never tried. Volunteer doctors may bring back items duty-free, so René also purchased a VCR with money a Miami Cuban friend of mine had sent. I was surprised when René asked our local parish priest to say a special Mass, since few Cubans are devout, though that changed somewhat after Pope John Paul II's 1998 visit.

René's replacement was Oscar, a fat middle-aged chain smoker, loudly touting his communist party membership and the superiority of all things Cuban. Shunned by patients and townspeople alike, he soon moved on to the Choluteca public hospital, where other Cuban doctors worked. "Good riddance" was the local reaction.

Falling Water

After two weeks of non-stop rain, Seth and I both hit a slump. Despite repairs, our roofs still leaked copiously, spreading damp and mold. We patched with duct tape, which didn't hold—Garrison Keillor, take note. The electricity was out most of the time, so no fans or lights, only candles and oil lamps. No phones either because the local system was solar-powered. Washed clothes never dried. Seth and I spent long evenings in rounds of cribbage, which I'd played as a teenager with my Dad.

Whenever it rained, Hondurans sighed, "Here comes the water."

I set out a barrel to collect roof run-off for washing clothes. Since Marina's patio had become a muddy swamp, I fashioned a raised brick patio and walkway. Frogs, crickets, beetles, and spiders all sought refuge inside my place. I poured Clorox on invading streams of ants, streets became rivers, and, although ducks supposedly like water, Marina's pet duck, Patita, hid out in the latrine. One dark night, forgetting that she lingered there, I recoiled when my bare toes touched something soft, warm, almost furry, soon realizing it was only Patita. Later, plump, trusting Patita mysteriously disappeared. Marina believed a neighbor had stolen and eaten her.

One day, skidding on wet ground, my bike collided with a bus. I fell face-down into a mud puddle, emerging covered with sticky goop from head-to-toe, my eyes staring out of a black mask. Kids pointed and smirked, "Loch Ness monster!" Grit even got into my teeth and I left a muddy trail crossing Marina's freshly mopped floor.

Then both Seth and I came down with intestinal upsets. We reverted to speaking English together, ignoring PC instructions to the contrary.

It didn't help that my late son's birthday fell during this season. After a lull in the downpour, I glimpsed a child's white coffin covered with flowers being carried by siblings singing plaintively in reedy voices, almost too much to bear.

Then rain pelted down even harder, accompanied by strong gusty winds, becoming Hurricane Keith. People panicked, remembering Hurricane Mitch. A major bridge washed out and supplies ran low. Feeling waterlogged and shut-in, I set out doggedly for Choluteca. Our bus halted at the washed-out bridge where an enterprising soul had rigged up a rickety footbridge, charging a dollar equivalent for each pedestrian crossing. On the other side, I caught another bus into Cholu, where the electricity was out as well.

Wading through ankle-deep water to the Choluteca post office to buy stamps, I found it closed for a military holiday. Drat! I feared the same at the bank, but it was open, a diesel generator operating the computers under flickering lights. There I ran into Kim, a fellow health volunteer. She recounted how the night before, while crossing a city street through muddy waters, she'd stepped into an unseen pothole right up to her neck. Her companions had managed to haul her out, completely soaked, unharmed except for a cut on her chin.

Excess water produced a bumper crop of mosquitoes, resulting in an upsurge in malaria and dengue. Another member of our volunteer group fell ill with dengue, but not the sometimes fatal hemorrhagic variety, often signaled by a sudden nosebleed. In late November, the rains stopped abruptly. Some trees flowered, while others shed their leaves. Grass soon turned yellow and dust churned up on roadways. Marina finally replaced my leaky roof tiles with corrugated asbestos. Was that safe?

While daytime temperatures in December and January were milder (high 80s) and the air was dry, we were shaken by a series of minor earthquakes. Neighboring El Salvador was devastated and adolescent boys went door-to-door with tin cans supposedly collecting for Salvadoran earthquake victims, but I had my doubts.

Although his roof no longer leaked, Seth became restless living at Reina's after Loni's departure. He moved into a cheaper, roomier apartment rented out by Miguelangelo and his wife. The only drawback was a large resident bat that left copious droppings and munched on left-over food. Seth fervently hoped he (or she) wouldn't start raising a family soon.

Seth's new landlady, Lupe, was an energetic soul who roasted and sold cashews, raised pigs and chickens, and cultivated an abundant vegetable garden. She also cleaned, cooked, and cared for three grandkids whose parents had gone to Canada. Her husband usually lay around in a hammock, smoking and guzzling beer, except when lavishly tending a half-dozen fighting cocks, bred from his own prize hens. His beautiful birds, long-necked, with multicolored plumage and proud white tail feathers, were trained to fight aggressively, first for practice with bare feet, then for real with attached razors in heavily wagered death bouts. Miguelangelo boasted that his roosters rarely lost, winning him most bets. Cockfighting is a cruel, bloody sport that I once watched years ago in Mexico with my daughter Melanie. We left sick to our stomachs after the first bird was killed. So when Miguel invited me to see his champions in action, I politely declined.

One weekend while his wife was away, he asked Seth for some condoms. Seth obliged, feeling it best to provide them.

Adiós Teresa

After several months on the job, the teenage maid Teresa begins picking fights with Marina. An attractive girl with freckles sprinkled over across her upturned nose, light-brown hair, and flashing blue eyes, Teresa starts returning late from family visits and sneaks out at night without permission. When scolded, she simply shrugs, sticking out her tongue. Under her breath, below the radar of her half-deaf boss, she chants a little ditty, something like "Liar, liar, pants on fire." She often sighs or sniggers when given an order.

Yet Teresa works hard. Rising at 5 am, she empties Marina's chamber pot, lights the cooking fire, makes tortillas, heats up beans, sweeps the yard with a broom she fashioned herself, cleans the latrine, feeds the chickens, gathers eggs, washes dishes, scrubs clothes, burns trash, and runs errands, usually taking her own sweet time once out the door. After finishing, she gets to watch evening soap operas on TV. She has every other Sunday off and earns about $25 a month, plus room and board.

Despite her unconvincing denials of earlier thefts of my belongings, I've grown quite fond of Teresa. Besides teaching me how to make round tortillas, she's shown me how to roll a hard green cylinder of laundry soap over my clothes to get them sparkling clean, then twist them until they're almost dry.

I've also come to appreciate Teresa's impish sense of humor, even when I'm the butt of the joke. She announces it's her birthday just to get a gift.

"Ha, ha, I tricked you," she grins, "it's not really my birthday."

She also likes to stand outside my window at night emitting a shrill whistle. When I go out, she hides and, in an eerie, quavering voice, pretends to be a *chupacabras* (goat sucker), a supernatural creature reputed to suck the lifeblood of livestock. We play this game often. Teresa always hides in a different place, sometimes climbing up a tree and leaping down with a blood-curdling shriek. When I go out to the latrine after dark, she jumps out at me, convulsing with laughter.

I begin teaching English to Teresa, who hopes to move to a city, maybe even work in a clothing factory up north where her sister lives. Her ultimate goal is to go *por allá* (over there), shorthand for the U.S., hence her motivation to learn English.

Matters finally come to a head between Teresa and Doña Marina. When Marina orders the girl to kill a chicken, she looks heavenward, vowing piously "never to kill any of God's living creatures."

"Nonsense, you've done it many times," Marina snorts.

"Well, never again," Teresa insists, "I'm a vegetarian now, like Seth."

Her sarcastic tone infuriates Marina, who throws a mango at her, missing badly. Teresa erupts into giggles. That's enough; Marina orders the girl to pack her things and get out. Smirking and winking at me, Teresa says she'll be more than happy to do just that.

From her room, behind a ragged curtain, Marina and I hear shuffling as the teenager stuffs her belongings into plastic bags. When she emerges, she's shed her drab housedress and flipflops for a low-cut blouse, tight jeans, and new leather sandals, with her finger–and toenails now painted a bright vermilion. Taken aback, Marina asks, "Just where do you think you're going, young lady?"

"To Choluteca," Teresa says archly, turning on her heel, slamming the front door as she dashes for a passing bus.

Marina paid Teresa only the day before and now regrets it. The poor woman, clutching her chest, feels heart palpitations coming on. I fetch daughter Reina, who takes up vigil at her bedside. It's several days before Marina feels well enough to bring on another maid.

The new one, Ixia, claims she's 11, but looks about 7 standing on a chair to wash dishes. I convince this child to attend night classes, although at her age, she really should be in day school. Ixia soon proves her mettle by stalking and killing a weasel-like animal sneaking around at night, biting into budding bananas and sucking out eggs, also leaving behind trails of bloody chick's feathers. She later cooks up the dead animal's carcass into a stew.

Ixia turns out to be just another in a series of maids who come and go. Born in rural villages, they use Marina's house as a steppingstone toward emancipation. After helping their mothers keep house, they now do the same for Marina, while earning spending money and entering the larger universe of El Triunfo, also leaving one less mouth to feed at home. After a few months, each either marries or graduates to a similar job in Choluteca, where higher wages and more attractions beckon. But Marina can always count on an unending supply.

My gifts to Marina's young maids are seldom reciprocated. Fifteen-year-old Delmi is no exception. She begs for clothes for her 10 brothers and sisters, including a newborn, and for reading glasses for her father, which I gladly provide. Since Marina won't let Delmi attend Sunday Mass unescorted, we go together, giving her a chance to see friends.

Once, walking home from church, Delmi asks me, "Do you like orange juice?" I nod, considering that her oblique way of asking me to buy her some. Instead, she purchases two small cartons of sweetened juice at a *pulpería*, a convenience store, and hands me one. Since she seems so proud, I dare not offer to repay her.

On her Sunday off, Delmi invites me to visit her family in a distant village. On the bus, when I ask her not to throw trash out the window, she looks puzzled, "Why not?" Her family is surprised to see me. They quickly change into the "new" used clothing I've brought and line up for a family photo.

Slave Labor?

Young rural women seeking escape from early marriage and frequent childbearing often begin as live-in servants like Teresa and Delmi. They work their way up to cities and, finally, if lucky, are hired by *maquilas*, foreign-owned clothing factories paying real wages, however small, enabling them to actually buy consumer goods. Of course, the ultimate prize is getting to the States.

Housewives too find factory work offers financial emancipation from husbands who often squander their own wages on alcohol, pool, and prostitutes. While Americans consider maquilas sweatshops that exploit workers, many Honduran women consider them their ticket to independence.

Although Honduran public employees strike frequently, that never happens in the private sector. Yet even the Taiwanese, reputedly the harshest of taskmasters, have no trouble finding willing workers. Often these are young mothers who leave their children unattended all day long, this, according to another volunteer starting a day care program in her factory town. So are maquilas bane or blessing?

Honduran Elections

U.S. elections are not the only ones taking place in 2000. December 3, 2000 is the date of Honduran party primaries, with final elections scheduled for the following year. The country's gender affirmative-action system, similar to one adopted later for Iraq, means that one-third of candidates must be women and at least one-fourth of elective offices must be held by women. A revolution in gender affairs would be created if our own country required the same.

According to the Honduran constitution, presidential candidates must be native-born of Honduran parents. Nationalist front-runner, Ricardo Maduro, a prominent banker whose 17-year-old son was brutally murdered by kidnappers, was actually born in Panama, but he had Honduran grandparents and had lived in the country since childhood. His chief opponent, Liberal Rafael Pineda, claimed to be Honduran-born, but questions were also raised about his true birthplace. The birthplace question soon receded after each won his party's primary.

As a former election observer myself, I approached these Honduran primaries with a practiced eye. Honduran voters never changed their voting residence, always going home to vote in their birthplace. Marina, Reina, and their family were staunch members of the Liberal Party, while most *triunfeños* were Nationalists.

I accompanied Marina to her polling place, a school guarded by stern, rifle-wielding male and female soldiers. They let me inside without any ID, as others were required to show, since I was such a well-known local figure. Of course, I couldn't vote.

The ballot displayed a color photo of each candidate with a box underneath to be marked with an X, making it user-friendly even for those unable to read. Each party had observers on hand. Voters marked their ballot behind a makeshift curtain in a classroom corner, then deposited it in a cardboard box, dipping a thumb in ink to prevent re-voting. All that was familiar to me. However, the ballot here was not called a *boleta,* as in other countries, but rather a *papeleta,* from the word *papel* for paper. Ballots were hand-counted with observers present. The Honduran voting system appeared more transparent than our own.

In 2001, Nationalist Party candidate Maduro won the presidency and, at first, was highly regarded. His beautiful, blond second wife made headlines by adopting two little brothers, but in her own name, since the couple had not been married the three years required by Honduran law. Soon the First Lady fled to her native Spain with the children, accusing her husband of adultery with an old flame. After a tense public standoff, she returned, all apparently forgiven and forgotten.

Child vendors plying their wares

CHAPTER 9:
FULL IMMERSION

Charlas

Giving health talks or *charlas* was my main official task. Designed to convey essential information, charlas also served as social events breaking up the monotony of everyday life. When talking about nutrition, safe birthing, or AIDS prevention, I always drafted local folks to help out. Although initially hesitant, after a little practice, they could carry on alone, earning them special status. Most instruction was hand-on. Just *telling* people what to do was not enough.

For me, actually traveling to and from outlying villages was the hardest part, involving hitchhiking, horseback riding, or just plain walking, laden down with bulky charts, magic markers, and obligatory snacks. I had a bicycle, but most villages were located uphill. It was especially discouraging after an arduous trek if my audience failed to show. I then offered local boys treats to go round them up. I also used a whistle to signal my arrival or to bring sessions back to order when side conversations got out-of-hand.

Approaching the hillside village of Matapalos, I encountered a waist-deep rushing river. Now what? Taking a deep breath, I plunged in, wading gingerly across holding rolled-up charts high overhead, with my feet slipping on unseen rocks below. Thirty women and their kids were waiting for me in an evangelical chapel inhabited by giant scary-looking fruit bats, actually harmless to humans. Bats typically sleep in daytime, but because my arrival had disturbed them, they fluttered aimlessly about. My inadvertent shrieks as they circled around provoked much shy laughter.

Wringing out my wet skirt, I tried to muster my dignity. Nutrition was our topic for the day, vital because 40% of Hondurans, mostly children, are malnourished. Malnutrition can trigger a downward spiral. Malnourished youngsters are less resistant to disease and, when sick, absorb fewer nutrients, leaving them still more vulnerable. The ladies helped me stick food cutouts on the appropriate places on my nutrition charts. Some were already growing their own vegetables and herbal remedies. We practiced making "super-tortillas" with chopped spinach, onions, and tomatoes, giving this food staple more nutritional heft and flavor.

Lea, the meeting's organizer, a local health guardian and midwife, invited me to stay for lunch and killed the fatted chicken in my honor. I did eat meat then, savoring the tastiness of free-range chicken.

Because of rampant animal rustling in the area, Lea admitted that pigs and chickens were kept inside homes at night—really quite unsanitary. Men took turns as night watchmen for cows and horses, each holding his trusty firearm at the ready.

Recently, a two-headed piglet had been born nearby, with both heads nursing greedily from the sow. But before the owner could charge admission to viewers, this rare creature died. "Some man," Lea solemnly opined, "probably the very same owner, must have had his way with the sow to cause that freak birth."

In neighboring La Peña, two women attending my talk had just given birth to triplets, one to three girls, the other to a boy and two girls. The babies were passed around amid admiring coos. Their mothers, while visibly proud, acknowledged the difficulty of nursing three hungry babies. "Only two teats," one sighed.

Still, I advised them to avoid risky bottle feeding and to consume plenty of purified water, powdered milk, and eggs themselves. I praised them for doing a very hard, very good, job since the babies all looked healthy. Just having one another made each triplet mother feel less alone.

"Ask your husbands to help out with the other kids," I urged, "and maybe some women here will also offer." Several hands shot up.

Triplets occur naturally in only one in 8,000 births and many U.S.-born triplets, despite advanced neonatal intensive care, either don't survive or experience life-long complications. American triplets often result from fertility treatment, hardly the case here. What are the odds that two sets of natural triplets would be born almost simultaneously, delivered by the same surprised local midwife—in a tiny rural village without electricity or running water—and still survive? These were truly miracle babies.

I gave the triplets' mothers first choice from my bag of used clothing. The rest, I passed out arbitrarily, one item to each person. It was too hard to match preferences, so, amid titters, the few men present got frilly underwear or dresses to pass along to wives and daughters.

Young Cecilia took me aside to confide that her newborn had resulted from a rape. I sympathized, but wondered if her story might have been concocted to assuage her own stern father. Yet surely some rape pregnancy stories were genuine and, while the perpetrator was usually known, as with 99% of all crimes, he was never reported. Cecilia vowed to love her baby regardless and to keep silent about the father's identity and the violence of the child's conception.

Health Priorities

AIDS prevention was a top priority because of the high incidence. In talks to both youth and adult audiences, I explained transmission through semen, blood, vaginal secretions, and breast milk, or from mother to unborn child, distinguishing between HIV, the virus, and AIDS, the resulting illness, since someone may unknowingly harbor the virus for years before AIDS actually emerges. HIV infection is not obvious, I emphasized, nor can individuals know about themselves without a test.

Except for needle sticks, direct blood transmission rarely occurred in Honduras, intravenous drug use being uncommon. Sexual contact was the main avenue of infection. In Honduras, as in Africa, while HIV was mostly transmitted by men who acquired it from prostitutes or other men, women were increasingly on the receiving end, with female incidence catching up with male. Practically speaking, wives cannot refuse husbands' sexual overtures or insist on condom use. Semen holds very concentrated amounts of HIV and women's interior mucous membranes can tear easily to absorb the virus. From a woman, HIV can be passed on to her child, either *in utero* or through breast milk. This whole cycle can largely be interrupted if unmarried people practice abstinence, couples remain faithful, and, otherwise, partners use condoms. A woman inventing a ditty incorporating these principles was drafted as my assistant.

She and I devised various AIDS games. In one, a volunteer from the audience was surrounded by others locking arms to represent antibodies warding off infection. Individuals designated as pneumonia, TB, and a fungus tried to break through, but the circle held fast. Then the deadly HIV virus, represented by a wickedly grimacing fellow, broke through the circle, driving out the antibodies, allowing the infections to attack their victim.

Grabbing my magic markers, eager participants made drawings of people kissing, shaking hands, swimming together, and being bitten by mosquitoes. These they stuck under a sign saying *"No da"* (this doesn't give it), while pictures of guys injecting drugs, a naked couple in bed, and a very pregnant woman all went under *"Sí da"* (this does give it—a play on words since SIDA is AIDS in Spanish). Of course, to transmit HIV, those depicted must actually be infected.

Only if pressed did I get into more esoteric points, such as that saliva and tears do contain the virus, but in concentrations too low for transmission. Still, I warned, "Don't let an HIV-positive youngster bite anyone. And never pick up used condoms or discarded syringes."

Training local people to give AIDS and other health charlas not only multiplied our manpower, but committed them more strongly to the message. Teens informing their peers about AIDS and play-acting resistance to drinking, drugs, and sexual pressure became invested and were more likely to model their own behavior accordingly.

Before I left Honduras, the UN global fund for AIDS, malaria, and TB began financing limited antiretroviral trials in major cities. Priority was given to pregnant women and those in advanced stages. AIDS education efforts, including our own, seemed to be bearing fruit, since the incidence of new cases and the death rate began leveling off.

My main advice to midwives, to prevent the spread of HIV and other infections, was to keep the birth area clean and use disposable gloves. The umbilical cord should always be cut with a sterile razor (sterilized by flame). And the failure of the placenta to be expelled within an hour requires emergency treatment at a health center or hospital. A local mother of six failed to expel the entire placenta after a stillbirth and, within hours, died of infection.

Dental care was another charla topic. A traveling public health dentist and I joined forces to promote dental hygiene. At elementary schools, we passed out toothbrushes donated by Colgate. The dentist, a genial, effeminate young man with a Mr. Rogers' manner, painted teeth with fluoride while I handed each child a toothbrush and small toothpaste to take home. Asked how they had brushed their teeth previously, some said, "with twigs," and most admitted, "never.

Peace Corps wisely advises taking a low-tech educational approach. A fellow volunteer, whose brother had brought several computers from the U.S., learned after his departure that all had broken down and the computer lab he'd started had closed.

To get to distant charla sites, I sometimes teamed up with Corcride, the local evangelical development organization directed by Reverend Jaime, who would drive me there in his pickup. I also went by horseback or, even, despite the prohibition, piggybacked occasionally on motorcycles wearing my trusty bicycle helmet.

I soon expanded my subject matter, going out with Corcride staff member José Luis to give disaster preparedness sessions. Hurricane Mitch had dramatically demonstrated the need for such advance planning. Out in the villages, we went house-to-house together, distributing illustrated booklets on home emergency preparedness. With local leaders, we mapped out each community's vulnerabilities, outlined concrete steps for improvement, and drew up a timetable for goal achievement.

After one such talk, I helped Lola, from Agua Fría on the Pacific coast, write a letter to the national health ministry about a fulminating cancer, apparently caused by water-borne pollution, which had already claimed several lives.

Although our disaster-preparedness sessions were adults-only affairs, much of my outreach involved kids. I had arranged with the teacher at a one-room school to give an all-day workshop on HIV and pregnancy prevention to 5th and 6th graders, encouraging them to engage in career planning and continue on to high school. But when I arrived at the appointed hour, the school door was padlocked. Students milling around outside explained, "Our teacher left to go run some errands." Swallowing my pique, I tacked my charts up outdoors and we held a very lively session out under the trees.

During AIDS charlas at the Triunfo high school, kids curiously fingered the colored condoms I passed around, inevitably blowing up and popping some like balloons. They hung onto my every word because *sex* was involved. Eager students drafted as my assistants actually appeared less embarrassed than most adults. Their knowledge also proved fairly good. When one grinning boy asked about "oral sex," I made another explain as girls rolled their eyes up toward the ceiling. In high schools, I also used a curriculum called *Como Planear Mi Vida* (How to Plan My Life), containing self-awareness and career planning exercises.

After classes, Triunfo high school students proudly showed off the computer room they were building themselves, complete with cinderblock walls, tile floor, and corrugated metal roof. Glaringly absent were any actual computers or air conditioners to protect them. Confident that computers would eventually materialize, the kids had left air-conditioner openings in the walls.

Most towns had elementary schools, but secondary schools were centralized. Triunfo's was a regional high school requiring students from outlying areas to travel the distance daily or stay in town with relatives. While most kids dropped out after elementary school, the Triunfo high school's rapidly growing enrollment reached over a thousand before I left.

Condoms were just one example of how material resources can affect behavior. If condoms are unavailable, it's futile to recommend their use. If daily brushing protects teeth, toothbrushes are needed. A balanced diet requires access to a variety of foods. Our conundrum as PCVs was educating people who often lacked the means to follow through.

To set an example, we planted gardens ourselves, gave out seeds, and invited tastings of new dishes, but lacking material resources, it was an uphill battle. My workshop mothers often constructed elaborate family menus, more fantasy than fact, mainly to impress me. Orfelina, a scrawny mother with five scrawnier kids, purported to feed them a hearty daily breakfast of scrambled eggs, reconstituted powdered milk, fruit, and tortillas. I only wish...

We also had to confront a culture of poverty arising from constant scarcity leading to widespread feelings of helplessness and hopelessness. The fatalism that helped folks withstand disasters also kept them from preventing disasters in the first place. "*Somos pobres ¿qué podemos hacer?* [We're poor, what can we do?]" was a frequent lament.

People first had to be convinced that they *could* improve their situation, then be motivated to take the necessary steps. Success breeds success, so once on a roll, they often continued on an upward spiral. Together we prayed, "Lord, give us strength to change what we can, to accept what we cannot, and the wisdom to know the difference."

Season's Greetings

December was celebration month, beginning with December 7, feast of the conception of the Virgin Mary, *la purísima*, the most pure, the festival's shorthand name. This was Reina's big day. She came back from the border loaded down with whistles, plastic jewelry, wooden tops, pencils, gum, and candy to pass out to kids going house-to-house, just like on our own Halloween. Besides distributing these goodies, she rigged up a spectacular display—a plaster statue of the Virgin tied to a rope pulley rigged to make her ascend bodily into heaven. Flowered branches hung with colored lights illuminated the scene. When the electricity went out, Reina remained undaunted, setting out candles and lanterns. A barricade held back revelers while Seth and I frantically passed out treats, enduring rough grabbing and shouts of "Gimmee, gimmee!" which is why this festival was also known as *la gritería* (the shouting). Cherry bombs and fireworks exploded day and night. (The following year, Reina mounted the same statue inside a giant clamshell, opened and shut it with pulleys from above.)

At 90 degrees in the shade, it was hard to get into the Christmas spirit. But, surely I exaggerate; it was only about 87 and dry, with few mosquitoes. Local residents, to the extent they even displayed Christmas trees, used artificial ones. No tree farms existed and cutting down live evergreens was illegal.

So what was on Marina's holiday menu? Roast iguana. "Hey, iguanas are a protected species," I protested, pushing my plate away. Marina's grandson, who had killed it, retorted, "Only females are protected."

He offered me a tiny bird instead, "One of Grandmother's parakeets," he grinned. When I again recoiled, he chuckled, explaining that he'd shot a brace of wild pigeons, hardly whetting my appetite.

When the great-grandkids began firing off rockets in the patio, the new young maid stood on the sidelines. I encouraged her to join in but she held back. Maids rarely ate with their employers and often were unwelcome in the family circle.

New Year's Eve brought even more fireworks. Giggling boys threw live firecrackers at each other, hardly funny. Pyrotechnics lit up the night sky as the whole town erupted in an orgy of explosions. Straw-stuffed dummies representing the Old Year were placed at intersections on broken chairs and set alight, while rockets and gunpowder thrown at them burst forth in all directions. Adults tossed in 100-lempira bills to show contempt for mere money. Daredevil boys approached, then jumped back as errant missiles shot out from the flames. Others zoomed bikes in close, circling around the burning dummies, daring fireworks to flare up in their faces. Kids kept passing the hat to buy more explosives. Youngsters with burns inevitably showed up at the health center.

Guns too were shot up into the air, but what goes up must come down. Several deaths from falling bullets occurred nationally, but none locally, thank goodness.

Christmas had finally come and gone and I was still in El Triunfo, triumphing, once and for all, over my old friend's Christmas curse.

Spare the Rod

Hondurans expressed emotions physically, alternating between fierce hugs and fisticuffs. Husband beat wife, wife beat kid, kid kicked dog. How often did I see this clichéd scenario re-enacted? A woman obeyed her husband and the children obeyed her simply because that was how it was always done. If it took a stick to keep order, so be it.

January 25, Women's Day, brought forth elaborate tributes to the fair sex, "man's faithful helpmate, the mother of his precious children, keeper of hearth and home"—no mention made of women's independent contributions, domestic violence, or abandoned wives raising kids alone.

But times were changing. The wife of the vice chair of the human rights commission went public with abuse allegations against her husband, unleashing a flood of similar complaints. The government stepped forward to create an institute for women's rights, immediately arousing a hue and cry among men alleging that their wives had battered *them*. The attorney general then invited men to bring their grievances to the same institute, to be seen exclusively by male attorneys.

What about children threatened with a belt, as in my first host family? Most mothers kept a switch handy, frequently threatening "pow, pow," representing the sound of descending blows. My suggestions of alternative disciplinary measures fell mostly on deaf ears.

Mini Population Explosion

While they might enjoy few rights, children remained strong in numbers. The government was using every means short of abortion to lower the birth rate and reduce population growth. The average number of children per family was five when we arrived in 2000, far exceeding replacement despite premature deaths. As health PCVs, we were tasked with increasing child survival and preventing HIV, two strategies which, if successful, would further augment population. A developed nation like our own needs more workers to support an increasing number of elderly.

But in Honduras, adults were supporting a disproportionate number of minors and pushing children into the workforce, while senior ranks were also growing, thanks to medical advances.

Although the Honduran Catholic Church stood firmly behind the abortion ban, it seemed to look the other way on sterilization and contraception. Nonetheless, babies and pregnant women abounded, especially in rural areas. Families with only one or two children were pitied, while those with 10, 12, even 15, children were openly admired. I met several families with two sets of twins, all conceived without fertility drugs. My friend Thelma—more on her later—had given birth to a total of 21 children!

Items Americans take for granted—deodorant, shampoo, chapstick, nail clippers, dental floss, bobby pins, scotch tape, paper clips—all these were simply unavailable in remote areas. Honduran peasants did make soap by combining pig's lard and ashes, but disposables like toilet paper, napkins, and tissues were luxuries largely beyond their reach. From women lacking sanitary pads (forget tampons, much too radical), I learned the origin of the expression "on the rag." Disposable diapers, of course, were virtually unknown.

Rural mothers diapered their babies with worn grimy rags tied in double knots, something I noticed after several had leaked copiously onto my lap. Once ambulatory, kids just went around bare-bottomed, squatting at will, giving them an immediate appreciation of their powers of elimination and promoting early potty training, but also exposing them to microbes in dirt and animal droppings.

For infants, I resolved to bring back cloth diapers and diaper pins from a trip to the States, ignoring PC injunctions, not waiting for people to identify this need themselves. In the U.S., cloth diapers proved elusive, but I finally located some at Sears and plastic-coated pins as well.

Diapers by the dozens perplexed Honduran customs officials examining my luggage when I returned. They threatened to charge duty until I declared indignantly that these diapers were not for sale, rather, were gifts for needy mothers.

The problem with giveaways, we had been sternly warned, was that they neither promoted self-sufficiency nor qualified as sustainable. I rationalized that a one-time gift of cloth diapers could be considered sustainable because women would wash out and reuse them. I passed out diapers sparingly, only to my immediate neighbors and new mothers delivering at the health center, asking them to please keep mum. But secrecy soon proved futile.

On the Saturday after my first "confidential" diaper distribution, I embarked on my weekly clothes-washing ritual, starting early to avoid getting stuck outside during peak temperatures. While soaping my dirty clothes in a plastic tub, I heard a rising crescendo of female voices beyond our compound's metal gate, "¡Doña Bárbara, Doña Bárbara!" Peeking out, I spied a crowd of women, each holding an infant, with additional toddlers in tow.

Shouts rang out, "*¡Pañales!* [Diapers!]"

Holy Toledo! An invasion! Quickly calculating, I shouted back that I could provide only two diapers and one set of pins per mother. Frantically, I started passing them out, as even more women gathered and Doña Marina emerged to investigate. I soon lost track of who had gotten what. Outraged cries ensued: "She got more," "Greedy pig," and, even, "You thief."

In the growing pandemonium, I felt like simply throwing all the diapers out to the crowd and retreating to my room. When the diapers were gone, I did retreat, leaving my clothes to soak until the coast was clear.

Soon, I heard a soft tapping on the gate. Hardly daring to peer out, I saw a skinny, barefoot girl about 13 clutching a naked infant who had wet all down her ragged dress, creating a rank ammonia smell. Almost inaudibly she whispered, "Please, diapers for my son."

My heart sank, "Sorry, no more diapers. But wait a minute."

Going back inside, I rummaged around, emerging with a plastic bag containing two T-shirts, a bar of Ivory soap, and a towel. At least she wouldn't leave empty-handed. Obviously, no matter how many diapers I might bring, demand would always exceed supply, even in this small corner of the universe.

Canadian Gringos

Taking a break from giving talks, I served as interpreter and guide for a dozen Canadian church people visiting Corcride, the local evangelical development organization. Regular grain contributions were being collected by churches all over western Canada, especially Alberta, where my dad was born into a wheat farming family. My maiden name, Currie, I learned, was common there. The grain was then either sent directly or sold, with the proceeds being donated. Whenever actual grain arrived, Corcride distributed it to those working on communal roads or to families building their own houses.

These visitors, who understandably bristled at being called "gringos," were driven around in borrowed air-conditioned vans, served only bottled water, and lodged in the fanciest local homes. Expensive pasteurized long-life milk was provided for their cornflakes. God forbid, Reverend Jaime fervently prayed, that any should fall ill. But, alas, some inevitably did.

The visitors were driven past crews of men, women, and children using picks and shovels to do roadwork, then taken to warehouses to snap photos of sacks of wheat, corn, and rice stamped "Canadian Food Bank Program." These generous, well-meaning guests imagined that they were really roughing it, while actually being coddled. And the road crews' appearance was hardly spontaneous.

Some shook their heads in disbelief when I said I'd be spending two years in El Triunfo. "What, living like this? You must be crazy!" one woman exclaimed.

I felt like telling her, "My dear lady, if you consider the royal treatment you're getting hardship, you should try the real thing."

Jaime grumbled when the visitors failed to close his office door tightly behind them, resulting in the theft of a radio and an electric fan. But he had to forbear. Canadian churches provided a lifeline to his organization. These visitors would go next to Nicaragua to see projects competing for contributions there.

Later, members of a Canadian youth group actually rolled up their sleeves to help villagers construct a water irrigation system, passing heavy buckets of cement and rocks hand-to-hand. One young man privately observed, "Back home, all this backbreaking labor would have been accomplished by machines in just a few hours."

I also helped escort American visitors to La Cosecha, an evangelical medical clinic supplied and financed by U.S. churches, then painstakingly translated package inserts on their donated medications. Once a prayer group from Iowa walked through El Triunfo, praying in turn for the health center, schools, and even the red-light district. Members passed out multiple copies of a bilingual pamphlet entitled "Four Spiritual Laws" and ate only their own MREs. After I revealed I was Catholic, one woman patted my arm, "Don't worry, dear, that's OK."

One-Year Mark

Just before May 2001—our one-year anniversary—at the smoldering end of the dry season, Triunfo's big sugarcane harvest began. Each evening, exhausted men carrying machetes trudged in from the fields, dirty sweat-rags tied around their foreheads.

At this point, our volunteer group suffered further attrition, shrinking to 38. Each time someone left, we questioned our own commitment. Worldwide, about one-third of volunteers drop out before completing the full 27 months, a figure even higher in the Corps' early years. Returned volunteers had told me that as many as half their colleagues had quit early. Why? Missing a significant other, illness, accident, rejection by local people, or just plain loneliness and depression. Those following in the footsteps of a revered predecessor might simply get fed up trying to match a legendary prior performance.

The chain reaction started by these departures slowly continued until eventually one-third of our original training group, consistent with worldwide averages, had left early. Of our eight health volunteers, only one besides me would remain for the full 27 months. Among those departing after one year, sadly, was my sitemate Seth, whose romance with Loni was still going strong, even though she had moved elsewhere. Seth was medevacked to Washington because of recurrent illness and advised not to return. I felt stunned and abandoned, as did Loni.

Seth had left in the midst of a persistent drought. The rains did not come. Newly planted crops withered and died; families subsisted on dry tortillas sprinkled with salt; wells were dug even deeper. With so many kids malnourished already, drought could tip the scales into frank starvation. Realizing the urgency, I helped Corcride obtain two $10,000 emergency grants to buy and distribute beans and tortilla corn. Another grant funded an irrigation system and tilapia ponds in the village of Matapalos, including uphill water storage tanks to collect excess flow during the rainy season, later to be gravity-fed to crops and ponds below.

Inheriting Seth's own water projects, I oversaw the installation of two wells in separate towns, making sure his name was stenciled on their metal covers in tribute. The water was tested and found pure. While my health talks had uncertain outcomes, I felt immediate satisfaction at seeing cool, clear water being pumped out of these new wells. Everyone brought buckets to fill and children drank greedily from cupped hands, now avoiding contaminated river water.

Under the Big Top

One sultry evening, to cheer me up after Seth's departure, Marina's son Roger invites me and our maid, this time Sarita, to accompany him and his two youngest kids to a traveling circus that's come to town. Sarita, at 15, is Roger's daughter's age. Wearing a new blouse and the Sarita-brand lipstick I've given her, she's excited, never having seen a circus before. Roger treats us all at $1.40 apiece.

This circus bears only passing resemblance to the three-ring Ringling Brothers' extravaganzas of my own kids' childhood, its refreshing, amateurish charm the very antithesis of an American hi-tech production. Inside the tent, a generator whirrs away, while the theme from Star Wars blares continuously from a lone loudspeaker. The single center ring is covered by a frayed red velvet curtain, opened to reveal, ta-dah! a singer impersonating the impossibly narcissistic and swishy Juan Gabriel. He circulates amid the audience in a shiny metallic suit clutching a portable mike in both hands, soulfully lip-sync-ing to coos from the ladies. Exiting offstage, he reappears as a big-footed clown telling dirty jokes, then as a trampoline acrobat.

Next, a sequined young contortionist balancing on one leg gracefully brings the other up over her shoulder, tucking her foot under her chin. I recognize her as the ticket taker. With both feet planted flat, arms folded neatly across her chest, she then bends over backwards to pick up a flower from the floor with her bare teeth and returns smoothly to full upright position, flashing a big smile with the flower still clenched between her teeth.

"She's made of rubber," Sarita murmurs in awe.

Where are the lions and elephants shown on the outside billboard? Apparently nonexistent, but there *are* performing animals: high-wire monkeys, a prancing pony, an ostrich ridden by a small boy, and a baby hippo fed from a bottle. Finally, a black-booted trainer emerges with two twenty-foot anacondas wrapped around his neck, each purportedly weighing 200 lbs. They slide languidly down to the floor, moving slowly toward a low barricade separating them from the audience. Sitting in the front row, we watch their quickly darting tongues as they slither silently toward us. The crowd screams and our own kids jump back. Roger and I stay bravely seated as the grinning trainer explains that while anacondas are not poisonous, they *can* crush humans to death in seconds, typically swallowing them whole.

Suddenly, the lights go out and women begin screaming in earnest. Before a riot ensues, the lights flip back on and the trainer deftly turns the serpents around. Presumably, they were fed before the show and are not particularly hungry. Still, we feel goose bumps from our close encounter, the 90-degree heat notwithstanding. A fitting finale to an entertaining evening.

Author gathering village women for health talk

Children being introduced to toothbrushes

*Usual bare-
bottomed
toddler*

*Boy helping
grandmother
carry home
donated food*

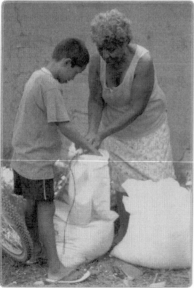

Circus arriving in town

CHAPTER 10:
NEWS & NOTES

Thinking in Honduran

After Seth's departure, my immersion deepens. My relationship to Spanish goes beyond incorporating Honduran slang—a subtle shift in perspective is occurring without my conscious awareness. I realize I've crossed the Rubicon when I start dreaming in Spanish. Before long, my tongue twists when switching back to English. I now take everything slower, no longer always busy-busy and rushed, like back in the States. And I automatically have Plan B ready if Plan A should fail, surprised when it actually isn't needed.

Speaking Spanish, I find myself gesturing vigorously and becoming more verbose. Even when there's a waiting line for the phone, getting right to the point in a conversation would be rude. I've become socialized in the language like an actor absorbed by a role: "Hello, Doña Rigoberta, how *are* you today? And your husband and dear parents? Your sweet little puppy? Listen darling, I'm calling to ask a *huge* favor, the favor of your gracious company—bring the kids, of course—at tomorrow's meeting at 7 pm at the Triunfo parish hall. We'll have plenty of refreshments."

She may answer that she'll be there *sin falta* (without fail), but that's really no guarantee, because something might come up and because, in Spanish, it's hard to ever say *no*.

We all wear cultural blinders. For example, Honduran kids, age 9 or 10, collecting bus fares on or working as servants, don't feel exploited, though certainly they *are* from our North American perspective. Universals do exist, physical needs for food, clothing, shelter, and health; the more intangibles of companionship, meaningful occupation, and freedom from fear. But there's considerable leeway in the expression of such needs.

Americans often recoil when I mention using an outhouse or bathing bucket, but where that's customary, it's really no big deal and has been the norm throughout human history. On vacation visits to the States, I view hot water and flush toilets as terrible extravagances. Honduran peasants would welcome electricity and running water, but their lack is not felt as a daily deprivation.

Most Hondurans are dyed-in-the-wool fatalists, answering my cheery "See you tomorrow" with *Primero Dios* (God willing). If they drop a cup, the cup (feminine) has fallen of her own accord, *la taza se cayó*. Likewise, the shoe (masculine) lost himself, *el zapato se perdió*. Because these items are gendered, their personification and willfulness become more plausible. The food ate herself, *la comida se comió*—exactly who ate it remains murky. And a pesky swatted fly killed herself, *la mosca se mató*. Human agency somehow seems missing in these transactions.

But fate, luck, or chance is relentless. Cows are stolen, the harvest is lost, a house burns down, a child sickens and dies. No stranger to fatalism after my own losses, I know that hard work, sobriety, and honesty carry no money-back guarantees, so how to overcome the paralysis engendered by this realization? Somehow, folks must be persuaded to increase their *odds* of avoiding illness and having healthy kids by observing some simple precautions: purifying drinking water, venting stoves, and making sure babies with diarrhea are kept well hydrated.

"If God calls my child to heaven, there's nothing I can do," a mother laments. "Perhaps," I agree, "but, remember, God helps those who help themselves. You can often delay that divine call by your own actions."

On Trial

It wasn't Judge Judy or Court TV, but when my friend Gustavo, a Choluteca judge, invited me to witness a murder trial, I thought, why not? But first I asked whether the courtroom would be air-conditioned, as I'd become quite enervated by the relentless heat and couldn't face hours of sitting inside a stifling chamber.

"*Naturalmente,*" Gustavo assured me, "otherwise we judges couldn't think clearly wearing our heavy black robes. At least we don't have wigs like the British." Whatever happened before A/C?

Juries don't exist in Honduras—too dangerous because of threats of retaliation. Instead, a defendant pleading guilty is sentenced by a single judge, while an innocent plea requires a three-judge panel, as in this criminal trial.

The only other spectator present in the gallery was a small, frumpy-looking woman my own age. The handcuffed defendant sat between a pair of stern-faced policemen while his attorneys occupied a nearby table. Two government prosecutors sat separately.

The youthful defendant, with unruly dark hair, a wispy goatee, and arms covered with tattoos, wore baggy pants and a backwards baseball cap. He smirked and grimaced throughout, as if finding the proceedings terribly amusing. He reminded me of Sean Penn playing a condemned murderer in the film *Dead Man Walking*. I wondered if such facial expressions were common among accused murderers whom Penn might have studied in preparation for his role.

After being sworn-in on the Honduran constitution (not a Bible), the defendant stared at the floor and spoke in a barely audible monotone, giving his version of events: namely, that on the day and time in question, while innocently tending his cows at a river near his home, he saw two masked strangers ride by on horseback.

The common-law wife of the victim—who had sustained 30 shots in the back—gave quite a different story. Dressed in a pink tank top and mini-skirt, she broke down frequently during her testimony. She said she had been sitting on her front steps, holding her infant daughter, when the defendant had ridden up on a bicycle, together with another man. When he asked for a glass of water, she went inside to get it, then heard him shout, "I've come to kill you, you SOB!", followed by a blast of gunshots.

She ran from the kitchen to find her husband lying bleeding on the ground. As neighbors converged upon the scene, the two men rode off together on the bike, with the defendant reportedly yelling, "At least I spared the woman."

"Is that man sitting here today?" the chief judge asked. "Yes," said the wife, pointing to the defendant, who stifled a laugh. He winked at the other spectator (his grandmother?).

A policeman then testified that he had found the murder weapon under a neighbor's bed.

Three defense witnesses were called, all young scantily-clad women who gave identical word-for-word testimony: that they were washing clothes down at the river where the defendant was bathing with his cows, that he never left their sight, and that they heard no gunshots in the area.

"What day are we talking about?" Gustavo asked one.

"March 23, of course."

"And why would you remember that particular date?"

"Because that's the date it happened."

"What happened?"

"I don't know."

She looked helplessly at the defense team. As witnesses, these women weren't terribly convincing.

In a Honduran trial, judges rely on a preponderance of evidence rather than proof beyond a reasonable doubt. The defendant was unanimously declared guilty and given a 25-year sentence. Honduras has no death penalty, at least not yet.

I'd noticed Gustavo addressing the female witnesses as *tú,* the familiar *you,* while the other judges, both women, used the formal, more respectful *usted.* All three judges had used only first names. I asked Gustavo later what the motive for the killing might have been. He said the victim had apparently tried to cut off gang ties after becoming a father.

Only the week before, Gustavo told me, the court's chief judge and her husband had been carjacked, stripped down to their underwear, and left out on a lonely road to walk back to civilization. Their vehicle was never found.

Reading Is Fundamental

Books provided a precious lifeline to us volunteers. *Cold Mountain,* covetously passed from hand-to-hand, mirrored our own raw experience: hauling water, chopping wood, plucking chickens, trekking to the outhouse at midnight. While re-reading *Jane Eyre, Wuthering Heights,* and other childhood favorites, I easily identified with riding in an oxcart, hiking across open fields, and writing letters by flickering candlelight. Here in Honduras, we were living in a veritable time warp.

I also read books in Spanish by Honduran authors, such as the late Ramón Amaya Amador, whose most famous work, *Jacinta Peralta,* written in the 1960s, now seemed curiously dated. Jacinta, a poor country girl exploited by lecherous men and rapacious capitalists, is inspired to become a labor leader after reading Marx, eventually traveling to Cuba to stand at the feet of her idol, Fidel Castro himself.

As a devoted bibliophile, I sought to reopen an abandoned local building, the Reverend Guillermo Aubuch Memorial Library. I especially wanted *children* to acquire the reading habit. Some folks read the Bible and students dutifully perused textbooks, but most regarded reading as the tortuous chore of deciphering odd squiggles on a page, a mentality I hoped to change.

After some sleuthing, I met a local musician and farmer, Pedro Joaquín, who had actually opened the library during the previous mayor's term, collecting some 800 books and organizing a volunteer staff. But, after taking office, the current mayor proved disinterested. "Her Grace didn't offer us even a bucket and mop to clean the floor," Pedro grumbled.

Even worse, she ordered the library shut down completely, citing lack of funds, after first removing the donated furniture for her own use. Pedro Joaquín quickly took home all the books for safekeeping.

Pedro, a slight, boyish 30-year-old, had five kids, including adorable blond, identical-twin baby girls. His wife carried them both around, one hanging onto each breast, while doing housework and tending to her three small boys. I gave her calcium and vitamin pills and advised her to cure tortilla corn with lime, not ashes, to provide more calcium in her diet. Nursing twins must have been quite a drain, but the babies looked plump and healthy. Pedro confided that his wife had "gotten her tubes tied" since their birth.

No progress was made on the library, despite smiling verbal assurances from the mayor, a former schoolteacher. Pedro and I organized a local committee, but she remained passively resistant, so we decided to bide our time until the next election, while continuing to collect books. We also invited the next mayoral candidates to join our committee, since one of them was bound to win.

Once the new mayor was installed, we pushed forward again and even explored outside funding. But soon after taking office, he ditched his pre-election promises, renting out the library building to cronies and personally pocketing the proceeds. Pedro's own Liberal Party affiliation may also have been an obstacle, since the mayor was a Nationalist. We invited *nacionalistas* to join the committee, but the new mayor remained obstinate, not seeing how a library would feather his own nest.

"He's also totally illiterate," Pedro observed.

Pedro's sister, Olivia, a bright, attractive, feisty middle-school teacher, was another library advocate. She once asked me confidentially, "Do you think I still have a chance to marry? I'm already 29."

Frankly, she had virtually educated herself out of the local marriage market. Few Triunfo men, especially single ones, were her equals in education and intellect. Marriage for the sake of marriage, yes, was possible, but I told her from experience that singlehood is preferable to being unhappily married. Olivia felt she was bucking nature by remaining single; everyone paired up and had children. Being unmarried was a calamity, not something she had freely chosen.

No News Is Good News

To catch up on world events, I sometimes bought a newspaper from a raucous barefoot boy, Arquimides, who balanced a huge stack on his head with no hands. Small, wiry, and 8 years old, with dark slanting eyes, a sly grin, and spiky black hair, he reminded me of a leprechaun. Most print news involved lurid crimes graphically photographed: dead bodies, machete wounds, severed fingers, weeping relatives. Murder victims were said to have been *ultimado,* providing a certain ring of finality.

Particularly grisly crimes attracted the most rapt attention, as in our own tabloid press. One was the murder of a 15-year-old girl, her burned remains discovered by a woman crossing through a vacant lot. The woman rescued a whimpering baby clinging to the dead body, her little hands bleeding from broken glass.

In another front-page story, a corpulent 47-year-old gringo salesman holding a million-dollar life insurance policy on his 25-year-old Honduran wife (met through an ISO ad) was arrested after her body parts turned up in discarded suitcases.

Public demonstrations often took bizarre twists, as when striking teachers conducted a group crucifixion, sans nails, draping themselves semi-naked onto wooden crosses in front of the legislative assembly. Since few Hondurans pay taxes, concessions to public employees were not particularly controversial. In another development, indigenous leaders opposing a hydroelectric project were dispersed with tear gas and one was murdered before dam work finally stopped. After citizens of Olancho province, opposed to the unregulated logging of mahogany, conducted a citizens' march to the capital, two were killed. (I would later help a member of this group gain political asylum in the U.S.)

I was watching TV news one evening with Marina and company when Fidel Castro was shown falling down. A spontaneous cheer went up. Castro may have his partisans in Latin America, but probably mostly among intellectuals. Ordinary Hondurans, notwithstanding their appreciation of Cuban doctors, soundly rejected the idea of communism for reasons they couldn't quite explain.

According to news reports, Cuban rafters had begun arriving at Guanaja, the country's northern-most Caribbean island. At first, Hondurans felt flattered that Cubans would seek refuge in their impoverished country. But 500 refugees later, the Honduran government pulled back the welcome mat, asking Havana to halt the flow, although neither country could afford repatriation costs.

Radio: Media King

Radio was the most ubiquitous communications medium. Most radios were battery-operated and small stations could broadcast cheaply. I often announced my health presentations via radio. Radio messages also substituted for phone calls: "Doña Xiomara asks her son to meet her at the bus stop to help carry home her purchases." "Joselito Obrador's parents advise that his surgery went well." "Don Artidoro Mercado's grieving family sadly announces that he succumbed to a heart attack. A wake at the family home will follow a 3 pm funeral Mass at the cathedral. May his soul rest in peace."

Broadcasts often highlighted agriculture, the main source of livelihood, including news of the worldwide crash in coffee prices after coffee production was introduced into Africa and Vietnam. Other programs warned of a fungus threatening the cocoa crop. New sales taxes were also announced via radio.

Every May Day, public employees were featured marching to protest globalization, privatization, free trade, neo-liberalism, and tax increases, while also demanding more jobs, higher salaries, and more benefits. Although trade agreements such as CAFTA (Central American Free Trade Agreement) would probably increase Honduran exports and raise overall GNP, farmers with small plots of marginally productive land would be the biggest losers, but rarely participated in demonstrations.

A debate raged on the airwaves about civil servants elected to office who were keeping both salaries, even though substitutes had been hired in their absence. Over bitter opposition from public employee unions, legislators quashed such double dipping, requiring the newly elected to choose just one salary. Nepotism sometimes became excessive, as when one official was revealed to have put 32 relatives on the public payroll.

At U.S. government urging, radio stations ran frequent spots about the risks of going north, including extortion, robbery, rape, and murder. "Fathers, mothers, don't leave—your children need you here at home." In one month alone, seven Hondurans were reportedly killed en route. According to these warnings, only one of every hundred migrants actually makes it to the States. Really? I suspect the success rate is actually higher.

Popular radio personalities included "internationally famous" Salvadoran preacher Rev. Dr. Blanco Mariaga whose revival meetings, according to fervent testimonials, cured everything from paralysis to chronic pain. A pastor of the Abundant Life church, after a gay rights parade, cited stern injunctions from Leviticus and Deuteronomy against men lying down with men or animals. American James Dobson's evangelical series *Focus on the Family* was broadcast in Spanish translation; in one episode, a wayward son was saved from homosexuality, in another, a wife pulled back from divorce.

Politicians ran frequent radio ads, including a presidential candidate referred to simply as "Jaime"—whose last name turned out to be Rosenthal, hence wasn't mentioned.

A physician hosting a medical advice program shamelessly touted his own private practice, complete with address and phone number: "*Señora, to treat your special problem, stop by my office today.*"

Reverend Chandía, a nonogenerian guru, advocated drinking urine to cure impotence, acne, arthritis, headaches, and memory loss, crediting his own longevity to the practice. Listeners also telephoned a seer to give them personal love tips on live radio.

Appropriately enough, condom ads were interspersed, "Darling, with brand X, I feel safe and they're so-o-o colorful, sweet-smelling, and delicious too," a sexy woman's voice cooed, "banana-flavored yellow is my favorite, yum." There was also, "Gentlemen, is your member flaccid and unmanly? Do you fail to satisfy your partner? Viagra is the answer!"

Late at night, I sometimes picked up Radio Martí, a Voice of America (VOA) program beamed toward Cuba, mostly music and weather reports. Some evenings, I tuned into static newscasts of VOA proper. Once, on VOA, President Bush was heard saying about Vladimir Putin, "He don't know me and I don't know him very well." On another evening, I was excited to hear Roberto, a Washington-based Argentine friend, discussing his country's economic meltdown. However, midway into my stay, without any prior notice, VOA shut down its transmitter to Honduras. Doña Marina's TV still yielded world news from Univisión, a Miami-based Spanish-language network, until that was discovered being pirated without proper payment. Before these sources went black, I maintained contact with events in the outside world.

9/11 and Beyond

For the 2000 U.S. presidential election, my own absentee ballot never arrived. Every few days, I tuned into the radio to find election results still in contention. Puzzled Hondurans asked, "How could Gore possibly lose if he actually got more votes?" *Agreed;* in my own foreign election observer experience, we never would have declared the minority vote-getter the winner. I was glad to be far away from the U.S. during much of George W.'s tenure.

The morning of September 11, I'm waiting in the PC lounge in Teguc for a medical appointment, watching CNN news with other volunteers. A replay flashes of the first plane crashing into the towers, then, as the camera pans back to the live scene of the burning building, another plane crashes into the second tower. Sitting there stunned and speechless, we all realize these were not mere accidents. Soon scenes appear of the Pentagon burning outside Washington, DC. Over a loudspeaker, our director tells us that the United States has been attacked so we may not leave the premises until further notice. A volunteer whose parents live near the twin towers tearfully tries to phone home but all circuits are busy. Bush's sagging poll numbers instantly shoot up. Even I am ready to give him the benefit of the doubt in this emergency.

Hondurans express shock that the mighty U.S. has been brought so low. That northern nation, representing the pinnacle of all human aspirations, seems to crumble before their eyes as the twin towers implode over and over on TV. Several Hondurans are reported injured or killed in the towers. On my bus ride home after we are allowed to leave, I hand a few lempiras to a barefoot tyke wearing a black felt hat singing in a sweet soprano voice about "the evil one, Osama bin Laden."

The subsequent invasion of Iraq garners little support. Protest marches take place in Teguc and also in San Pedro Sula where a number of Arab merchants live. PCVs are expressly prohibited from taking part. Honduran troops on their way to Iraq are prominently profiled in the media, including a young female soldier whose father proudly extols her bravery. By April 2003, Honduras's first Iraq casualty is announced.

One outside news item that cheers me is the awarding of the Nobel Peace Prize to former president Jimmy Carter. I have vivid memories of the Carter presidency from when my then-husband did consultant work for his administration. Carter always impressed me as an unpretentious, honest, kind man, a true visionary, faithful to his wife and to his word, though perhaps a bit too attentive to detail and too sincere for the political life. His presidency was often pronounced lackluster by pundits. Yet, since then, Carter has devoted time and energy to a variety of humanitarian and democracy-building efforts, in stark contrast to Bush's empty rhetoric of "compassionate conservatism."

I clearly recall Carter's finesse and sensitivity after Violeta Chamorro's unexpected victory over the Nicaraguan Sandinistas in 1990. I was one of few election observers not surprised, aware that most tradition-minded Nicaraguans resented the Sandinistas' heavy-handed efforts to mold them into "new men." Some of us had gathered on election night at Doña Violeta's home, awaiting the returns. Around midnight, Carter strode through the front door, acknowledging her victory in his twangy Spanish. But he asked her to delay announcing final results until the next morning, giving him time to calm down the losers, thus showing himself to be a real peacemaker in action. (In 2006, when the tables turned, Carter again played a conciliatory role after Daniel Ortega's comeback.)

Other long-distance news proves less inspiring. In Chile, General Pinochet, who used an Alzheimer's and physical frailty defense to leave Britain, upon arrived in Santiago, arises miraculously from his wheelchair to wave gleefully to his cheering supporters. I'd been an election observer in Chile when he lost the 1988 plebiscite and appeared on TV almost in tears.

And John Negroponte, wryly dubbed the "Ostrich Ambassador" locally because of claiming ignorance of the Honduran military's human rights abuses during his ambassadorial tenure, is named Bush's UN envoy.

Youthful paperboys

CHAPTER 11:
OF MEN AND MOSQUITOES

Knock, Knock

Knock, knock sounds insistently at our gate.

"Who's there?"

Peering out, I spy a paunchy, balding figure extending a half-dozen mangos in his grubby hands. He's naked above the waist, with sweat gleaming on his ample torso. Body odor mingles pungently with the sweet smell of the fruit. I manage a wan smile.

"*Señora,* a neighborly gift for you," he murmurs.

Awkwardly, I reach through to accept the mangos—red, green, gold— all plump and shiny. "I live nearby," he says, "so please ask for anything you need."

I thank him, taking the mangos inside to soak in chlorinated water before biting into their juicy, succulent interiors.

Mango gifts don't stop there, but continue arriving throughout the season. I do enjoy eating mangos, especially since vegetables are practically non-existent, but enough's enough. Soon, I'm overflowing with mangos, even after giving Marina her share. With misgivings, I notice a dozen trees in the man's yard, all still heavy with fruit. He sends his sons up to toss down mangos before bringing me his copious offerings. Not knowing his name, I dub him Mango Man. Once he proudly tenders a super-sized mango that barely squeezes through as I remain firmly ensconced behind the locked gate.

One morning, he brings a basket of eggs, *huevos de amor,* love eggs or fertilized ones, winking to emphasize their significance.

"You know," he says, reaching through the fence opening for one of my outstretched hands, "I'd do anything for you, *mi querida* [my dearest]." He's addressed me for the first time using the familiar form of *you*. I shrink back immediately and he almost drops the eggs. I march straight to my room and slam the door, leaving him still standing there. After that, I ignore his plaintive knocks and whistles, but he continues leaving gifts with Marina to pass along.

Coming home alone late one night, I can't arouse Marina's maid to open the front door. Then I notice that the gate's padlock, usually left inside to prevent tampering, is hanging outside, signaling me to enter there. My key jams stubbornly in the rusty lock. Instantly, Mango Man materializes out of darkness and my heart leaps with fear. He grabs the key and turns it easily with his meaty hands, whispering fake English into my ear, "I luff yoo."

From then on, I avoid passing Mango Man's house. Once, however, when the coast looks clear, I'm walking briskly past when he suddenly emerges from behind a mango tree to toss me a kiss. His wife glares out from an open doorway, kids clutching onto both her legs.

Days later, my bike tire is flat, so I slather on sunscreen and, donning hat and sunglasses, set out doggedly on foot to hand carry some bulky medical donations to the health center. Mango Man rides up stealthily behind me on his bicycle, almost causing me to drop my cargo. Screeching to a halt, he offers me a ride. I know I should refuse, but already flushed and perspiring, I throw caution to the winds, placing most items in the front basket, holding the rest tightly against my chest as I balance sidesaddle, since my skirt won't let me straddle the front bar.

We zigzag down the road, bouncing off stones and potholes, avoiding other cyclists bent on collision. I protest that he's taking the long way around. "Don't worry, my darling," Mango Man says, pressing his flabby moist naked torso against my back.

I cannot pull away without losing my precarious balance and precious goods. I grit my teeth until the end when, arms still loaded, I hop—feigning nonchalance—off the cross bar only to endure a sloppy wet kiss on the cheek. Fortunately, I'd turned my head just before it landed on my lips. Ugh! I wipe off my cheek with the edge of my shirt. No more accepting rides from Mango Man, no matter what! Just as there's no free lunch, there are no free rides either.

Mango Man is not my only ardent suitor. By no means. Being well past 60 and virtually invisible to the opposite sex in the States, I'm unprepared for this pesky onslaught of attention, but my green eyes and fair skin do make me stand out. A man will often press his lips to my hand, a gallant greeting until the kiss lingers too long. I never make eye contact with men. On a bus, I always try to sit next to a woman and, if left standing in the aisle, avoid turning my back on a guy who might sidle up against me. Still, I attract catcalls and wolf whistles and even get a half-joking PC award for attracting the most *piropos*, flirtatious remarks.

One early morning in Teguc, awaiting an outbound bus, I'm dogged by a scrubby fellow in a straw hat, who backs me toward a charcoal fire where a young albino woman stands grilling ears of corn. (Hondurans eat tough, feed-grade corn, roasted and salted, finding our sweet corn too soft.) "Kindly calm down, my dear," he intones, "I'm inviting you to rest a spell in my hotel room at no cost to you whatsoever."

Imagine that! Just then a grocery bag I'm clutching too tightly bursts, scattering cans under the tires of passing cars. That's enough. "Halt! No touching," I order, pushing my upturned palm toward my harasser's face, "Stay back one meter; remember, that's the rule." Momentarily confused, he backs off.

My rescue appears unexpectedly in the form of a group of ladies I recognize, just returning from a religious retreat. Wearing headscarves, aprons, and calf-length dresses in bright hues, they wordlessly close ranks around me in a colorful protective sisterhood, their backs turned toward my tormentor who wanders away muttering. I shed tears of gratitude at the way they have immediately sized up the situation and moved in unison to protect me.

It's even worse for young female volunteers, who frequently endure unwanted pawing and poking. Fair-skinned women are especially vulnerable. An attractive volunteer cuts her long blond hair into a boyish bob to deflect attention. (Even with my graying mousy brown hair, I'm considered "blond.") Fair-haired male volunteers are also subjected to persistent flirtation by Honduran women and even approached by some fathers, begging them for blue-eyed grandbabies. Might that be the origin of the occasional blond appearing among Honduran kids?

Yet, some female volunteers appear overly impressed by sweet talk. One confides, "Imagine, we've only just met, but already he's telling me, 'I *love* you.' American guys never say that."

Marina's son Roger, loud-mouthed, mustachioed, often chewing on a toothpick, is a notorious philanderer. Thank goodness he never makes a pass at me, but he does feel duty-bound to fix me up. One prominent candidate, his 45-year-old half-brother, sports gold front teeth, a goatee, and dragon tattoos on both biceps. He's wearing a black muscle shirt, cowboy boots, and a silver cross around his neck. "Just hasn't met the right woman yet," Roger remarks, "but now he has met you and *you* are that woman. *Muy gaupo* [quite handsome], don't you agree?"

He turns his brother around to show off this studly specimen from all angles. The brother laughs nervously and I laugh too, "Yes, your brother *is* very good looking and surely a great guy, but, really, he's too young for me and I'm certainly too old for him."

Don Juan

One evening, Roger drags over a sad-eyed shrunken man with several days' white beard stubble, a guy about 5 feet tall with the leathery, wrinkled skin of an outdoorsman. Roger announces, "Meet my good friend Don Juan [his real name], a prosperous farmer. You simply cannot leave here without a husband. Since you found my brother too young, here's a mature man, 70 years old, a hard worker his whole life. Poor fellow, just lost his wife—God rest her soul—so he's sorely in need of female companionship, someone to cook, clean house, and warm his bed" (wink, wink).

We eye each other warily. Juan's Adam's apple bobs up and down as he clears his throat, but no words come out. "Speak up, man," Roger growls, elbowing the reluctant suitor.

"*Buenas noches, mi señora,*" the poor guy murmurs, bowing stiffly without removing his hat. He extends a rough, gnarled hand, which I shake briefly. No kiss on my hand from him. We stand there in awkward silence.

I make up a white lie, "Respected Don Juan, I'm so very sorry for your loss and will pray for your wife's immortal soul. But, actually, my dear fiancé is waiting for me back home." He visibly relaxes and even manages a shy, toothless smile. "I do hope you find another woman as wonderful as your late wife," I add.

Roger spits out his toothpick, muttering, "You're simply impossible."

Later on, in August 2002, when I'm moving away from El Triunfo, Mango Man, noticing a pickup loaded with my belongings, runs over breathlessly, his hands full of mangos, "What's this? Leaving without even saying goodbye?"

Poor Mango Man. Observing his hangdog look, I accept the fruit, awkwardly extending my right hand, which he shakes vigorously in both of his, then lurches forward to kiss me, but stops short, noticing my driver looking on.

"Thanks so much for all the delicious mangos, which I'll always remember," I say quite sincerely. Perhaps his attentions to me, however annoying, allowed him a fantasy escape from his humdrum life. As I climb into the pickup's front seat, I wave to him and to all the neighbors gathered to see me off, some waving white handkerchiefs in return.

Field of Dreams

In Honduras, my dreams soon appeared more vividly, clinging stubbornly in memory, no longer like Alzheimer's waking moments, mere gossamer wisps, but rather a hyper-reality repeated nightly. They even lingered in a sort of twilight dream at dawn.

This was due to the effects of two weekly tablets of Aralen (chloroquin), a bitter malaria prophylactic. The night right after taking it, dreams often transformed into nightmares. (Another malaria prophylactic, Larium, stimulated even more bizarre dreams.) The real-life scorpion that had so painfully pinched and stung me morphed into a creature armed with giant pincers. Bats throwing shadows nightly on my candlelit walls now displayed sharp teeth, grim faces, blood-red eyes. Animal and human features combined in living things with humanoid hands, long fingernails, furry tails. Some nights, I closed my eyes with trepidation.

In a scene inspired by the film Fantasia's diaphanous swimmers, I watched in horror as lovely, unsuspecting creatures swam right into the rapacious jaws of a giant clam. But not every dream was scary. A cartoonish, characteristically smirking G.W. Bush popped up in cowboy hat and boots. Other images were breathtakingly lovely: flowers in kaleidoscopic patterns and psychedelic colors, ephemeral and ever-shifting like Mandelbrot fractals. Who needed LSD? Aralen had created some sort of neural short-circuit; I was really tripping.

Among slumber's enhanced pleasures was partaking of a festooned buffet groaning with rare delicacies: lobster, raw oysters, asparagus, artichokes, kiwi fruit, and key lime pie, all in mouthwatering contrast to my daily fare of dry tortillas and unsalted beans. Their very aroma was delicious. At these sumptuous feasts, I joyfully encountered loved ones and old friends.

Often the years simply melted away as I romped again with my four young children and our frisky black Lab, Claire, out at our country cabin. In dreamland, I relived a real-life event when Claire dove into a pond with her eight pups following behind her like little ducklings. My late son, Andrew, a shy boy who had climbed into my bed after seeing the movie "Jaws" before growing into a bold young man, was again alive and well, joking around, just as when I last saw him. Flooded with joy and relief, I touched his solid, muscular arm to make sure it was real. "Hey," I chided, "Why on earth did you tease us by pretending to be dead?" "You only dreamt that I had died," he laughed. I awoke with my cheeks wet with tears.

The most puzzling recurrent dream involved a flaming love affair with a frequent collaborator on humanitarian projects. This reserved, bookish, and generous fellow, living in a distant city, was at least a decade my junior, not per se an impediment to romance. However, although I was quite fond of him, he was not someone who in my sober waking moments I'd ever remotely considered in that regard (doubtless a feeling that was mutual). At first, I found these dreams absurdly amusing. "Water, water everywhere, but not a drop to drink," was how I viewed the constant proposals (propositions?) of Honduran men. Yet, even as I rejected my immediate fleshly suitors, why had my unconscious now fixated on someone thousands of miles away? Did I secretly lust after him in my heart? Because of the platonic nature of our long friendship, the idea seemed ludicrous, almost incestuous.

Our dreamland romance began innocently enough as we ambled hand-in-hand across Prague's Charles Bridge, where I'd actually once walked with another man. In my dreams, my friend and I were our best selves—kind, insightful, tender, and whimsical. We engaged in deep philosophical discussions and debated serious moral questions. Our sweet nocturnal relationship soon moved on from heart-to-heart talk into a more graphically passionate realm.

Things started really heating up, getting pretty darn exciting! I felt like the protagonist in a virtual reality soap opera. Closing my eyes to sleep, instead of dreading nightmares, I now shivered in delicious anticipation. One afternoon, still during this torrid dream series, I found myself sitting wide awake before a computer screen at a Cholu cybercafé staring at a surprise e-mail. The message was from my real-life friend, announcing plans to fly down to visit me. I looked again. Omigosh! Fantasy was colliding with reality. I flushed with embarrassment as others tapped away wordlessly beside me. What should I say when he arrived? Should I reveal, even in a playful manner, his secret exotic and erotic hold on my nightly slumbers? Or would that forever place an awkward barrier between us?

As it turned out, a death in my friend's family aborted his travel plans and I didn't see him again until after leaving Peace Corps. By then, I was no longer taking Aralen and the dreams had faded. We enjoyed a warm, anticlimactic reunion, no sparks or fireworks. I never mentioned his role in my Honduran slumbers. So please forgive me now after reading this, dear friend, if forgiveness is in order.

Itty Bitty Bite

Don't ever belittle a mere mosquito bite. While Aralen enlivened my dreams, it didn't actually prevent me from getting malaria. Prophylactics merely suppress the plasmodium parasite lurking inside the liver, where it may still manage to break through. Having had the illness as a girl, I was familiar with its symptoms. Malaria confers no subsequent immunity, afflicting the victim anew with each exposure.

Childhood memories came flooding back one early morning, when I awoke feeling achy and nauseated with alternating chills and fever. I realized this was no bout of what we volunteers commonly referred to as "Lempira's revenge," dysentery supposedly inflicted by indigenous peoples on European invaders (called "Montezuma's revenge" by tourists to Mexico). No, something far worse.

My temperature shot up to 104 degrees. Too weak to even crawl out of bed, but recalling my childhood bouts, I began whispering softly, "Mama, please help me, I'm so sick, maybe I'm even dying and won't ever get to see you again."

My now-frail mother, so far away and nearing 90, would hardly have been able to help me even if she'd been standing right by my bedside. For a brief moment, I *did* see her there in a younger incarnation, which gave me solace. I recalled once rejecting the approach of a traveling coffin salesman, assuring him I wasn't planning on dying in Honduras. Well, maybe I'd been too hasty—I might actually need that coffin after all. At least my family would know I'd died doing what I had always wanted to do.

The room began turning in slow motion and the door looked impossibly far away. Too far to reach. Existential thoughts sprang up. Hadn't Descartes said, "I think, therefore I am"? I mulled this over. A scary notion then arose: that I was the only conscious, perceptive, sentient being in the entire universe, utterly alone, all my experiences mere figments of my overactive imagination. Can any of us prove otherwise? Can anyone truly communicate with others? What is truth? What is reality?

I was further assailed by a variation on a childhood fear that changelings had assumed my parents' forms, namely that now all my humanoid companions, as in science-fiction films, were only programmed robots. No use calling out to Doña Marina and her maid—mere evil cyborgs masquerading as humans.

Barely able to lift my water bottle, I wet a cloth, placing it on my burning brow while shivering uncontrollably. Blindly recalling the bitter quinine Mama used to give me for malaria, I desperately swallowed several doses of Aralen. It helped. By evening, I was able to sit up, change my sweaty nightgown, stumble out to the privy, and even shuffle to Marina's house, where the phone mercifully possessed a clear dial tone. Marina searched for the key to unlock the phone, while I stood there wrapped in a towel, my teeth chattering in the 98-degree heat.

Shakily, I dialed Doctora Jeanette, praying that she would be home. She finally answered after seven rings. Whew! In a trembling voice, I told her I was sure I had malaria and that several doses of Aralen had helped.

Reviewing my symptoms, she agreed, "Sounds like malaria all right." But she advised me to reduce the Aralen, "only two tablets daily and take another medication, Primaquine."

Gathering up all my strength, I dressed, and, using a stick for balance, staggered a kilometer down the road to the pharmacy, where, thankfully, it was still open and the second medication was available, no prescription necessary. Marina's maid had refused to accompany me for fear of contagion, doubting my assurances about mosquito transmission.

My dreams while I was taking both medications were real humdingers! In one, I'd actually died of malaria. My rough-hewn coffin, blanketed with flowers, was lowered into a grave right at the local cemetery. I beat my fists frantically on the lid, protesting that I must be buried next to my son back in the Virginia countryside. I soon felt better, thankful to have overcome yet another setback and determined to keep moving forward.

My death would not have been such a farfetched outcome, since an estimated 500 million people come down with malaria annually and a million die in a largely ignored epidemic. Mosquitoes transmitting the disease have become insecticide-resistant and malaria parasites are also growing impervious to drugs used in prevention and treatment. But recent vaccine trials do offer some promise of protection.

Another mosquito-borne plague afflicting some volunteers was dengue, a viral illness with no known preventative or cure, but with symptoms similar to malaria and, like malaria, with an especially lethal hemorrhagic version. Also called "break-bone fever," it typically inflicts severe aching, especially around eye sockets. A local couple's three-year-old daughter appeared to be suffering from hemorrhagic dengue, so I warned them against giving her aspirin, which would only increase her bleeding. Dengue has four variations and victims must survive them all for complete immunity. An American friend working with USAID had come down with dengue three times, so had only one more version left to go. Dengue is caused by the tiny female *aedes* mosquito, while malaria's carrier is the larger *anopheles*.

Still another dreaded insect—the *chinche* bug—transmits chagas. Measuring more than an inch long and looking like a flying cockroach, it inhabits thatched roofs, emerging at night to fall down onto defenseless sleepers, depositing feces under the skin. If the bite is noticed and treatment started right away, survival is likely. Otherwise, the disease gradually attacks internal organs and eventually the heart, causing death. A village health guardian brought a jar of live chinche bugs into the Triunfo health center for testing, the first time I had actually seen them. Several turned out to carry chagas.

More benign, but still annoying, were bedbugs that some volunteers picked up in hotel rooms. Also fleas. Fleas can carry typhus, but we'd had shots for that.

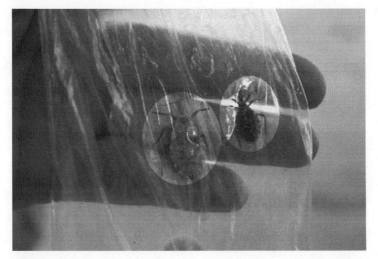

Live chinches

CHAPTER 12:
DOCTORA BÁRBARA

Everybody Knows My Name

In Honduras, I scarcely have a last name. Ditto in the States, where people often ask, "Say, Barbara Joe, what's your last name?" The last name "Joe" actually comes courtesy of my dearly departed Korean father-in-law who chose that English spelling. Since my kids have it too, I kept it after being divorced, as did my daughters after marrying. In Honduras, I'm simply Doña Bárbara, AKA Doctora, Licenciada, or Profesora Bárbara (Doctor, Graduate, or Professor Barbara), no last name required. My PC colleagues are also addressed on a professional first-name basis: Architect John, Engineer Elizabeth, Nurse Sandy, titles honoring their particular credentials.

Doña is a term of respect reserved for mature married women or widows, that is, officially sanctioned non-virgins. Because of my age, Hondurans automatically address me as Doña and by the formal you, *usted*.

Better-read folks often compare me to the protagonist of the 19th-century Venezuelan novel *Doña Bárbara*, about a feisty horse-back-riding woman who out-machos the men. My name has such staying power that even after I leave El Triunfo, my successor PCV, 40 years my junior, much slimmer and way prettier, becomes annoyed at sometimes being called Bárbara herself. Babies are even named in my honor.

Asked about my husband, I explain that we were divorced, evoking surprised murmurs. Honduran men may openly consort with "other women," but legal divorce occurs mainly in soap operas. In rural areas, legal marriage is not so common either. Most shocking is that my husband, divorced or not, "let" me go so far away alone.

"Well, actually, he died."

"Oh, that explains it. And how many children do you have?" The answer is *three* and I show them photos, unless they also have lost a child, then I mention Andrew.

"So why did you come to Honduras—for the high salary that surely the North American government can afford to pay?"

" No, I earn less than a nurse or teacher here, certainly less than in the States."

"Then maybe you are actually a CIA spy?"

"Hardly, I just came to help."

That makes no sense; what's the hidden agenda? Hondurans express fierce family loyalty, but the idea of traveling to another country to assist mere strangers is pretty hard to fathom, hard for many Americans too. I try to explain, "We're all God's children in the same human family, going back to Adam and Eve, and all related despite time and distance."

It's also hard to convey the notion of empowering people to *help themselves,* rather than offering direct assistance. *Sustainability* is our mantra; we want people to carry on without us after we leave. Some folks nod at hearing this, others look dubious. In water and sanitation or agriculture, volunteers do provide direct technical assistance. But health volunteers are not supposed to render treatment, only offer training and advice. For respiratory infections, the main killer of children under five, that means urging parents to keep youngsters well nourished and take them promptly to the health center if their fever soars. For diarrhea, the second biggest child killer, we emphasize continual hydration and purifying drinking water for prevention.

So, do I ever stray over into treatment? At first, as a proper health volunteer, I strictly avoid treatment. When addressed as "Doctora Bárbara," I issue a prompt correction, insisting I'm no doctor. Soon, I give up. If I have the means to alleviate suffering, I cannot stand back on a technicality. So, yes, like community health guardians (not doctors either), I do work off-label and without credentials—disbursing from my personal medical kit Tylenol for headaches, condoms upon request, athlete's foot medication for a man with a fungal skin infection (it works), cortisone ointment for fingers burned in hot lard, and envelopes of rehydration salts for diarrhea. I also teach mothers how to make their own salts. And I help suture wounds.

Don José, my 86-year-old neighbor, has had a stroke. He drags one foot, but, using a stout stick, still takes a daily walk. The fingers of his right hand are missing, lost in a sugarcane grinder accident decades ago, creating an inconvenience to be sure, but nothing serious. I give him ibuprophen for his aching bones and some reading glasses, as he can't see well. He invites me to his home, a dirt-floor hut shared with relatives. We sit inside on tree stumps still rooted to the ground.

"May heaven reward you, as I cannot repay you," he sighs.

"Your friendship is more than enough," I assure him.

I also help deliver babies, clearly beyond my scope of duties. I reason that if the choice is between me and nobody, at least I'm a warm body conversant with safe birthing practices and certified in first aid. And I never act alone.

One morning, I'm busy discussing TB prevention at the health center with waiting patients when Loni calls out from the maternity room. I rush in to see tiny feet emerging from a prone woman's body, indicating a breech birth. Forceps might help, but we have none. The teenage patient's own mother mutters that she's never witnessed such a birth.

The young laboring woman screams in pain as we push and pull, hoping the infant will emerge alive, but soon his thrashing legs go limp. Eventually, he's dislodged, barely breathing. Loni applies mouth-to-mouth resuscitation and cardiac massage, but to no avail. A small life ebbs away as the faint heartbeat slows and stops.

While Loni matter-of-factly fills out the death certificate and hands the tiny body over to the grandmother for burial, I choke back tears and try to comfort the young mother. Loni is unsympathetic; when the girl and her mother came to the health center the previous night, she told them the baby was breech and to go to Choluteca for a hospital C-section. Due to lack of transportation or failure to appreciate the risks, they returned later to the health center with the child's feet already showing.

Functional Therapy

Rehabilitation has always intrigued me because of my previous work in occupational therapy. The Honduran government has established a few regional rehabilitation centers, each called Teletón after their annual fundraising telethons. Since few Hondurans possess either checking accounts or credit cards, contributors toss cash into baskets set up at local banks. Promotional TV footage often shows a child emptying a piggy bank into a bank's collection basket.

I find that three years earlier, the Honduran government established a school of functional therapy combining elements of physical and occupational therapy in a 2 ½ year curriculum. The few local health workers now actually labeled *occupational therapists* were trained in other countries and occupy a higher rung on the career ladder. The term "functional therapy" seems eminently understandable, unlike "occupational therapy," which is often misunderstood, even in the U.S. Although American therapists each jealously guard their own turf, the combining of physical and occupational therapy does make practical sense, especially in an impoverished country.

A recent survey showed 14% of Hondurans to be disabled, leading to the establishment of the new functional therapy school, which I visit just before the graduation of its first class of 70. The approach there is strictly hands-on, similar to the two-year course for U.S. occupational therapy assistants. Only recently has rehabilitation in Honduras even been defined as health care. Health care's definition everywhere is elastic and culturally determined, as evidenced by its expansion in our own country.

Disability, like illness itself, is also culturally defined. The usual differentiation between illness and disability is that disability is permanent, illness temporary. Rates of disability tend to be greater in Honduras than in the U.S. because people ride around in open trucks, don't have birth defects corrected early, fail to have broken bones set properly, and seldom buckle up. On the other hand, those with severe impairments usually don't survive long and are not maintained indefinitely on respirators and feeding tubes. A disabled Honduran faces multiple environmental obstacles, often without wheelchair or crutches.

In the United States and Honduras alike, rehabilitation enjoys lower priority than acute medical care. Rehab can be a lengthy process of incremental gains, perhaps significant to the individual and family involved, but hard to measure in terms of societal or financial benefit. The ability to dress, eat, and bathe independently may increase personal self-esteem and reduce the care-giving burden, but not end up saving any money. In Honduras, nearly all personal care is provided by relatives, who often encourage dependency, "*Papi,* don't get up, I'll bring you your supper."

I volunteer to assist an organization called Central America Medical Outreach (CAMO), working in Santa Rosa de Copán, near the famed Mayan ruins. Directed by former PCV Kathy, a nurse whose lack of Spanish fluency has proved no impediment, CAMO not only regularly brings surgical teams and equipment to the public hospital there, but also assigns visiting physical therapists (PTs) to the local Teletón rehabilitation center.

I interpret for a group of American PTs tactfully demonstrating new techniques to Honduran practitioners: "You might like to try this," or "We've found this exercise useful in developing trunk strength."

I also help fit prosthetic limbs made on the premises, including for a couple of one-legged jail inmates brought in under armed police escort (injured fleeing arrest?). And I donate used splinting materials and slings I've brought from the States, feeling gratified when a stroke patient reports instant relief from chronic shoulder pain thanks to his new sling.

We distribute used wheelchairs as well, donated after the original owners have died or graduated to new chairs. CAMO arranges to have used wheelchairs shipped in empty banana cargo containers returning from stateside deliveries. These chairs are all manually operated—electric wheelchairs would be impractical—and run the gamut from child to adult sizes. Sometimes parts must be exchanged between them to accommodate a given patient. The PTs and I create a Spanish-language checklist for proper wheelchair assignment. The simple outfitting of a wheelchair with a front tray evokes cries of gratitude from a mother trying to manage her disabled child within a busy household. Remember, these mothers have no access to automobiles, electrical appliances, or supermarkets.

Among adult wheelchair patients, men predominate, mostly gunshot or accident victims. Not ever having owned a chair before, each must learn to use it. A young Misquito Indian recounts in halting Spanish how he became paralyzed when nitrogen bubbles entered his spinal cord during a too-swift pearl diving ascent. The only female gunshot patient, a mother of four, lay sleeping when a random bullet entered through her open bedroom window. A teenage girl was paralyzed by what sounds like chicken pox.

Another teen, after a series of mysterious seizures, has been left with emaciated, contracted limbs. She constantly thrashes and screams. Her weary peasant father, believing she's under an evil spell, begs the therapists to remove it. Therapy offers little hope for this girl, who appears unlikely to survive long in her remote rural village. Yet, when placed upright in a well-cushioned wheelchair, she suddenly stops screaming and looks around for the first time with luminous and seemingly curious eyes. In severe cases like hers, families hoping for miracles must learn to find satisfaction in such almost imperceptible signs of progress.

I do express misgivings about one aspect of CAMO's wheelchair giveaway. As patients roll out proudly in their new chairs, an evangelical

American couple hands each a Spanish-language Bible. So far, so good.

But then, laying a hand on each dark head, the husband solemnly inquires, "Do you agree to be born again in Christ Jesus and saved from eternal damnation?" Of course, they all answered *yes* and bow down to receive his blessing.

"Praised be the Lord," the husband later reports, "everyone surrendered to Jesus; no one refused."

Little Brothers and Sisters

With a hired driver, a group of volunteers visits Nuestros Pequeños Hermanos (Our Little Brothers and Sisters), a rural children's institution established in 1954 by a Catholic priest, part of an international chain serving 1,800 children in several countries. It once served only children with AIDS; though the number of HIV-positive children in Honduras has decreased, some still reside there, along with other disabled youngsters. However, most of the 500 residents are kids whose parents simply cannot afford to feed and care for them. A few have been removed by court order, while others have been abandoned or surrendered directly by parents.

Kids are encouraged to think of Pequeños Hermanos as their permanent home. The facility allows parental visiting, but makes little effort to reunite families and opposes adoption. In any case, adoption in Honduras, even domestic adoption, is exceedingly costly, complicated, and rare. I know a certain Honduran lawyer who found it too difficult even for himself; instead, he and his wife simply took the newborn from the hospital with their own names written on the birth certificate.

We are shown triple-decker-bunk-bed dormitories, each accommodating 18 children, divided according to age and gender, so siblings are separated. Each dorm has a communal shower and an attendant sleeping there. School classes are held on the premises.

From what I observe, the kids receive adequate food, clothing (uniforms), and shelter, and probably a better education than in regular public schools, but all under highly regimented conditions. In California, I once licensed children's institutions as placements of last resort, so I now view this facility with a more critical eye than do my fellows, who seem taken in by what our guide, a bubbly psychology fieldwork student, describes as its myriad benefits. I want to ask, "Why not give the money invested here directly to parents to care for their children at home instead?"

But realizing the difficulty of raising funds for direct parental assistance, I hold my tongue. Orphaned and abandoned children do tug more poignantly at donors' heartstrings.

Out on the playground, youngsters swinging and climbing under adult supervision appear eerily quiet and unsmiling. Suddenly, a boy spies a fallen orange tree limb and the kids rush over excitedly to gather up the fruit. Their flustered minders order them to drop it immediately and shoo them back to the playground, where their animation fades as they return to dutifully swinging and climbing.

Deliberately letting the others go on with the guide, I fall into conversation with five giggling "tween" girls just excused from class. Jostling each other, they all latch onto my arms, typical behavior for institutionalized kids starved for affection.

They pepper me with questions: "Are you married? Do you have children? How old are you?"

They complain bitterly about living so far from town. "I can't wait 'til I'm 18 and can leave this boring dump," a girl named Evelín grumbles.

We amble along, legs entangling as they cling to me. Soon, we encounter our waiting driver, leaning up against the front fender, idly blowing smoke rings. Evelín grabs the keys from the ignition and jangles them in front of him, begging, "Take us into town."

When he refuses, she jumps right into the driver's seat and presses a button that sets off an alarm. Frightened, she drops the keys. The girls then huddle briefly, chattering agitatedly in a Spanish pig Latin called *caliche*. I can decipher just enough to know they fear getting punished.

As the guide and other volunteers approach, the girls run off. The guide gives me a disapproving look, though I'm not sure how much she actually saw. The driver and I exchange glances in an unspoken pact to keep mum about why the keys lie on the ground and why the car alarm went off.

Surgical Brigades

I soon begin escorting children to surgery performed free-of-charge by visiting American brigades. Though not officially sanctioned by Peace Corps, participation provides tangible and lasting (sustainable?) benefits. Furthermore, Honduran physicians scrubbing-in on the surgeries learn new techniques.

During a supervisory visit, my program director, filling out a routine questionnaire, asks me to name my most significant achievement. Hands down, it's participation in medical brigades. "I can't put that," he protests, "it's not a Peace Corps program." "OK," I say, "then put AIDS education, which I consider next in importance."

Most brigades provide only one type of surgery in an assembly-line fashion, often for clubfoot or harelip/cleft palate, both prevalent, perhaps due to frequent intermarriage among cousins and inadequate prenatal nutrition. Research now indicates that many lip-palate malformations could be prevented with adequate folic acid intake during pregnancy, and spina bifida as well. Surgeries are performed skillfully and expeditiously, but families, PCVs, and local health clinics are left to deal with any post-operative complications.

When inviting families to surgical brigades, I require and permit only one responsible adult to accompany each child, usually the mother, but if she's pregnant or tending a newborn, then a grandmother, father, or older sibling may substitute. Although Honduran fathers rarely care for children, when pressed into duty, they rise to the occasion—changing wet pants, preparing bottles, and sleeping with the child, as is customary.

Occasionally, a father objects to his child's surgery, exercising his authority as paterfamilias, forbidding his wife to "abandon" the family by traveling for that purpose. When a man digs in his heels, I don't press further, fearing retaliation against the unfortunate mother. I always invite such a dad to accompany his child instead, but he usually refuses, having already taken his stand. I have plenty of willing families and don't try coaxing recalcitrant fathers since every surgery carries risks, especially under sometimes makeshift operating conditions, requiring parents to carefully weigh risks and benefits before making a decision.

At a Cholu pizzeria, a tiny girl with a severely twisted foot begs among the tables. I slip a note to her mother into her apron pocket about an upcoming clubfoot brigade. But she shakes her head, "Mamá won't let them fix my foot because then I can't earn any money."

Many surgical brigades are held in either La Ceiba (dictionary translation: "silk-cotton tree") or San Pedro Sula, both on the north coast, where visiting physicians have easy flight access and can indulge in water sports on the northern islands during breaks. From the distant south, we must therefore make an arduous 15-hour journey on a series of buses, shepherding disabled children between terminals in major cities along the way.

To my first brigade in La Ceiba, named for a large tree at the city's entrance, I escorted 20 youngsters and as many parents, sticking a nametag on everyone to keep track. We started out from Triunfo at 4:30 am. A shouting woman carrying her clubfoot baby chased our bus for two whole blocks until I noticed her running alongside in the predawn darkness and made the driver stop. We changed buses in Choluteca where Dr. Loni met us, as I'd invited her along, although she'd already left El Triunfo.

When our final bus arrived in La Ceiba, I sent my families out from the terminal in pre-paid cabs to a shelter where Sandy, a former health PCV, had arranged for us to stay. Volunteers from all over the country showed up with patients, although none with as many as I had brought.

We set up camp in two large dormitories equipped with metal bunk beds and plastic-covered mattresses. Most kids came with their mothers, including one mother only 17 herself. Loni and I laid claim to a corner bunk, with her on top, as I didn't feel like climbing up without a ladder. Each dorm had a common bathroom where Sandy had thoughtfully laid out bars of soap that immediately vanished. Numerous complaints also arose about thefts of toothbrushes and combs. I used my fanny pack, containing cash and ID, as a pillow.

Before dawn, we escorted our patients to the private hospital where the brigade would be taking place, joining long lines of waiting locals notified by radio. At 7 am, surgeons began walking along the standing rows, triaging potential patients. Babies had priority, their bones and tissues being softer and more malleable. If a cleft palate is repaired on an infant, the child starts eating normally and learns to talk more easily; after clubfoot surgery, a baby will walk with little problem. But for older children, surgical risks increase and chances for satisfactory outcomes diminish. Time permitting, older kids would have operations later in the week.

Pre-op screenings observed the common rule of 10: the child must weigh at least 10 pounds, be 10 weeks old, and have a 10 hemoglobin count since low hemoglobin increases hemorrhage risk. Dr. Loni had shown me how to roll back an eyelid to check on hemoglobin, a lesson I never forgot after a woman in labor, whose inner eyelid showed completely white, bled to death in childbirth. For those rejected for low hemoglobin, I advised feeding them an egg a day and using iron cookware. I also wrote out requests for iron drops available from their local health center.

While babies had priority, one of my most successful patients was 10-year-old Jorge, one of 12 children. Because of a fast-growing aqueous foot tumor, he couldn't wear shoes, was teased by classmates, and had trouble walking. His dad had left his cornfields to accompany him while his mother stayed home nursing newborn twins. Loni and I both assisted in the operating room during his surgery. The nonmalignant tumor was removed, leaving a wonderfully ordinary-looking foot. As with many clubfoot patients, Jorge's biggest challenge would be rebuilding muscle mass in his previously affected leg, weakened by relative disuse.

Another successful patient was two-year-old Norland, whose mother had been bottle-feeding him a watery corn-based solution because of tongue and swallowing defects. After these were corrected, the mother was advised by a Honduran physician assisting us to start serving the boy eggs.

"But my chickens all died," protested the single mother of seven. The doctor ignoring her remark, told her, "Go get your tubes tied, so you won't be getting pregnant every time your husband comes around."

Her risk of pregnancy derived not only from her estranged husband, but also from her after-hours profession, as she often greeted me sheepishly wearing high-heels and lipstick while standing outside a certain cantina of dubious repute. Norland, finally able to eat solid food, filled out and started walking for the first time, but never fully recovered developmentally.

One couple brought three children with lip/palate problems. I had allowed both parents to travel with us, since three separate surgeries would be involved. Another couple brought two children with clubfoot.

Some parents arrived completely unprepared. I bought underpants for one girl when her mother feared their absence would be noticed. We made sure all kids were bathed and shampooed with anti-lice solution before surgery.

Youngsters awaiting surgery were not allowed to eat or drink after midnight, a wait that often stretched into the next afternoon. Sympathetic parents fasted as well, while babies whimpered constantly. One brigade nurse allowed infants to breastfeed, but most preferred to err on the side of caution, since aspirated vomit can prove fatal. A woman waiting to have her son's clogged tear ducks opened adamantly refused to withhold sustenance and simply left. Later, back in Triunfo, when I noticed her child's eyes still oozing, she turned away, avoiding my gaze.

Parents typically slept with their children post-operatively, with up to six families occupying each hospital room. Since the hospital fed only the children, we provided for their parents with funds Sandy had collected in the States. When one ward's cribs filled up, a mother and baby stretched out together on the floor. We turned over pain medication we'd brought to Honduran nurses on duty, but after the drugs mysteriously disappeared, we gave them directly to parents to administer instead.

Once home, kids had to be monitored for pain and infection. Because the Triunfo health center had run out of antibiotics, I bought them for the mother of a double-clubfoot patient with an infected foot. Later, I learned that the mother had also hit up the mayor's office, so when the father asked a third time for money for the same medication, I told him the boy was being overdosed.

Marina warned me, "Don't be too trusting, especially of poor people."

Later, when a girl's corrected clubfoot began turning inward, I referred her to a Cuban orthopedist in another town. He recommended special shoes, but declined to treat her further. His terse return note to me read: "Let the gringo doctors who operated on her foot fix her up now."

Opposable Thumb

One of the most remarkable surgeries I witnessed was not for a child, but for a young farmer whose thumbs had been severed by a machete-wielding rival, the usual unreported crime. This man had a hard time providing for his family without thumbs.

In an hours-long operation, visiting surgeons managed to shorten and transplant his forefinger into the thumb position, meticulously reconnecting muscles and nerves, a delicate task that left the patient with an opposable thumb and three functioning fingers on a fairly normal looking right hand. The doctors decided not to tempt fate by also operating on the left hand and the man was hardly anxious to repeat the painful procedure.

While these surgeons were fueled mainly by altruism, they also enjoyed the professional challenge of treating more complicated cases than they usually saw at home. In the U.S., most anomalies are corrected early, preventing them from advancing to stages found in Honduras.

The Brightest Smiles

Lip-palate kids experienced less pain than foot patients, healed faster, and had fewer complications. Parents would often bring them by later to show them off.

Marina was impressed, "No one has ever done what you have."

Little Alejandrina, barely able to smile previously, now displayed a broad, toothy grin. Another girl proudly repeated the name of her Aunt Tina, "Tía Tina" being impossible to pronounce before. A boy demonstrated his new prowess at whistling and sucking through a straw. A baby's opening up to her nostril remained as only a faint scar on her upper lip. A few kids developed small post-op palate fissures, repaired at the next brigade.

Soon, I found venturing out in El Triunfo downright embarrassing. Folks fell into step beside me, lavishing extravagant praise, and strange children ran up to kiss my hands. I was a small fish in an even smaller pond, famous for being famous. Before I left Honduras, dozens of youngsters, probably more than 100, had received life-changing surgery because of my efforts. Of course, my role was only peripheral: identifying patients and escorting them to brigades. After surgery, I followed up: removing stitches or keeping a steady hand to cut away a cast without nicking tender flesh.

But I'm scarcely any sort of heroine. Real credit goes to former volunteer Sandy, arriving annually from her California home to cover patients' food and lodging costs with private donations. And top honors still belong to the skilled and dedicated surgeons and nurses so generously providing their time and expertise.

Some maladies proved simply beyond surgical remedy. Hopeful parents brought me children with Down Syndrome, legs of different lengths, or permanent paralysis, trusting utterly in the reputation of American medicine. But I was no miracle worker.

Too Late

Occasionally, even my best efforts failed. I took 8-month-old Yunis, her parents' 9th child, to the public hospital in Choluteca, accompanying them for hours in the stifling pediatric emergency room until she began to breathe easier and her fever abated. But on the radio the next morning, in a notice to her family back in the village of Las Chácaras, I heard that she had died. Distraught, I rushed back to the hospital, but her parents had already taken her body home on the bus.

Some brigade patients who might have benefited earlier also arrived too late. José Alberto, almost 18, had had either polio or meningitis as a child (he and his mother disagreed). His painfully thin legs twisted like pretzels as he hobbled along, leaning on a broken tree limb and smiling to feign a sunny outlook. With his older brother as brigade companion, he marveled at La Ceiba, the most exciting place he'd ever seen, never before having traveled farther than Choluteca, the south's main city. With other patients, he splashed for the first time in the ocean just outside our shelter, enjoying the Caribbean's lukewarm waters, which buoyed him up along with others unable to keep balanced on dry land.

A brigade surgeon examining José shook his head, "This boy should have been seen years ago; it's too late now. With a dozen surgeries and rehabilitation, his legs might still be straightened, but only in the States."

José was too old for a humanitarian visa. "Using a younger brother's birth certificate, could he still get a visa?" his mother later asked.

But I couldn't go along with such a ruse. It was not only a matter of his birth date, but the maturation of his leg bones. Instead, I referred him to Teletón, the under-funded rehab agency in Choluteca, though it proved hard for him to get there very often.

Since I noticed that Teletón sorely lacked equipment, I later managed to bring yard-sale crutches, Play Doh, and inflatable beach balls from the States, but wheelchairs were the greatest need. The facility's two decrepit wheelchairs were required for in-house transport, leaving none available to loan out to patients. Paralytics had to be carried bodily to and from appointments. I realized, however, that disabled preschool children *could* use ordinary strollers, sometimes available locally. We mounted a radio campaign asking for donations of outgrown strollers and a few better-off mothers actually complied.

I soon made friends with José's mother, Thelma, who operated a soft-drink concession at a rural bus stop. As we shared her shop's hammock, surrounded by her four youngest kids, Thelma reminisced about her eventful life. At age 42, after giving birth to 21 children, she looked none the worse for wear with her hennaed hair, bright lipstick, and chipped purple nail polish.

Robust but not fat, with a smile revealing gold-capped teeth, she patted her stomach, "If only my old man hadn't up and disappeared, I might have had a couple more kids left in me yet." Shaking my head, I remarked, only half-joking, "Let's hope he stays away."

All her offspring had survived except a newborn twin, accidentally dropped by a teenage helper. "It was so sad losing that perfect baby," Thelma sighed, "I regret ever letting that girl carry her. But I still have other children left to comfort me."

Yes, she certainly did. Her three oldest had migrated to the States and regularly sent back money to sustain the rest.

Casa Rosada

If he'd been younger, José might have actually had corrective surgery in the U.S. In Santa Bárbara, Dolores, a former PCV in her 70s, operated Casa Rosada (Pink House), a center for dispatching kids to the States for surgery, a complex process involving obtaining a humanitarian visa, temporary foster care, and a hospital and doctor willing to operate *pro bono*. No family members were allowed to accompany the child, who was escorted by a reliable non-relative. Dolores spoke only limited Spanish, but had fully mastered the intricacies of the U.S. immigration bureaucracy.

When I visited Dolores, two children, just back from treatment in Pennsylvania, were being reunited with their families. One, a boy age 5, had been gone for a year for orthopedic surgery and rehab that now allowed him to walk for the first time. He was understandably shy with his parents after his long absence, but eager to show off his new walking skills. The other was a girl the same age, away for four months for ear reconstruction surgery. Both children spoke fluent, unaccented English and seemed hesitant in Spanish, something that would soon pass.

Girl awaiting
clubfoot surgery

Author with double
clubfoot patient and
mother

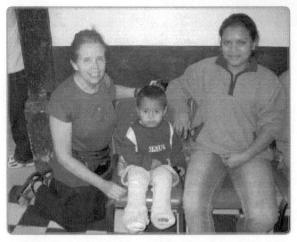

*Boy shows
self-portrait*

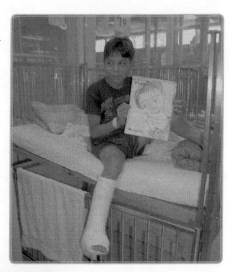

Boy with foot tumor

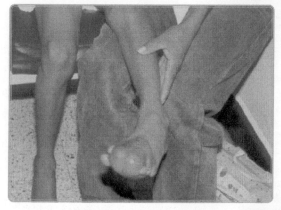

*Same boy's foot
after surgery*

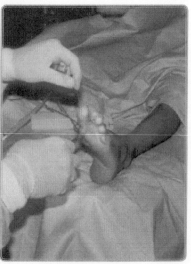

Yunis, 8 months old, who died in the hospital overnight

Thelma, mother of 21 children, with her two youngest

Three Triunfo siblings after lip/palate repairs

CHAPTER 13:
IN GOD WE TRUST

A House Divided

C hristianity is the only conceivable faith in Honduras, but there's nothing ecumenical about it. No one is unchurched, religion is imbedded in the very fabric of everyday life, yet religious rivalries within Christianity remain strong. In Triunfo, I'm vigorously courted by both Catholic and evangelical churches, but strive to avoid favoritism. Despite my own affiliation, I end up working mostly with Corcride, the local evangelical development organization.

It's no secret that the fundamentalism represented by Corcride, thanks to U.S. missionaries, is making serious inroads into Latin America's Catholic ranks. Honduran Catholics have only to look to the example of neighboring Guatemala, where one-fourth of the population is now either evangelical or Pentecostal. Gaining adherents as well are Adventists and Jehovah's Witnesses (*Testigos de Jehová*, also slyly referred to as *Testículos de Jehová*).

While more than 90% of Hondurans still identify themselves as Catholics, evangelicals are gaining ground, especially among the poor. Theirs is a fiery Old Testament God, softened by a gentler, more forgiving Jesus. Young, autonomous fundamentalist faith communities reject hierarchy, with women assuming highly visible roles. Eschewing dry sermons, traditional rituals, and esoteric theological arguments, believers seek to be moved, feel faith in their bones, and become transported beyond everyday travails.

I notice the Honduran Catholic church fighting back with charismatic Catholicism involving laying-on of hands, clapping, prophecy, biblical literalism, and even speaking in tongues. Lay Catholic men and women venture out into the hinterland to promote these new observances.

Escorting groups of visiting American fundamentalists, I privately lament the lack of Catholic visitors, knowing that many of my co-religionists back home would love a chance to serve in Honduras. A Protestant mission from Kansas visits El Triunfo periodically, delivering medicines to an evangelical clinic and engaging in "prayer walks" to strategic locales. During a prayer walk, participants don't proselytize or even speak to those in their prayers. "It really works," the group's leader insists, "We've witnessed many miracles among folks who never even knew we were praying for them."

Separate but Equal?

Charismatic Catholicism notwithstanding, a deep religious divide persists. On any given Sunday or holy day, Triunfo's cathedral is packed to overflowing. Inside, ornate gilt statutes, most centuries-old, offer glaring contrast to the plainness of an evangelical meeting-place.

Local Catholic religious pageantry peaks during Holy Week. A torchlight Good Friday procession is accompanied by a rich-voiced *a cappella* choir of white-robed women and girls displaying the long, abundant tresses so envied by us fine-haired females. Crowds of candle-carrying marchers shed genuine tears. A ritual procession held after the blazing sun has set moves from one "living" Station of the Cross to the next as costumed players act out the roles of Pontius Pilate, Jesus bearing the cross, Roman soldiers, Mary Magdalene, the Virgin Mary, and the two thieves. I wince as boys throw stones at a straw effigy of Judas, excoriated as "the Jew." The procession ends with the symbolic burial of an ancient statue borrowed from its cathedral niche—a reclining Jesus in a glass casket, wearing a bloody crown of thorns and red velvet loincloth, his blue glass eyes half-closed.

Meanwhile, on ordinary weekday evenings, it's not unusual to pass a whole string of evangelical services being held in unadorned living rooms, with singing and electronic music spilling out and intermingling through open doorways. These services, like those in Nueva Armenia, last for hours with no loss of fervor. I never see, as in Catholic churches, folks sneaking out early.

Walking by one night, I happen to overhear an evangelical minister preaching to just four stalwart brethren, "Yeah, verily, according to the Hebrew calendar, our Lord Jesus was actually born in February, not December, as the papists allege."

Evangelicals, who sway and emote vigorously in church, are usually circumspect outside. A big celebration is held for Corcride's accountant, Deris, and his wife, now being married in religious rites by Reverend Jaime—ten years and three children after their original civil ceremony. Folks bring gifts, drink sodas, and sing hymns, but imbibe no alcohol and never get up to dance. When kids begin drumming fingers rhythmically to gospel tunes, parents reach out to quiet them.

Jaime soon tumbles from grace after a widely rumored affair with a female employee. Although male infidelity is commonplace, Jaime has enjoyed such a straight-arrow reputation that his transgression proves immensely shocking. He prays publicly for forgiveness, but many quit the church where he is pastor.

Once, when a fierce rainstorm obliges me to stay overnight with village health volunteer Blanca, her kids cheerfully vacate a bed for me. The family gathers around a scratchy battery-operated radio to hear the evening news. Then the children, ranging from elementary-school age to adolescence, take turns inventing religious stories. Mercedes describes Jesus' birth and model childhood. Jhony envisions black sooty devils erupting from volcanoes as white-gowned angels swoop down to rescue frightened earthlings. Young Betulia's tale involves a family saved from the ravages of Hurricane Mitch by the Virgin Mary herself. Bedtime prayers are then recited aloud, the magical mood enhanced by flickering candlelight. I can't help thinking that when electricity eventually arrives, a blaring TV will replace these charming stories and group prayers.

Personal Crisis of Faith

Religious rituals comforted me after my son's death. But upon hearing about the pedophile scandal in the American church, I fault not only the errant priests, but the hierarchy's blatant cover-up. Feeling betrayed by my lifelong faith, I'm glad to be in Honduras where the church still seems relevant. I've always believed, along with many fellow Catholics, that allowing married and women priests would not only enrich and expand the applicant pool, but also reduce the risk of pedophilia and other abuses.

I met Pope John Paul II in 1979 at the Carter White House and even kissed his ring, respecting his vast command of languages, anti-war and anti-capital punishment stances, advocacy for the poor (though he himself lived in luxury), and role in communism's downfall. Around the world, I have encountered Catholics of every nationality and ethnicity and have yet to visit a city on any continent without finding an active Catholic community. I've seen remote church-sponsored humanitarian missions serving people of all faiths and feel privileged to have met many dedicated priests, nuns, and laypersons, including Sister Helen Prejean, an eloquent witness against the death penalty. An avid student of the church's glorious and inglorious 2000-year history, I also love the beauty of traditional religious music and rites. Yet, influenced by my American upbringing, I nonetheless consider our church, over one billion strong and still growing, to be excessively hierarchical, authoritarian, and anti-female. I long for the days of John XXIII.

In Honduras, I come to admire Cardinal Oscar Rodríguez, a relatively young, outspoken prelate of part indigenous heritage, who organizes 15,000 lay men and women, Delegates of the Word, to fan out to baptize children, perform marriages, give communion, and bury the dead. He also leads an anti-corruption campaign after Honduras is identified as the third most corrupt nation in Latin America. Later, when Joseph Ratzinger is elected pope, Hondurans express deep disappointment. With over half of the world's Catholics living in Latin America, Rodríguez does receive some votes at the papal conclave, but falls far short.

Angel statue wearing cloth dress

Statue of San Martín de Porras (also known as Porres), descendant of African slaves

CHAPTER 14:
FRIENDLY VISITORS

Tourist Alert

H onduras is not particularly welcoming to foreign visitors, except in the northern islands and the Mayan ruins of Copán, scene of my earliest memories. The Mosquitia's eastern jungles, home of the Misquito Indians (chronicled in *The Mosquito Coast* by Paul Theroux, himself a former PCV), are largely inaccessible, but wild and beautiful. Everywhere, transportation and communication are difficult and accommodations often fall short of tourist standards. Volunteers try to promote tourism by mapping out a trail modeled after Peru's Inca Trail, but lack of a tourist infrastructure hampers its success.

Peter, a PCV tasked with reviving tourism on a Pacific island called *El Tigre* (The Tiger), appeals to fellow volunteers to visit there. Before the advent of trailer-truck containers shifted port activities to the mainland, it was a busy shipping hub, becoming a ghost town overnight with its warehouses and guesthouses left empty and abandoned. Twenty-five years earlier, Marina remembers cruising to the island and being serenaded by local musicians waiting on the docks.

To support Peter, several of us volunteers visit there, entering an island restaurant only to find its welcoming sign badly out-of-date. With no customers expected, no food has been prepared. The owner offers to send out a fishing boat, but we decline to wait. That night, rain pouring through a leaky roof soaks us all in our beds. Creating a viable tourist industry requires investment and none is being made here. Only the wealthy have cash to invest; others cannot get loans. Banks seem to profit mainly from buying dollars low and selling high.

So Honduras generally is unsuitable for FOPs, those "fresh off the plane." But for those seeking to avoid the beaten path, it offers a genuine and memorable experience.

Tan bonita, tan simpática

My first stateside visitor was younger daughter Stephanie, who flew all the way from her home in Hawaii, alarmed by my various calamities. She was aghast to find my weight down from 135 to 120 pounds (alas, this loss proved only temporary).

Stephanie and her husband are biologists who once worked in the rainforests of Cameroon assisted by Baka (pygmy) tribesmen. So Steph was no stranger to roughing it. But after an all-night plane ride, she wasn't quite up to standing-room-only bus travel and fell asleep on her feet grasping the overhead rail.

In Cholu, where we stopped briefly by the post office for stamps, stamps had run out. I left my postage payment and letters with a clerk, asking her to please mail them when stamps arrived. Meanwhile, another employee handed over a sheaf of letters addressed to me.

"You know me?" I asked, surprised. "*¡Cómo no!* Of course!" she replied. That's what comes of being famous. Stephanie was impressed.

Bless her heart, my daughter brought several very practical gifts, including a rechargeable battery-operated lamp and a portable water filter, both immensely useful. She readily slept in my hammock, used the pila and latrine without complaint, and never even mentioned Triunfo's oppressive heat. She was once conversant in Spanish, but had since acquired an overlay of other languages, so people had trouble understanding *her,* though she mostly understood them. She also brought several pairs of reading glasses, which I asked health center nurses to distribute to needy patients, but soon noticed the nurses wearing the glasses themselves.

Because Steph's father was of Korean descent, she has some Asian features, both puzzling and fascinating to *triunfeños,* who unabashedly referred to her as *la chinita.* A red-leafed oak pattern of her own design tattooed on her back invited frequent touching and I also had to keep the inevitable bunch of lecherous young men at bay. Marina's maid often stood with her nose pressed up against my mesh window to stare in at Steph.

One evening, Stephanie helped Loni deliver a baby. While Loni ordered the teenage mother to push, Steph held the flashlight and offered her hand for squeezing during contractions. The loss of blood left my daughter slightly queasy, but as the crying infant slid out, we all cheered.

In Spanish, giving birth is *dar a luz,* giving into light. This child emerged from darkness into life and light, albeit in a darkened room. Loni wrapped up the 7-pound baby and handed her over to my daughter, who proudly showed her to the woman's waiting mother, sisters, and aunt—no man around. The family dressed the infant in a brand new outfit. Steph, noticing that the disposable gloves I'd brought engulfed Loni's slender hands, later sent her smaller ones.

Before leaving, Stephanie visited Teguc with Loni and me, all of us staying overnight in a tiny apartment rented by Loni's brother, sister, and cousin studying there. With just two adjoining beds in the only bedroom, one single, one double, we five women arranged ourselves cross-ways on the double bed, feet hanging over, while a whimpering puppy licked our bare feet and peed on the floor. Next morning, Steph and I hiked with Loni in a tropical rainforest park outside Teguc called *La Tigra* (The Tigress), encountering only one other hiker, a Swede. We then ate lunch at Pizza Hut, less of a thrill for my daughter than for us.

Stephanie fit in well in Honduras. She has a sympathetic quality that transcends culture—and I'm not just saying that because she's my daughter. After she left, triunfeños professed their admiration, *"Tan bonita, tan simpática* [so pretty, so nice], when will she be back?" Even a year later, they were still asking for her.

Mother et al.

After Stephanie's departure, five family members arrived together, including my elderly mother. I'd arranged for the services of a driver, Arístides, the incumbent mayor of Santa Lucía, who took time out to make a few extra dollars (and insisted on payment in dollars). He owned a double-cabin pickup that accommodated us all in some discomfort, alleviated by our taking turns riding out in the rear truck bed on dry days. The vehicle leaked oil and the tires had seen better days, but went flat only once.

I put together a tour starting out in Tela, a north-coast city where we stayed at Telamar, a seaside compound once occupied by American banana-company executives. There we feasted on fresh fish, visited a botanical preserve, and toured a Garífuna village where we were bitten mercilessly by no-see-ums. Garífunas are black Hondurans, mentioned earlier, who have kept their own traditional dress, dishes, language, and dance, all with strong African overtones.

We interrupted our southward travels for a fresh fish dinner at Lake Yojoa. The next day, we visited Valle de Ángeles, where Irma, my host during training, prepared us lunch. We then continued on to Santa Lucía, where our mayor-driver gave us an insider's tour, including to the erstwhile PC training center, the white-washed 16th century church, and the venerable cemetery. At her local eatery, Comedor Maribel, friend Maribel prepared us a typical meal. After that, it was on to Choluteca, where my family stayed at the best hotel, Gualiqueme, a converted hacienda complete with swimming pool and window air conditioners.

After one look at El Triunfo, Mother refused to stay there overnight. Only my sister and her husband, PCVs years ago in Colombia, ventured to remain, while the others were driven back and forth from Choluteca. They all made daytime rounds in El Triunfo, including attending an afternoon party in their honor with food prepared by Marina's daughter Reina, although my brother and his companion didn't eat, fearing contamination. Among the guests were postmistress María Elena, elderly sisters Mariana and Mercedes, and Marina's large extended family. Loni and other health center colleagues arrived as well, but not Dr. Jeanette, often a no-show, both on and off the job. Children dutifully embraced and kissed my visitors on both cheeks. Imagine an American child doing that!

Everyone was surprised by how well my people spoke Spanish, including Mother after all these years. She was showered with gifts, including ornate vases and figurines, which she accepted graciously and promptly gave away at our next stop. Mother's main complaint in Triunfo, apart from the heat, was about the latrine and toilet paper the consistency of crepe paper.

The trip's highlight was a visit to Copán, where in 1941 my architect father had assisted Swedish archeologist Gustav Strössner. In the village square, I met a 90-year-old man who had once worked at the ruins and claimed to remember my dad. Mother was allowed free entry into the archeological park after giving the director copies of Dad's early drawings and photos of the ruins. She marveled at the manicured lawns, chiseled stonework, and clear pathways that had emerged from the raw jungle of 60 years before.

Mother was not up to walking, so we rigged up a sedan chair to carry her regally around the various pyramids, ballparks, and stellae. She sat outside while the rest of us entered underground tunnels to view the ruins' lower depths. The Mayas periodically built a new city atop the old, so Copán has at least three levels. In the town museum, we admired the maize god statue that our father had assembled so long ago. We also visited Las Sepulturas, a Mayan burial site, and a lesser-known set of ruins called El Puente. I've seen larger Mayan edifices in both Mexico and Guatemala, but find Honduran ruins more pristine and esthetically pleasing. According to ancient Mayan myth, human beings were created by the god Popol Vuh, who after trying out different materials, successfully formed humans from mud and maize, a creation story represented in several carvings.

Our stay at the magical *Hacienda San Lucas* enhanced our Copán experience. San Lucas, a century-old house located in a wooded area, overlooks the ruins below. Owned by Doña Flavia's family, it includes its own Mayan site, *Los Sapos* (The Toads), a birthing stone near a waterfall where native women once reclined to shorten labor. Flavia, mother of three U.S.-born children, including a former PCV son, returned to Honduras after a divorce from her American husband to reclaim the abandoned family estate. We enjoyed exclusive occupancy of the two-bedroom old stone dwelling. Nighttime illumination was provided by lanterns and candles, with bath water heated by solar panels. Traditional indigenous dishes, made with native plants, were cooked over a wood fire in the ample kitchen by local Mayan descendants.

Wherever Mother went, she created a mild sensation, since elderly American tourists who speak Spanish are indeed rare. Hotel maids patted her snowy white head exclaiming, *"¡Qué preciosa! ¡Qué divina!"* blowing her frequent kisses. Their attitude, while maybe too cute and patronizing, was better than being ignored, the fate of many American seniors.

Pals Old and New

Another stateside visitor was Anna, whom I hadn't seen since we were teenagers together in Colombia. After almost 50 years apart, we scarcely recognized each other, but with our first embrace, it was like old times again. Valiant Anna, who still remembered Spanish, joined me on a medical brigade to La Ceiba, where a child's father admired her beautiful blue eyes and begged her to marry him despite being already married, a rather minor detail.

On a side trip, Anna and I passed by some spikey pineapple fields en route to a mountaintop resort, Pico Bonito, where wild monkeys and toucans chattered overhead, then visited a Garífuna fishing village called Sambo Creek, and ended up eating at a Ceiba watering hole called Expatriates' Bar. Next day, at a butterfly farm set among fragrant-blossomed orange trees, a crested lizard darted across our path, black birds with yellow wings flitted up to high-hanging nests, and flocks of wild parakeets chirped noisily overhead. We sampled bitter cocoa fruit and seeds, scarcely resembling processed chocolate.

Back in El Triunfo, Anna contributed $35 to outfit Marina's maid Sarita with prescription eyeglasses. When Sarita first donned the glasses, she marveled at the crisp, tiny details of flowers and insects never seen before.

With old friends visiting from DC, Jo and Dean, I shared a memorable wild ride on an ocean-going motorboat that nearly capsized.

Jay, a young American medical student seeking hands-on experience, arrived later. Unlucky Jay, his first delivery was of a breech infant with spina bifida and hydrocephaly. Despite his heroic resuscitation efforts, the baby died. Then there was Denise from California, more on her later. I also hosted several older trainees making initial volunteer visits like I once made to Helen. So while I theoretically lived alone, I spent very little time in solitude.

During my service, I posted monthly letters and photos on a website that visitors consulted in advance. They felt a special thrill on meeting local folks in person and joining in adventures they'd only read about. Popular magazines touted reality tours as the latest travel fad. Heck, visiting me was even more authentic and much cheaper.

"Better than Disney World," Jay commented half in jest. Yes, it was real.

Author and daughter Stephanie hiking in rainforest park

Fisherman showing off his catch

Reina's daughter offering author's mother bouquet

Former Copán laborer claiming to remember author's father

Author's mother carried in home-made sedan chair

Author and her mother at visit's end

CHAPTER 15:
DEATH'S DOMINION

Day of the Dead

On November 1, Day of the Dead, families festooned loved ones' graves with fresh-cut flowers and left homemade toys for deceased children. Some graves were decorated with crude wooden crosses, others displayed ornate sculptures and laminated photos of the dearly departed.

If in Honduras I had hoped to escape the Grim Reaper, I was sadly mistaken. Untimely death was commonplace and openly lamented, with women abandoning themselves to a cacophony of wailing at funerals, flinging themselves down in paroxysms of rage and grief while men stayed rigidly stoical.

Marina's house stood near the cemetery. Often at daybreak, to avoid the scorching sun, a procession of mourners passed by carrying shovels and a homemade casket. With no refrigeration or embalming, bodies required prompt burial.

I joined the funeral procession of one of Reina's daughter's classmates killed in a freak accident. To publicize a school fund-raiser, women had been tossing candy out of a pick-up to kids running alongside when the girl fell under the wheels. I also witnessed the burial of a 101-year-old matriarch, her gnarled, withered face visible through the wavy glass window of her casket.

Too many deaths were premature: mothers in childbirth, newborn babies, fathers shot in robberies. So much sadness. Each death revived my own sense of loss. I readily identified with the bereaved, knowing that grief cannot be shut off and a loved one's memory pushed aside. Whenever someone's son or daughter died, I expressed genuine sympathy based on our shared experience.

On each death anniversary, Hondurans held a remembrance honoring the deceased with religious rituals, food, and small prayer cards bearing the loved one's image. By focusing their sorrow on this annual ceremony, survivors seemed better able to function during the rest of the year.

Living and Dying with AIDS

Dr. Fredys, our neighbor and a prominent Triunfo physician rumored to be gay, died suddenly of AIDS. Undaunted, his sisters left his shingle hanging outside their house and began offering medications and medical advice themselves. Others believed to have AIDS were shunned and families fed them from separate dishes.

Two of Marina's twenty-something grandsons, both local residents, also died of AIDS while I lived there. I can never forget the younger one, looking so impossibly pale and gaunt, sitting in the front cab of a pickup on what turned out to be his final journey to a Teguc hospital. He claimed to be suffering from a kidney infection. But with a stab of recognition, while shaking his limp hand, I felt a sudden chill despite the heat, seeing in his fearful sunken eyes those of my foster son, Alex, who had succumbed to AIDS years before. This grandson died two days later at age 25. Doña Marina admitted privately, when I asked her point blank, that in fact he had suffered from AIDS. I gave her daughter, the young man's mother, my condolences, telling her, "My foster son died of the same disease"—no need to mention its name.

Marina consulted me about preparing her grandson's body for burial. I gave her disposable gloves to protect against touching bodily fluids, especially if there were cuts or abrasions on the hands. She hinted that he was bisexual, "Don't tell anyone, but he was punished for breaking God's law."

His mother-in-law, a nurse at the health center, must have been worried about her own daughter and newborn grandchild, but said nothing. At the wake, a sister, a born-again Christian, burst forth with a rant against homosexuality and promiscuity, embarrassing the whole family.

I also met two unfortunate women partners of Marina's other grandson, who likewise died of AIDS. Each had three children, all born before their mothers became infected. One woman often visited Marina and, though I knew of her illness and she knew I knew, we skirted the subject to protect her kids, always clinging to her, somehow aware that they would lose her.

One day, the other woman sought me out alone, riding up on her bicycle. When she asked for me, Marina immediately guessed why she had come. With the woman pushing her bike along, we walked outside together to speak privately. Tearfully, she revealed that she was only 30 and furious with her dead partner for his infidelity and for infecting her. "At first, I considered doing away with myself, but now I'm just trying to stay alive for my kids," she confided.

My burdened confidant hadn't told her children the nature of her illness and had given up all intimate relations to avoid infecting others. She experienced frequent chills, fever, and severe headaches despite taking AZT donated by an international agency. Something that had lifted her spirits, making her feel less alone, was a recent excursion for 30 AIDS persons to the Copán ruins, sponsored by the same international agency. Of the 20 men and 10 women in the group, some were admittedly gay, "but it didn't matter. We all felt a strong kinship and relief at not having to pretend we weren't ill and dying." It was her first overnight stay away from El Triunfo, "and I didn't have to cook or do anything."

She ended up passing away a few months later, leaving her parents to care for her children. Her death gave new urgency to my AIDS education efforts.

I met several others secretly living with AIDS, receiving treatment only for opportunistic infections. At Triunfo's health center, AZT was provided to HIV-positive expectant mothers to prevent transmission to their babies and, after giving birth, they were advised against nursing because breast milk contains the virus. This, in turn, involved risks in preparing formula and sterilizing water and bottles.

Every international AIDS Day, Dec. 1, I joined an annual march and helped train young people as AIDS educators. But AIDS persons rarely participated, fearful of being identified.

Before I left Honduras, 100 patients each in San Pedro and Teguc were selected for a pilot program providing antiretrovirals through the UN global fund. If this trial proved successful, these medications would be made more widely available. Otherwise, most AIDS victims would die within two years of showing symptoms.

Lethal Potions

In Honduras, as in the U.S., psychiatric illnesses had low priority and were often misunderstood, even by health workers. People with apparent schizophrenia were completely shunned and considered possessed by the Devil. Sometimes, maladies with psychiatric aspects were tackled indirectly. Ana, a nurse, got an almost catatonic woman to open tightly clenched fists by gently massaging them with lotion.

While I sometimes counseled volunteers experiencing depression and panic attacks, Hondurans almost never expressed such complaints. An exception was a young father, a pillar of the community, whose wife was unaware of his depression, although I urged him to confide in her. He trusted me to keep his secret and I doubt that an anonymous mention here breaches that pledge. He had undergone childhood hardships, including his father's desertion, but that alone seemed insufficient to account for his current collapse, which had left him unable to perform at work, hesitant to lead prayers at his church, unresponsive to his children, and feeling life was not worth living.

After e-mail consultation with a psychiatrist friend in Puerto Rico, I advised my young man to focus on the brighter aspects of his past and present circumstances, remain physically active, stay on his job, get ample exposure to sunlight (no problem in Triunfo), avoid alcohol and excessive sleep, and consume sufficient vitamin B. He followed this advice, but couldn't shake his melancholy mood. He told me that except for religious scruples, he would surely take his own life. Alarmed, I suggested he try Prozac, available at a Cholu pharmacy without prescription, but also urged consultation with a psychiatrist. After circuitous maneuvering, he located one in Teguc, deliberately far from home to avoid detection. This doctor recommended an antidepressant called Rowexetina manufactured in the Dominican Republic at one-fourth the cost of Prozac. Five weeks later, he was almost back to normal.

I counted him as my only mental health success. With others, sadly, I never learned of their depression until after they had taken their own life. Young people usually committed suicide by drinking insecticide, kerosene, or diesel fuel, compounds readily at hand. Most grieving families blamed a lover's rejection, perhaps indeed the final trigger, but suicide rarely has a single cause. One father attributed his son's suicide to the influence of heavy metal music, whereas his penchant for such music was probably as much symptom as cause. A mother insisted her daughter's death by insecticide was an accident, "She would never have intentionally hurt us; she was such a virtuous girl."

Even where worrisome signs had appeared beforehand, families vehemently denied them, "He was always whistling a happy tune."

Teodoro, an effeminate 21-year-old neighbor, wore blue eye-shadow, flowered shirts, and curls plastered to his forehead. He sat outside evenings with his mother, greeting passersby in a friendly, high-pitched voice. He always called me *jovencita* (young lady), making us both laugh. Once returning to town after a short absence, I noticed his mother sitting out alone, dressed all in black, her face tearstained. Her precious Teodoro had died after drinking pesticide.

Dr. Fredys' shingle still up after his death from AIDS

CHAPTER 16:
MOVING ON

April, Cruelest Month

While friends back in Washington are busy celebrating cherry blossoms and spring flowers, no April showers fall in Honduras. Central America's rainy season spans six months from May to November, which also marks the end of the hurricane season. The rainy season is called "winter" *(invierno)*, although days are slightly longer then—Honduras being above the equator—and temperatures may actually get hotter than in the dry season or so-called "summer" *(verano)*. In mid-July, still nominally winter, there may be a few dry weeks called little summer—*veranito*—analogous to our Indian summer, usually not long enough to threaten crops, except in drought years. School vacation lasts from mid-November to early February.

After November, especially in low-lying areas such as El Triunfo, no rain falls again until May. As daylight hours grow marginally shorter toward year's end, temperatures cool somewhat. In December, January, and even early February, the high may reach only into the 80s with nights down to 70° F. We then breathe easier.

But around March, with longer days and no cloud cover or cooling rains, the south heats up again. Choking dust covers every surface. I drape a sheet over my bed to keep out grit. The only redeeming feature is abundant watermelons and cantaloupes. Then in April, high temperatures peak daily at over 100° F. My mind grows fuzzy. I bathe several times a day, not bothering to dry off, and keep changing into clean, still damp clothes.

One especially torrid April afternoon, after visiting village volunteer Blanca in Río Grande #1, I'm sitting out on a rock by the roadside, waiting for the bus back into town, fanning myself with a large leaf. Because of tomorrow's commitments, I have to get home. The temperature is 110° F, give or take, with the air thick and eerily still. Feeling almost suffocated, I take in only shallow breaths. Two hours later, drenched in sweat, with still no bus in sight, I decide to set out on foot. Except for the bus, no vehicles traverse this lonesome road. Triunfo is 8 kilometers away, so even in intense heat, walking is not physically impossible, though dangerous because of unpopulated stretches. I wait for reliable walking companions to show up.

Soon, a middle-aged peasant couple appears carrying bundles of firewood, she on her head, like most women, he on his back, as men do. I fall in beside them, feeling safer with a woman present. Although nearly my own age and bearing heavy loads, they move along briskly. I can barely keep up, panting on the upgrades. My eyes sting, my bare sandaled toes stub on rocks and roots, my skin is glossy with perspiration. A snake slithering across our path gives me a sudden start but doesn't phase my companions who plod wordlessly forward. "Please," I pray silently, "let the bus finally come." But only the loud cackling of birds, perhaps complaining of the heat, sounds high overhead.

Out of breath, dizzy, with my calves cramping, I have to stop to rest. My tongue feels thick, I'm nauseated, my head throbs, and my heart is pounding. My companions stop too, but only briefly, aiming to reach town before nightfall. Without setting down their loads, they lean up against the vertical road bank while I squat on the ground. I'm weak and feel strange goose bumps, but dare not fall behind, lest I faint or be attacked along the way. What if I died or simply disappeared along this lonely road? Remembering that a volunteer vanished in Bolivia, I ask, "How far?" *"Una legua,"* the man mutters in a guttural voice. (Consulting a dictionary later, I find a *league* is three miles.) After a swig of now-hot water, I stand up and promise not to stop again.

Finally on the outskirts of town, I signal to the couple to go on ahead. Falling back alone, bedraggled though I am, I'm taunted by guys standing outside cantinas chugging beer: "Marry me now, baby," "Gringa, you need a real man," "Give me a kiss, darling."

Kids thrust out their hands, begging for *un peso, un dólar,* and for once I have no snappy comeback. I just stagger on toward Corcride's office, closer than my own place. There, I collapse, red-faced and breathing hard, onto a plastic chair, smack in front of an electric fan turned on high speed. The secretary brings me a plastic bag filled with cold coke, which I swallow in a single gulp. Reverend Jaime offers to drive me home.

Our group's departure date in August 2002 is not far off. Then my 27 months will be up and I can honorably leave. While my life in Honduras has hardly been the Cuerpo de Paseo (Vacation Corps) that some colleagues first envisioned, it's been a pretty good run. My commitment was never casual or lukewarm, but passionate, which helped me when the going was tough. I'm proud to have stuck it out.

Then I panic at the thought of leaving so much unfinished business behind. Should I quit now while I'm still ahead or would it be tempting fate to actually stay on even longer? Thinking it over, I decide to take the chance. So, while my South 5 fellows count down the days, I request at least a year's extension, but in another locale. No way can I remain in El Triunfo without risking heatstroke!

I'm the only member of our group granted a full year's extension. In September 2002, I'll be assigned to the country's only Peace Corps regional office, located in La Esperanza (The Hope) in the mountainous west. The name alone fills me with renewed optimism. There I can start out fresh, but return to El Triunfo as needed. I'm excited to be embarking on a whole new set of tasks without severing connections with the old. So much for my old naysayer friend as I now head toward my *third* Honduran Christmas. However, I must partly credit my success—my tenacity—to the challenge of disproving his dire prediction.

La Esperanza's elevation is about 6,000 ft. and its weather is cool, sometimes even downright cold. Though never reaching freezing, a temperature of 40° F is not uncommon there during our own winter months, with fierce winds increasing the wind chill. According to a newspaper article, the *average* year-round temperature, day and night, all months combined, in Esperanza is 60° F, while in Choluteca, it's 90. During an April exploratory visit to La Esperanza, I find clear skies and high temperatures in the low 80s, with gentle breezes wafting through the pines. Later I will find that April weather is atypically balmy.

Before departing from El Triunfo, I'm given a big sendoff by Corcride. A little neighbor girl, Neris, who saves all my greeting cards, attends with her mother and siblings. Pedro Joaquín, the library advocate, throws me another farewell party, as do elderly sisters Mercedes and Mariana. All are so gracious, I almost change my mind about leaving.

Potato Capital of the West

La Esperanza, my next home, is a charming colonial-era town of over 12,000 with cobblestone streets, red-tile roofs, and spectacular mountain vistas. It's also the potato-growing capital of Honduras, where potatoes are served baked, boiled, fried, pureed, and even distilled into vodka-like potato wine. The town holds an annual four-day potato festival complete with sample dishes, floats featuring potato themes, cockfights, displays of horsemanship, and the crowning of a white-garbed potato queen.

The cool, wet climate is hospitable not only to potato cultivation, but to the production of apples, grapes, and green vegetables unavailable in the south. Bananas and oranges also grow locally, but no mangos, coconuts, or cashews.

All references here to La Esperanza include Intibucá, on paper two separate towns, but so intertwined that only a surveyor could discern their exact division. Each municipality boasts a separate mayor and city council housed just blocks apart and, despite periodic merger proposals, each governing body jealously resists being subsumed by the other. In colonial days, La Esperanza was Spanish-town, while Intibucá was for indigenous people. Each side built its own cathedral, likewise only a few blocks apart, and while the ethnic groups once worshiped separately, now congregations, like residential areas, are thoroughly mixed. But separate graveyards still remain.

Half of urban—and 80% of provincial—residents are indigenous Lencas who speak a distinctive, staccato Spanish, their original language having been lost. They act deferential, reserved, and shy, unlike ebullient southerners. Men typically wear broad-brimmed hats, white shirts, white trousers, and machetes cinched to their belts. Women's flowered pleated dresses are set off by bright woolen headscarves and elaborate lace-trimmed aprons with zippered pockets for hiding money.

Since most Lencas are farmers, "Intibucá Farmer," a radio program broadcast at 5 am by the local Catholic station, offers daily tips for pest control and better yields. Someone in the role of an agricultural extension worker talks earnestly in standard *ladino* Spanish to farmers who respond in choppy Lenca speech. On a visit to the station during my exploratory trip to La Esperanza, I listen to actors performing on the air, often inserting humorous adlibs.

On September 2, 2002, when I first get off the bus in my final move to La Esperanza, I ask directions to the Pepsi warehouse, since the PC regional office, where I am to report for duty, is located nearby. Following these directions, I soon find myself in front of the Coca-Cola warehouse instead. Retracing my steps, I run smack into a forbidding-looking provincial prison wall bearing this stark warning: "Absolutely forbidden to do your necessities here, subject to fine." I am lost.

The sky suddenly darkens and rain pours down in torrents, plastering my long skirt against my legs. The electricity goes out all over town. As I wander, dripping and shivering, dragging my suitcase over cobblestones, this place seems impossibly large and unfamiliar. No one here recognizes me—there are no excited calls of "Doña Bárbara," no outstretched hands. I'm on the verge of tears when a local PCV notices me and guides me to the office.

Our regional office is located in a house owned by the father of Luis, one of my two Honduran colleagues. Luis, a genial, plump, loquacious guy in his late twenties with curly brown hair, is floating on cloud nine after his recent marriage. He occupies a reception desk at the office entrance, answering the phone (yes, a phone!) and amiably greeting visitors.

Another colleague, Agustín, the office manager, is short, compact, serious, and in his early thirties. Of pure Lenca descent, with straight black hair and a deep olive complexion, he grew up in a nearby village and is the first high-school graduate in his family. Echoes of Lenca-speak are apparent in his diction. He has taken several university courses and also studied English, once serving as a Spanish teacher for PC trainees. In fact, I recognize him as having grilled me orally when I first arrived in Honduras.

Agustín's two daughters attend public school, but his son is enrolled in a private bilingual school where the teachers' English is rudimentary at best, something I observe during award ceremonies held there. In addition to his immediate family, I meet Agustín's sister-in-law, a mother of four, tending her brood alone while her husband works in a Texas carpet factory to support them, planning to remain there until he's deported.

Agustín and I alternate using the office vehicle to visit volunteers in the western region. When not out in the field, we help Luis manage volunteers seeking medical care and supplies and signing up to use two Internet-connected computers. We also use the computers ourselves after hours, a wonderful convenience. My Honduran colleagues proudly wear their PC-employee ID badges everywhere, even for local errands, and laboriously unlock the gate guarding our official vehicle, preferring to drive rather than walk even a few blocks, honking and waving at envious friends as they pass by. Luis's family owns the whole block where the office is located and Luis is building an adjacent house, combining his own labor with that of hired help.

I've rented a small two-bedroom house with an indoor bathroom and had my furniture moved there beforehand. The place comes with a table-top refrigerator and a stove powered by a portable gas cylinder, its burners lit with matches, providing real luxury after El Triunfo, where I was basically just camping out. Though the rent is higher, these amenities allow me to prepare meals jointly with other local volunteers who lack them. But first I have to get rid of copious mouse droppings, ants, and sow bugs—also, a bunch of empty liquor bottles left by the previous tenant, which I give to some potato wine brewers. The *electroducha*, like the one back in Valle, is on the fritz, so no hot water, but I can heat up water on the stove to wash my hair.

Baby, it gets cold both inside and out! By late October, when nighttime temperatures fall into the 40s, I sleep in two nightgowns and three pairs of socks. At the office, answering the phone or working on a computer, I don knitted gloves with finger openings. During rainy weather, it can take almost a week for washing to dry out. But when I grumble, an ag volunteer assigned to an even higher elevation in a village without electricity or running water, declares I've got it easy. He uses a down sleeping bag from October to February, never changing clothes or bathing except on visits to La Esperanza because the village temperature actually falls below freezing. "If I get undressed," he confesses, "I'm afraid of freezing my balls off."

Even more than in Valle, I feel the lack of warm clothing and soon adopt a layered look, wearing items obtained from a *ropa americana* store, selling used clothing donated from the U.S. Except for houses with a *fogón* (woodstove), there's no indoor heat. I sometimes turn on my gas oven, resting my feet on the open door, and also nail heavy plastic over a grate where cold air rushes in. When I still can't get warm, I go over to the landlord's woodstove where coffee bubbles all day long. Barely sipping the coffee, I keep my hands wrapped around the nice warm cup. Occasionally, I take a weekend trip south just to warm up. So, be careful what you wish for!

I speculate about total energy use in Honduras if every household, following our lead, acquired central heating, air-conditioning, car, refrigerator, stove, and washer-dryer—imagine the extra energy consumption in just this small corner of the globe! Multiplied worldwide, it would be completely unsustainable.

Esperanza's electricity frequently goes out without warning, so I don't fill up my refrigerator with perishables in warmer weather. And because my house is located on a hill, spigots opened down below often use up all the available water. Whenever I'm at home, I leave the kitchen faucet turned on with a bucket underneath to collect water whenever it flows to save for bathing and flushing the toilet. I wash clothes in a backyard pila.

The landlord, his wife, and their four children, along with two fierce-sounding dogs, live next door, with the wife's mother and younger sisters occupying another house in the same compound. So, as at Marina's, I can choose either company or privacy, depending on my mood.

At the Office

Despite the cold, or perhaps because of it, La Esperanza has more drunks lying out on the sidewalk, day and night, than I ever saw in El Triunfo. I often step over their limp bodies walking to and from the office. Passing daily by the Pepsi warehouse, I'm usually greeted by the machete-wielding guard keeping stacks of returned bottles under strict surveillance, looking almost more menacing than the usual rifle-bearing watchman.

One rainy evening, while shutting up the office by myself, I dash out across the central patio to the rear computer room to close the door, which locks automatically. But suddenly, a gust of wind slams the main office door behind me shut. With both doors now shut and locked, I'm trapped out in the middle of the enclosed patio without a key. My jacket and umbrella are inside and I'm getting completely soaked.

Shivering and desperate, I call out, pounding on the metal gate protecting our official vehicle. A few laughing kids sharing an umbrella pass by, but continue on. My knuckles start feeling raw; my voice is hoarse. I envision spending the whole night outside alone, wet and cold. Finally, a man stops. I beg him through the closed gate to please alert Luis's father, the building's owner, living right next door. Soon Don Luis rescues me with a spare key. His wife graciously prepares hot tea to warm me up before my homeward trek.

On another evening, walking home alone through narrow darkened streets, I freeze when moonlight glints off a knife coming straight toward me—is it wielded by a drunk, robber, or lunatic perhaps? Where to run? Unlike *triunfeños*, folks here don't sit outside after dark, instead keeping their doors tightly shut against inclement weather. I feel my luck may finally have run out. I think about my mother, my kids. But no, the stranger stumbles right past, knife still pointed, lurching along unsteadily. Heart pounding, I run all the way home. One more close call. Each time I survive a peril, after the fear subsides, I somehow manage to feel even a little stronger than before.

During most of my stay in El Triunfo, I'd been the only PCV and only foreigner living there. But several NGOs work in La Esperanza, and two other PCVs live in town, with others visiting regularly on weekends. Saturday night parties feature loud music, dancing, and lots of booze. At a party, a young volunteer asks me, "Barbara Joe, how many beers can you drink tonight?" When I say just one, he says, "Aw shucks" and opens it with his bare teeth!

Our new PC country director—a take-charge, Donald Trump kind of guy—runs a pretty tight ship, periodically, calling for a surprise head count to make sure no one is playing hooky. We're supposed to be on duty 24/7 and, for security reasons, everyone must be accounted for, even on weekends and holidays. The only allowable absences are for pre-approved vacations. Punishment for being AWOL ranges from forfeiture of vacation days to ET (early termination) or even AS (administrative separation), typically invoked for vacationing in a neighboring country without permission. During such a countdown, our regional office is responsible for verifying, within 72 hours, that all volunteers in our jurisdiction are at their designated posts. For volunteers in towns without phones, this means sending out messages on buses or even traveling to remote sites in person. Fortunately, a few sites have short-wave radios.

On the Road

The only thing scarier than being a passenger in Honduras is being a driver. I reach this conclusion after driving alone to visit volunteers in far-flung locales. The office car is a manual-shift, four-wheel-drive Land Rover, a formidable looking vehicle with twin diesel fuel tanks. Despite its outward heft, a diesel-powered vehicle doesn't have much "oomph," especially going uphill. The car does sport MI (international mission) license plates, which help in getting through checkpoints. Following Agustín's example, I always offer a gun-toting teenage soldier a little cash for a sandwich and a drink, not exactly a *mordida* or bribe, merely a courtesy. After all, he earns so little. And whenever I park the vehicle, I give a little boy a few lempiras to guard it for me.

Most PCVs are prohibited from driving in Honduras, even in rented vehicles during approved vacations, after several unfortunate accidents, including one where a vacationing volunteer killed a Honduran woman exiting a bus. Exceptions are made only for third-year volunteers like me.

Before actually being allowed to drive, I first must take a road test with the head of the PC motor pool in Teguc. I'd learned to drive on a stick shift, but years ago, so I'm nervous. Everything soon comes back and I pass the road test with flying colors.

Although maps are scarce, there's usually only one road to a particular place, so once I get on the right track and keep on going, I'm OK. However, road signs are few and local folks often give unreliable directions, so actually arriving at a destination is chancy. Since there's only one lane in each direction at best, it's easy to get stuck behind a slow-moving truck spewing out black diesel fumes or a wide oxcart that leaves no room to pass. I once grazed the side of a cow in a herd blocking the roadway, though I prefer to think that she grazed *me*. Rural roads are mostly unpaved and so rough that it's sometimes easier just to drive off-road while keeping the roadbed in sight for orientation.

For fear of lawsuits, Peace Corps forbids carrying unknown passengers, but I do sometimes pick up a woman with heavy bundles and a small child on her back, as the experience of cars passing me by in the south has made me sensitive to the plight of foot travelers. I'm allowed to use the car only for authorized trips within the west, not for traveling back to El Triunfo, which would be handy.

Because of road conditions, our Land Rover's tires often go flat, sometimes even while the vehicle is parked. I drive in constant fear of flats. Not only would changing a tire on such a heavy vehicle be difficult, but alone and exposed out on an empty rural road, I'd be a sitting duck. However, luck stays with me and it never happens. The same fear prompts female PC program directors to invite me to accompany them on their fieldtrips.

After living in the south, I'm surprised while driving around the west in December and January to see leaves on oaks and other deciduous trees turning russet before finally falling off. These trees don't display the brilliant colors of a North American fall, but still react to cooler temperatures. Although tree cover in the west is greater than in the south, I often stop to pick up tree seeds from seed banks for volunteers to distribute in their communities.

Driving into a village called Guajiquiro near the Salvadoran border, I arrive during three simultaneous funerals: a grandfather dead of natural causes, a middle-aged father killed in an auto accident, and a teenage boy shot by gang members in Teguc. The women's colorful dresses, as the three funeral parties converge at the cemetery, create a rainbow effect contrasting with the somber mood of the occasion. No one is wearing black. Just then, almost in a mirror image, a radiant real rainbow appears in the sky above.

In Guajiquiro, I visit a young health volunteer who introduces me first to the mayor, campaigning with her to convince local farmers to stop burning their fields after harvest, then to the lone policeman, reporting the only recent crime as the theft of a pair of shoes, worn openly by the thief. The victim has declined to prosecute. This volunteer is one of my stars, someone who has mastered the language and become a trusted member of the community.

On other field visits, I find volunteers needing a little push to get up and go. "Just go hang out with townspeople," I urge, "it's the only way to improve your Spanish and gain acceptance." I also explain the volunteer's role to troublesome local officials, efforts that sometimes fail.

One of my economic development volunteers has helped a local savings coop win a $10,000 grant from a Dutch charity anxious to clear its books by year's end. But, to his dismay, instead of using the money for agreed-upon community projects, the coop director unilaterally diverts the money into an arcane lecture series, featuring himself as sole speaker, with exorbitantly priced snacks conveniently provided by his own sister. The Dutch charity doesn't seem to care, prompting the discouraged volunteer to seek a site change.

With local women farmers, I visit an organic farm run by Don Gregorio, a stocky 60-year-old, and his wife Cándida, both taught by previous volunteers to read and write. Gregorio proudly shows off his elegant script.

Seven adult children and their offspring also live and work on the farm, which rotates crops on a 20-*manzana* plot (a manzana equals 3.5 acres). These crops, produced both for family sustenance and sale, include yucca, squash, onions, tomatoes, carrots, oranges, lemons, pineapples, papayas, and melons, all planted in harmonious combinations, with beans weaving among cornstalks, coffee bushes shaded by banana trees, and pest-repellant chili peppers sprouting among vegetables.

"If one crop fails, we still have others," Gregorio smiles.

The farm has no working animals, only chickens, and no motorized machinery, just hand-held shovels, rakes, and machetes. Insecticides are shunned in favor of reliance on pests' natural enemies. Fields are never burned; instead, old stalks are chopped back and converted into mulch. Family members make their own soap and grow herbal remedies. There's no electricity, but storage tanks collect creek and rain water for household and irrigation purposes. The only concession to mechanization is taking a bus into town to sell excess produce.

We visitors are served a completely home-grown lunch of scrambled eggs, squash flavored with delicate spices, blue-corn tortillas, refried beans, corn-on-the-cob, fresh fruit, and, of course, coffee. The fruit includes hard crunchy pears, as well as *maracuyás* (passion fruit), my favorite, with a purple outer shell and yellow tart interior dotted with edible black seeds. Our portions prove so abundant that I pass my leftovers to the woman sitting beside me to take home. Discarding uneaten food would be impolite.

Towns I visit in the line of duty often combine Lenca and Spanish colonial origins. Their euphonious names include Yarula, Belén Gualcho, San Marcos de Otopeque, Jesús de Otoro, San Pedro de Azacualpa, and Gualala. Although crime is rare in this remote western region, every municipality has its own *calabozo* (calaboose), a bare, dirt-floor room with wooden bars and an external padlock located on the main street in full view of passers-by. Inmates are displayed inside like caged animals to deter crime.

Rumor Mill

When Hurricane Mitch devastated Honduras in 1998, volunteers were temporarily evacuated to Panama, but some refused to abandon their communities in the emergency, choosing to quit the Corps instead. Volunteers often become fiercely loyal to their assigned locales, but a few just never click, perhaps because entrenched leaders feel threatened or townspeople simply reject outsiders. *Chisme*, rumor, can become a potent weapon in breaking a PC career.

One day at the Esperanza office, I happened to take a call from an irate woman, accusing a female volunteer in a neighboring village of having an affair with her husband. I'd planned to talk with the volunteer before reporting the call, but my officemates, overhearing my end of the conversation, immediately notified PC headquarters in Teguc. Two high-ranking staff drove right out to the unsuspecting volunteer's site, swooped her up bag-and-baggage with no time for goodbyes, and put her on the next flight out, despite her loud protests and copious tears. She insisted that the accusations were malicious lies, angry that they would now appear to be true, imagining the conniving wife's satisfaction in thus getting rid of her so easily. But Peace Corps officials considered the truth less important than the danger posed by the beliefs of the accuser and her family. If this volunteer's term had not been ending soon, she might have been moved to another site, but with only weeks left to go, she was sent summarily home.

According to chisme, another comely volunteer caught the fancy of an older, married, high-ranking Honduran official. That young woman was also removed from the country.

Elsewhere, a male volunteer was threatened at gunpoint by a furious father who accused him of violating his daughter's virginity. The volunteer fled to his sitemate's house, where the latter called headquarters on a cellphone fortuitously in his possession. Both volunteers were evacuated that same afternoon to a distant locale. Better safe than sorry.

Author at her desk in Esperanza's Peace Corps office
September, 2002

Man standing on corner near Esperanza office

Inebriated man lying outside Esperanza office

Don Gregorio, organic farmer

Sisters harvesting coffee

CHAPTER 17:
FRIENDS AND FOES

Around Town

A lthough my regional office duties were primary, I also served the Esperanza community by giving occasional talks at the health center and assisting with surgical brigades. At a Lions Club eye brigade, I helped patients select from over 2,000 pairs of discarded glasses sorted by strengths. I also checked for eye infections and injuries, dispensed eye drops, and made referrals for cataract and strabismus surgery as indicated. After cataract surgery, performed on only one eye, patients sat quietly on plastic chairs for several hours with their eye bandaged. When the bandage was removed—presto!—each marveled at being able to see again. A few, dizzied by the unaccustomed barrage of sights, quickly donned dark glasses.

I also recruited local youths, ages 12 to 19, to give AIDS workshops before the December 1st AIDS Day commemoration, emphasizing that our goal was to change behavior, not simply instill rote learning. The ability to recite that HIV stands for Human Immunodeficiency Virus and AIDS for Acquired Immunodeficiency Syndrome (in their Spanish equivalents) was less important than knowing how the disease was transmitted and prevented.

Since rote learning pervaded Honduran education, I also encouraged volunteers to introduce secondary students to a problem-solving competition called *Odyssey of the Mind*. Students were typically less interested in acquiring knowledge or critical thinking skills than in obtaining a coveted credential leading to a sinecure with a steady paycheck. *Odyssey* was designed to alter that mindset and stimulate a love of learning for its own sake. Participants were amazed to discover a whole new challenging intellectual world.

After I met Claske, a Dutch child-development specialist just learning Spanish, we joined forces to help a troubled three-year-old, completely neglected within her large family that included demanding twin babies. With our encouragement, she began talking, walking, and asserting herself for the first time. We took pains not to appear critical of her harried mother and grandmother, hoping only that after noticing her response to our attentions, they would follow our example.

With Deborah, a 50ish municipal development volunteer, I sometimes hiked through piney woods above La Esperanza, the altitude leaving me slightly winded. Our usual route took us by a communal laundry area fed by a spring spurting out from a rock, then past public open-air shower stalls where spring water gushed forth continuously. Once, we surprised two naked men bathing there. In cold weather, water still flowed, but the showers remained empty.

One evening, Deb invited me to share a batch of wild mushrooms picked by her neighbor, gorgeous meaty mushrooms, fully seven inches across, with bright-red tops and yellow undersides. They looked enticing, but nothing like our own familiar edible white mushrooms. Were they safe? We tested them out first by placing tiny pieces on our lips, waiting for a reaction. Finding none, we fried them up and served them over rice, enjoying a hearty meal accompanied by homemade plum wine. The sense of risk heightened our enjoyment. At least, we'd go down together if the mushrooms turned out to be lethal.

I regularly attended Sunday Mass at the larger cathedral, where soft drinks and snacks were sold openly inside and bats swirled frantically around the belfry. The interior was dark and dank, smelling of incense and hot wax from candles blazing before a statue of the Virgin clad in blue silk cloth, while women kneeling on the bare floor prayed aloud for her intercession.

I helped organize a kids' vacation-library reading program in the church rectory next door. I also met the cathedral's stooped, white-haired rector, Padre Clementino, who held a weekly children's Mass where he hopped rather nimbly around the altar, acting out gospel stories, asking for responses to such questions as, "When I don this cloak and pour water over the head of Jesus, who am I?" Answer: "John the Baptist."

Sympathetically inclined toward this man, I was taken aback when a young acolyte publicly accused him of molestation (shades of the U.S. clergy scandal!). A local radio station reported the priest's defense: a doctor's statement attesting to his impotence, which sounded pretty lame.

I soon befriended members of a Lenca women's cooperative selling crafts, jellies, coffee beans, and pastries in a shop near our office. I often bought pickled pears there, also homemade blackberry and *arrayán* (myrtle-berry) wine. These women eagerly recycled all my glass jars and bottles. I never bargained, figuring their profit margin was slim enough. Besides, they always offered me a special price. To expand their product line, two other volunteers and I went out to the coop's country kitchen where we added pineapple-upside-down cake and banana bread to their repertoire. The ladies, in turn, showed us how to make tender green-corn tortillas called *cipras*.

At the bustling Esperanza market, I encountered a cornucopia of fresh fruits and vegetables: plums, strawberries, carrots, radishes, cucumbers, cauliflower. After barren El Triunfo, I was in seventh heaven!

One of my marketplace pals was Antonio, a 27-year-old lottery-ticket vendor, rendered paraplegic by a gunshot, though he strenuously denied any gang ties. Antonio had constructed an ingenious wheelchair using bicycle parts—a three-wheeler hand-pumped by pedals where the handlebars would normally be. Two paraplegic friends had copied his design. These vehicles all sported knobby tires well suited to Esperanza's cobblestone streets.

Another market friend was Doña Chunga, real name María de Jesús, whose nickname approximates Madam Jester. Chunga, known for her puns and jokes—only clean ones—was an ardent evangelical and mother of 13. According to my officemate Luis, she ran a cantina before she got religion. After her conversion, she and her husband sold clothing together until he was killed by robbers twelve years earlier on a sales trip to El Salvador.

Undaunted, Chunga took over their market clothing stall by herself, standing there 12 hours a day, 364 days a year, with Christmas her only day off. Sometimes her youngest daughter and namesake, Chunguita (little Chunga), just a baby when her father was killed, helped her out. The other kids brought them their daily lunch, but nothing to drink, since there was no bathroom handy. Chunga gave me *anonas* (soursop) from her own backyard, their white delicately sweet fruit wrapped around mahogany-colored seeds shining like bright necklace beads. She also made me a tablecloth embroidered with colorful flowers and both our names.

Chunga proudly showed me Chunguita's $50 Education Ministry award given to a needy student with outstanding grades. One evening, the daughter invited me to a play at her evangelical church where she starred as a misguided young woman who drank, smoked, used drugs, and surrendered herself freely to men. She also danced, something strictly forbidden by her church. Predictably, her character was "saved" and abandoned her wanton ways. When I asked Chunguita later how she was allowed to dance onstage, she assured me, "Oh, it's OK to dance if it's only make-believe."

On New Year's Eve, straw old-year effigies were burned, just as in Triunfo, several prominently affixed with the name of President Ricardo Maduro, who had carried the city by a landslide. Now, midway through his four-year term, Maduro's popularity was waning. Detractors described his performance as *más hoja que tamal* (more leaf than tamale), referring to that food's traditional banana-leaf wrapping.

I accepted an invitation to a midnight supper with officemate Luis's extended family, featuring a very tough, scrawny turkey that his parents had raised themselves. I brought along a bottle of local potato wine, but found my hosts were teetotalers. New Year's fireworks exploded non-stop all night long.

January 15th saw the festival of Our Lord of Intibucá, a semi-pagan celebration whose exact origins remained murky. Fireworks were combined with religious ceremonies and townspeople danced in the streets to the music of curbside musicians, warding off the cold with frequent swigs of potato wine.

Almost Going Postal

In Triunfo, I didn't need a street address, since everyone knew where I lived, and mail never went astray, thanks to faithful postmistress María Elena.

In Esperanza, it was a different story. Here, I used the official regional office mailing address: *Oficina Regional del Cuerpo de Paz, una cuadra al norte del depósito Pepsi, contiguo a Luis Knight* (Peace Corps Regional Office, one block north of the Pepsi warehouse next to Luis Knight), Luis Knight—last name courtesy of an English grandfather—being, of course, the owner of our building and father of his namesake, our amiable office receptionist.

Innocently, I imagined that having my mail addressed to an actual office would serve a protective function. Not so. The blatant larceny of the Esperanza post office almost provoked me into going postal myself.

After experiencing María Elena's absolute integrity, I initially extended my trust to this post office, located in an official government building staffed by two full-time uniformed employees. Accordingly, on a short visit to the States before moving to La Esperanza, I mailed myself several boxes of useful items, fully confident of their arrival. When they failed to appear, I began comparing notes with other local volunteers.

What a torrent of woe my inquiry unleashed, not only about lost packages and letters, but, even worse, those that had been opened, then clumsily re-sealed—and adding insult to injury—handed over only after payment of an unauthorized postal "storage" fee. A volunteer whose friend had enclosed a $10 bill inside a letter still got the letter, but without the money and with the envelope haphazardly re-sealed, leaving the postmark askew. Another volunteer, whose mother had sent homemade brownies, found only crumbs inside. A large package airmailed from England at a cost of $100 contained a single pair of undershorts. Tampering with volunteers' mail verged on sacrilege and some actually broke down in tears after finding their packages rifled.

My office colleagues hesitated to act because of their friendship with the postal clerks, but I decided enough was enough. So, I informed the country director in Teguc, who convened a meeting with postal authorities there.

My retaliatory comeuppance for tattling came when I went to pick up mail to forward to departed volunteers: the postal ladies grimly questioned the veracity of my signed forwarding authorizations. Only after Luis's polite intervention was I allowed to collect their mail and then only via a laborious process involving numerous stamped, sealed, and signed documents, with my name and identity card number prominently affixed to each. The whole procedure, conducted with grim smiles, took almost an hour. I had demanded accountability, so now I was getting it in spades!

Japanese Peace Corps

Although less well-known than our own Peace Corps, Japan also assigns volunteers to work in developing countries. Seventy fresh-faced young men and women are sent from that safe, orderly, clean, punctual, and polite society to encounter just the opposite in Honduras, not to mention that the transition from Japanese to Spanish has to be a lot tougher than from English. And home is really far away.

Japanese International Service, as it's known, begins with three months of language training in Japan, followed by 21 months in-country. Most volunteers are in their twenties, as in our own ranks. The few over 40, I'm told, have lighter duties and receive higher living allowances (hear, hear).

Japanese volunteers assigned to La Esperanza are completely new to Spanish. Although their accent is pronounced, we communicate entirely in Spanish, since they don't know English. Among them are roommates Junko and Yuki, both bleached blondes, carpentry and sewing teachers respectively. Junko, not particularly eager to return to Japan, hopes to go next to Cambodia. Yuki, who left her fiancé back home, also plans to see more of the world before settling down.

Yuki becomes discouraged when few of her sewing students try to mount a home business, the stated purpose of her instruction. Most are aiming for maquila jobs, enrolling in her class only to get a small government stipend.

Japanese volunteers are enthusiastic participants in all our PC bashes, so different from the low-tech, family-friendly outdoor gatherings in the south. Here, as colored strobe lights flash against a shimmering mirror ball, Japanese and American party-goers each gyrate alone rather than in traditional male-female pairs, often colliding in a frenzied jumble on the crowded dance floor.

I immediately gravitate toward these volunteers because of my admiration for all things Japanese after a brief Tokyo stop-over and doing extensive research for NHK, a prominent media network. I also once had a Japanese beau. Before meeting Japanese volunteers in Honduras, I never even knew they existed.

The Odd Couple

Honey and Leo (not their real names), first met on a shopping trip in La Esperanza, I secretly dub the odd couple. Honey, a hefty woman my own age with fair skin, heavy mascara, and hennaed hair, is an American nurse from a southern state. She speaks only pidgin Spanish, which doesn't stop her in the slightest. An unflappable optimist, she's a veritable steam engine always chugging full speed ahead. Her sidekick Leo is an indigenous Lenca, dark, taciturn, stoic, and obedient—Tonto to her Lone Ranger. His leathery face, bearing a prominent scar on one cheek, is topped by bowl-cut straight black hair. He's a few inches shorter than she, 25 pounds lighter, and as many years her junior. In fact, his mother, whom I also meet, is younger than Honey. Leo takes a lot of flack from Honey and never argues. Reputedly lovers, they still refer to each other by the formal you, *usted*—she, because she's apparently unaware of the familiar form, he, because he regards her with such awe and respect.

I learn that Honey, a fervent evangelical, initially came to Honduras with a Christian medical brigade. Soon after that, Jesus Christ himself directed her to build an orphanage to care for and impart the Gospel to needy children. Unlike PC volunteers, she didn't have to consult with the community first to see if such a facility was wanted or needed, since the Lord had spoken. With an inheritance, retirement income, and donations from her church back home, she bought 40 acres on a remote mountainside and started construction. Modestly, she named the site God's Ranch.

Soon after the land purchase, Honey hired Leo—a neighboring farmer with a third-grade education—as her second-in-command. The Almighty, who works in mysterious ways, further decreed their complete unity of body and soul, overriding any merely human objections to their unmarried state. Their romance soon hit a snag when Leo's wife, the run-away mother of his pre-teen son—tracked down by Honey—refused to agree to a divorce, at least not until being offered better terms. The son, meanwhile, was being cared for by his paternal grandmother, with Honey covering all his school expenses.

I observe that Honey and Leo complement each other, each benefiting from their collaboration. She has acquired a younger bosom companion and loyal worker, he a lifetime benefactor. I envision Leo faithfully caring for Honey in her old age and one day mourning her demise. He seems a little dazed by his current good fortune and by the obvious envy of his pals. If local peasants are at all scandalized by the relationship, they give the benefit of the doubt to this rare alien being standing above the rules applied to ordinary mortals.

Honey invites me to spend part of Holy Week out at her ranch. Since our office is closed anyway and all business at a standstill, I gladly accept. She picks me up in a heavy-duty 1990 four-wheel-drive Ford truck. Her fiancé, as she calls him, always sits next to her as she drives, with me on the outside. Honey frequently grabs Leo's arm in a proprietary manner and leans over to kiss his cheek. He doesn't flinch, but looks uncomfortable, his

Lenca reserve strained by this outward show of affection.

After Leo gets out twice to change a tire en route, we park the truck where the dirt road ends. Three tied-up horses stand in wait. Although I've ridden occasionally in the south, I'm a reluctant horsewoman. Honey has promised me a docile little mule named Carolina, but there's no mule in sight, only full-sized horses. Pobrecito (Poor Little One) is assigned to me. Leo helps me mount and hands up my overnight bag, which I balance awkwardly, trying to quell my skittishness to avoid spooking my horse. The path ahead looks narrow and precipitous, so I immediately start feeling queasy, having remained slightly off-kilter ever since that Triunfo thunderclap. Honey tells a funny (to her) story about a 300-pound Canadian church member's unceremonious fall into a river when that very same animal lost his footing on slippery rocks. Christopher Reeve, whom I met after he became paralyzed from an equestrian fall, immediately comes to mind.

Pobrecito has no reins and a clipped mane, so there's nothing to hang onto. Honey says not to worry, the horse knows the way. "It's not far," she insists, as we proceed in single file with me in last place, my sweaty hands grasping onto the saddle horn. I'm back at age 3, fearfully clutching the saddle horn on that dark night so long ago. The distance turns out to be 15 excruciatingly long up-and-down kilometers through unpopulated terrain and across rivers and streams. Whenever we descend, only inches away from a particularly steep slope, Pobrecito inevitably shakes and whinnies, provoking my involuntary shrieks—always to Honey's great amusement. She offers some good advice: lean back going downhill, forward on the upslope.

After an hour and a half, when I've almost turned to jelly, I see a large white cross looming up ahead and, beyond it, what looks like a base camp. Relieved, I announce I'll make the last lap on foot. My companions decide to dismount too and Leo briefly takes my arm to help me down. With a little frown, Honey abruptly pulls him toward her. (Don't worry, lady, I'm not trying to steal your boyfriend.)

We stand there together for a brief moment, just watching the setting sun. The view of the valley below is breathtakingly empty and peaceful, no sign of human life as far as the eye can see. The sound of a distant waterfall adds to the ambience. Maybe this spot is truly blessed after all.

The altitude here is about 500 feet above La Esperanza's and, after my anxious ride, I feel slightly dizzy hiking up to the old adobe ranch house and outbuildings. Several horses tethered Wild West style stand out in front. This is only the first outpost of a much more grandiose project, Honey explains. Construction of the orphanage itself, still only a wooden skeleton, has stalled temporarily because custom-made windows transported laboriously by foot and horseback turn out to have a major flaw: glass in what were to be vertical double-hung windows was installed horizontally instead, preventing them from sliding up and down. Honey says they simply must be returned and fixed.

The two-room dirt-floor ranch house, with a wood-burning stove in one corner, is furnished with several rough-hewn bunk beds. The room I'm assigned to share with the teenage cook doubles as the kitchen. She offers me her bottom bunk and agrees to take the top. Honey and Leo share a narrow bunk in the next room, while workmen occupy bunks right next to and above them. I can't help being curious about their intimate relations at such close quarters.

A transistor radio tuned perpetually to an evangelical station hangs from a rafter. Outside, clucking chickens encircle a tied-up pig called Chuleta (Pork Chop), spared the ax so far only because there's no refrigeration. Our supper, prepared by the youthful cook, includes blue tortillas, beans, and fresh vegetables from the garden. We eat with handmade three-tined forks. The ride here has given me a good appetite.

Adjacent to the main house is a bathing room outfitted with another woodstove for heating bath water. To prevent rapid latrine build-up, Honey has decreed that toilet paper not be thrown in, but rather burned with other combustible trash. After each use, a mixture of sawdust and dirt is tossed down the latrine opening, not only to control odor, but to create mulch.

That first evening, Honey sends out runners to convene everyone to a meeting on the open floor of the unfinished orphanage. She reigns over her territory like queen of the mountain, giving orders all around. I feel a grudging admiration for this woman who, despite her rudimentary Spanish and relative innocence of local culture, has moved her project relentlessly forward in such an inhospitable environment. When I praise her phenomenal progress, she gives the Lord full credit, "I am only the instrument; God is moving on this mountain."

Honey's home congregation has just sent numerous boxes of clothing, toys, and household goods. But before the contents can be distributed, the hundreds of folks gathered must watch a video—dubbed in Spanish—about Jesus' life, death, and resurrection. They sit crowded together on wooden benches and the bare floor as Honey leads them in a brief opening prayer, after which they cross themselves, revealing a Catholic habit. A generator is fired up to power a TV set and the film begins.

Two hours into the story, all the kids have either fallen asleep or left to play together in the dark. The generator runs down precisely at 11 pm during closing credits. Kerosene lamps are then lit and the distribution of donated goods begins, but quickly degenerates into a free-for-all, with some grabbing extras and others going empty-handed. Honey tries to restore order by passing out small plastic cups of sweetened coffee to children and adults alike, along with sugared buns brought from La Esperanza. The cups are then collected for reuse and people disappear into the darkness, many grumbling that they came for nothing. Honey appears not to hear them.

Back at the ranch house, I crawl fully clothed under scratchy wool blankets and fall fast asleep, only to be awakened periodically by a cat walking on my face and men entering to pour coffee from a pot left brewing on the stove. At 5 am, my bunkmate is already up, hauling in new firewood. Dragging myself out of bed, I find my arms and legs are covered with itchy red welts.

At sunrise, Honey announces a trip into town, not to Esperanza, but to a closer village, San Juan, to celebrate Leo's son's 12th birthday, Good Friday notwithstanding. I groan at the prospect of another horseback ride. After riding back to the parked truck, we tie up the horses and take their saddles with us for safekeeping. The truck's brakes soon give out, obliging Honey to ride the emergency brake all the way down to town.

Once there, we briefly watch a rodeo with bucking broncos. I then duck into a quaint 16th century church. Since it's a Catholic sanctuary, Honey elects to remain outside teaching Leo and his son to drive in an empty lot, using only the emergency brake to stop. Next, we pick up a teenage ranch hand, Bartolomé, the cook's boy friend, who sits out back with the son. After a celebratory meal, we're returning to the ranch when the truck grinds to a halt. Honey manages to turn it around and coast down to a mechanic's house. Alas, only the wife and kids are home, the mechanic having gone to see his "other woman." Honey decides to stay overnight at a guest house to have the car fixed in the morning, but directs Bartolomé and me to go fetch the horses and return to the ranch.

We hitch a ride in a pickup already packed with passengers. I'm helped into the rear truck-bed by a young man who hangs on a bit too long, so I sit down next to Bartolomé for protection. The tropical sun sets quickly as dark and chill descend. Suddenly, we realize we've left the saddles behind; bareback may be fine for Bartolomé, but not for me. Too late now, we're already on our way. A couple of passengers strum guitars, and I chime in on familiar songs, like Cielito Lindo and Guantánamera.

To make room for newcomers, two teenage boys edge Bartolomé aside and squeeze in next to me, including the one who'd helped me onto the truck. He introduces himself as Carmindo. His friend is Heriberto. Before I know it, they're competing vociferously for my hand in marriage. After all, if Leo could get himself such a sweetheart deal, why can't they?

"Wait a sec, boys, I'm 65 years old, my granddaughter is your age for heavens sake!" No matter, Carmindo reassures me, "we Hondurans are very mature."

Not to be outdone, Heriberto promises: "I'm a more passionate lover." He stretches an arm possessively around my shoulders. "Whoa! Now, that's going too far!" I stand up abruptly, almost losing my balance on the bumpy road, and call out to Bartolomé, who comes to my rescue.

The two smirking boys soon jump off and we continue on up the mountain until reaching the driver's turnoff to his own house. He asks each passenger for about $1. I offer him more if he will take us up to where the horses are tethered, but he's out of fuel and can only coast downhill. So Bartolomé and I begin trudging uphill in the pitch-dark moonless night as a light drizzle begins to fall; I clutch my companion's arm, unable to see much ahead.

We're almost up to the horses when a single headlight flashes behind us. Surprised, we turn around to see the Ford approaching at full throttle. It turns out the mechanic returned home and, untwisting the fuel hose, put the vehicle back in working order. I'm glad to see the saddles and don't complain during the dark, damp ride back to the ranch. Bartolomé doubles up on a horse with Leo.

Honey is a real dynamo, an unstoppable force, taming the wilderness with the help of her trusty companion—and, she would insist, with divine intervention. After my return to the States, she e-mails me that Leo's divorce finally came through and they have gotten married. I send best wishes.

Midnight Marauder

In my scariest robbery yet, nothing is actually taken. This happens in La Esperanza, reputedly safer than El Triunfo. Surrounded by a cinderblock wall, my little house has a roof of handmade red tiles laid atop wooden slats. It wouldn't be too hard for someone to climb up the wall, remove the tiles, and slip into the dwelling below.

I'm fast asleep when someone actually does just that, landing on a small table, shattering a lamp. I sit up with a start, hearing distinct footsteps and heavy breathing. My sleepy eyes make out a figure creeping straight toward my bed, a mere silhouette, barely illuminated by the moonlight shining through the window. Is this just a dream or is it real? Jolted suddenly wide awake, I open my mouth, but nothing comes out. I then emit a series of screams worthy of *Psycho,* leaving me completely hoarse. Fired by adrenalin, I jump out of bed, giving chase barefoot in my nightgown, crazy if the guy is armed, but at a time like this, who's thinking? Apparently I scare the would-be robber as much as vice versa, as he dashes out the front door. From the open doorway, I watch him vanish into the darkness.

Trembling, with my heart galloping 200 kilometers a minute, I flip on the light—the electricity is working—to reveal a gaping hole in the ceiling, as well as my radio, flashlight, scissors, and duct tape gathered all together on the floor, a rather pitiful collection of loot. Still barefoot (it's July and no longer cold), I dash over to the landlord's where the dogs greet me with effusive licks—where were they when I needed them? The family is already awake, having heard my screams. The landlord calls the police. Two uniformed officers arrive on foot and survey the roof hole with a flashlight, whatever good that does.

My roof is repaired the next day. I'm still jittery, but since I'll be departing soon, it's too much hassle to move out now, so I start immediately giving things away. First, my bike, which goes to the maid who mops our office floors four times a day. She's thrilled, as she lives at quite a distance. (I've questioned Luis about her incessant mopping, but he says she needs a job and would get bored if not kept busy.)

Afterwards, especially when walking out alone after dark in bright moonlight, I give a start whenever a human shadow overtakes me. Sometimes, it's only my own shadow.

Woman outside Esperanza's provincial prison waiting to visit her husband inside

Gunshot survivor Antonio selling lottery tickets from homemade wheelchair

Straw-filled New Year's dummy ready to be set alight

CHAPTER 18:
NICARAGUA REVISITED

Surprise Rift

Near the end of my 13-month Peace Corps extension, I traveled to Nicaragua to say goodbye. I'd first been there in 1941 as a toddler, during that same early Central American trip. In the 1980s, I'd made several investigative forays to Nicaragua and had kept in touch with friends there ever since. On visits during my PC service, I found *nicas* to be a stubbornly cantankerous lot, still arguing bitterly among themselves since the 1980s. Unlike largely apolitical Hondurans, they kept lobbing nasty barbs across the ideological divide. American political polarization pales in comparison. PCVs in Nicaragua had to carefully avoid taking sides.

Nicaraguan politics also made strange bedfellows. During my final visit there in mid 2003, I found Sandinista Daniel Ortega teamed up shamelessly with disgraced former Liberal Party president Arnoldo Alemán, now serving house arrest for massive fraud and corruption. Together, they organized demonstrations protesting Alemán's "persecution" by President Enrique Bolaños, a man I once knew and considered basically honest. Arriving at Managua's outskirts on my last visit there, I found roads blocked by pro-Alemán protesters burning tires, filling the air with dark acrid smoke. Ortega was not only courting Alemán's followers, but fending off accusations by his step-daughter, Zoilamérica, that he had raped and impregnated her while she was still a child, shipping her off to Moscow to have the baby.

In Nicaragua, prices were marginally higher than in Honduras, the *córdoba*, being worth slightly more than the lempira. Among other differences, the Nicaraguan population was a million less in somewhat larger territory. The country demonstrated close economic parity with Honduras, but had many more NGOs, some 1,200 in all, a legacy of the Sandinista era.

Nicaragua won hand-down on passable roads, constructed decades ago by dictator Anastasio Somoza using enduring blocks manufactured by his family business. Nicaraguans drank instant Nescafé, something Hondurans would not tolerate, and their phone and electrical services had been privatized, which Honduran unions would never permit. Nicaraguans loved baseball, while Hondurans were strictly soccer fans.

During my farewell visit to Nicaragua, I walked unwittingly into a bitter power struggle between two one-time friends who once ran a charitable foundation together outside Managua. Unexpectedly caught between impassioned charges and countercharges, I struggled to remain neutral, covering my ears to shut them both out. My reconciliation efforts proved futile.

Their dispute was partly ideological, going back to old Sandinista times, partly current. I was shown phone records of mysterious calls to Afghanistan and other far-flung places not obviously related to foundation affairs. Accounting discrepancies, lies, bribery, and embezzlement, even child abuse, were all alleged.

One of my combative hosts was Alberto, the foundation's Italian director, the other Larry, a Nicaraguan former board member, both in their early fifties. Since they were no longer on speaking terms and refused to cross into each other's territory, I shuttled awkwardly between them.

Larry lived in an extended family compound on a major highway in a half-built dwelling—unfinished after 25 years—shared with his wife and two adult sons, including the older son's wife and baby. The cinderblock structure consisted of one enormous room with curtained partitions and a corrugated tin roof. The walls were decorated with the usual prints of da Vinci's Last Supper and JFK, as well as a crucifix, an outdated calendar, a clock stopped at midnight (or noon), and faded photographs of my own family from 20 years before. I was assigned the younger son's hard, narrow wooden bunk, but never found out where he slept meanwhile. "Don't worry," I was told.

Tethered pigs lounged in the shade of abundant fruit trees. White gardenias sweetened the air around an outhouse and outdoor shower stall open to the sky, its rustic ambience marred only by giant hairy tarantulas scurrying up and down.

Across the road, a Taiwanese clothing factory hummed away day and night. Horse carts clopped along and trucks rumbled constantly past. Next door, drilling and soldering sounds emanated from a cousin's workshop. Altogether, a lively, noisy place.

The older son's wife made me an embroidered washcloth and gave me some rubber flip-flops she called *chinelas (chancletas* in Honduran). Larry's pregnant sisters-in-law, sharing another house in the same compound, informed me earnestly that duck soup was an abortifant and coconut milk, a fertility aid. Among the gaggle of nieces and nephews playing outside together was Heidi, a sweet-faced ten-year-old using only sign language. Larry's wife said she had lost her hearing after an adored older cousin died from drinking insecticide. Heidi, then 3, took one look inside the open coffin and fainted, never to utter a single word again.

Larry, who bedded down each night with his wife, nonetheless introduced me to his "other woman," with whom he had five children. He also took me to visit old human rights and labor leaders who instantly recognized me, embracing and kissing me warmly after almost two decades. With Larry, I attended a wake, visited a mass burial shrine to victims of a volcanic eruption, participated in political meetings—including of his own resurgent Neo-Liberal Party—and applauded a parade featuring *las gigantonas,* giant female papier-mache folk figures manipulated by guys hidden under bright flowered dresses. I was often served unpalatable chicken sandwiches, also popular in Honduras, consisting of white bread spread with mustard and ground up chicken, including crushed bone fragments that stuck between the teeth.

With Alberto, it was a quite different story. We consumed Italian wine and imported pasta out under the trees. We visited the foundation's schools, including a beauty school where two female students gave me a pedicure. They washed and massaged my feet and painted my toenails atomic pink, quite a sensuous experience, while a student in a wheelchair styled my hair. I also helped out with a free medical clinic conducted inside a small Catholic chapel and inventoried the contents of a shipping container of donated goods from Italy.

At an evening community meeting, I protested when Alberto introduced me as "a personal friend of Nobel Laureate Jimmy Carter," dismissing my disclaimers as false modesty. (I had once casually mentioned having met Carter during election monitoring missions.)

After the meeting, I talked with a blind couple with a squirming sighted two-year-old, clutching her tightly to keep her within their "sight," finally letting an older girl take charge of her.

At the foundation's headquarters, I met a beautiful mysterious woman of 20 named Exania. Slender, with long, lush hair, stylish clothes, and an enigmatic Mona Lisa smile, she carried around a cute, chubby baby rumored to have been fathered by a visiting Italian priest. In her bedroom, which she generously vacated for my use, I came across photos of her in Italy with an older man (the priest?), Italian cosmetics, and an Italian-Spanish dictionary.

Through Alberto, I also met 75-year-old Don Santos, founder of a village named for a deceased Italian priest, Padre Rafael Fabreto. Santos told me a rather unique fish story. While angling out on Lake Managua, though lacking upper teeth, he used to bite into the gills of each new catch to put it out of its misery. Once, a squirming fish slid right down his throat, choking him. When frantic efforts to dislodge the creature failed, Santos thought himself a goner. Before collapsing into a faint, he prayed to his friend, the late Father Rafael, promising to establish a community in his name if he survived. A passing woman came upon his prone figure and got him to a hospital, where he recovered, later fulfilling his vow.

Out one afternoon with Alberto, I'm driving his car along a country road outside Managua when a Vespa rider up ahead stops to pick up a female hitchhiker. They speed off, but around a bend, we come upon the cycle overturned and both riders lying in a ditch. The man is awake, but his left arm is oddly bent. The woman is unconscious and bleeding.

To avoid aggravating a possible back injury, we gently lay the injured woman on the back seat and I turn the wheel over to Alberto to drive to the hospital. The woman soon dies of head injuries and her family threatens to sue the cyclist, whose burst front tire caused the accident. At her family's insistence, the man is arrested and shoved roughly into a jail cell, further injuring his broken arm. When I tell Larry, although he has split with the Sandinistas, he flashes an old photo of himself guarding Daniel Ortega and Fidel Castro to Sandinista guards now running the jail and gets the man released. This accident especially upsets me, as my niece died of head injuries in a Florida motorcycle crash.

In a bizarre coincidence, around that same fateful highway curve, with Alberto now at the wheel, we encounter an overturned *moto-taxi*, a three-wheeled two-passenger vehicle. The unconscious driver, still breathing but smelling strongly of alcohol, lies pinned underneath. We're unable to lift the heavy vehicle off his body. Two soldiers in a jeep soon stop and we leave them in charge. We learn later that the man has died.

Glue Addicts' Lair

Another emotional jolt comes from visiting glue addicts living in appalling squalor in a decaying building in the heart of Managua's market district. Called *resistoleros* for a brand of glue called Resistol, or simply *huelepegas* (glue-sniffers), their communal abode is an eerie, phantasmagoric place—a hollow, crumbling, dank, cave-like structure, once opulent, but long ago abandoned. I've removed my watch and earrings beforehand and hold tightly onto Alberto's arm as we enter.

Before our eyes can fully adapt to the gloom, we almost gag on the choking stench of rancid urine. I suppress a shriek as a large gray rat darts past and an army of shiny brown roaches scurries underfoot. Shadowy human figures of all ages, some only half-clad, all gaunt and filthy, emerge from the shadows as our eyes adjust, several of them moving languidly, others lying stock-still in a drug-induced haze, each clutching onto a baby-food jar of glue. The blaze of an untended cooking fire in one corner provides the only illumination for this Boschian scene. Undernourished babies with smudged, tear-stained faces, highlighted by the fire, crawl aimlessly about the littered floor, sucking on fingers and whimpering softly. A young mother with papery sallow skin, awakened by her crying infant, reflexively pulls a jar out of her bra and gives the child a whiff to shut her up.

Returning now two years after my first visit here, I see many of the same people, miraculously still alive, but more emaciated, with even more children, and still sniffing glue. When I grab the upraised glue hand of a pregnant woman, protesting that she's harming her unborn child, she blubbers, "I really *want* to stop, but I just *can't*." Then she and another expectant mother burst into giggles.

A woman named Flor tearfully complains that relatives have taken away all her children. Another confesses that her toddler has been hospitalized after drinking kerosene.

Alberto tosses out canisters of powdered milk for the children to a forest of grabbing hands. We then edge slowly back toward our parked car, where our driver is standing guard. We manage to slip inside as addicts press against the doors and bang on the fenders. I wonder how often Alberto visits this wretched place and whether he's deliberately trying to shock me by bringing me here. He doesn't seem to be doing anything for these people except distributing milk—maybe that's all he *can* do. How do they survive anyway? By theft, prostitution, begging? It's distressing to see fellow humans living this way, producing children who know no other life.

Dumpsite Kids

Our next stop is a garbage dump community outside Managua. I've encountered trash scavengers before, but it's always heartbreaking to see wizened, undernourished kids—some only 5 or 6, barefoot, with dirty, calloused, and bleeding fingers—waiting for parental permission to dash over to the dump before all the good stuff is taken.

A perpetual odor clings to these youngsters, who wake up before dawn in shacks tacked together with scavenged cardboard and surrounded by fetid wastewater. Bypassing makeshift latrines, younger kids just pee on their home's dirt floor. Dogs, cats, chickens, and crawling babies mix freely in the muck, while vultures attracted by the nearby trash pit circle endlessly overhead. I keep my mouth tightly shut, warding off dense clouds of pesky black flies.

Once given the signal, shouting and jostling children race toward the dump—ominously dubbed the *crematorio*—dragging along empty gunnysacks, separate ones for metal, paper, plastic, rags, and glass. A boy named Felicio proudly hauls back a bent metal bedspring, too big for a sack.

Parents, too, join in, pooling each family's daily take to sell as scrap. They keep some items for home use: old pots, plastic soda bottles, pieces of tarp, half-burned candles. Worn clothing, scuffed shoes, a broken doll, a wobbly chair, all are recycled within a household. A bike with a missing wheel is set aside awaiting the appearance of another wheel. Homemade crutches and a wooden leg are saved in case of future necessity. A mother adorns her very floppy baby, obviously disabled, with bright ribbons and gaudy earrings found at the dump. Nothing is wasted. Families even consume discarded fruits and vegetables.

But it's hardly a free lunch. Scavenging obviously poses serious risks for children, keeping them out of school and exposing them to insect bites and cuts, as well as toxic car batteries, kerosene cans, and pesticide containers.

After this last shock excursion, Alberto drives me back to the border, where I get out and walk across the Japanese-built bridge separating Nicaragua and Honduras. As I set foot in Guasaule on the Honduran side, folks run up to greet me by name. I feel relieved to be back "home" again.

Crossing into Nicaragua on bicycle transport

*Outside Managua, roads being blocked with
burning tires*

Glue-sniffer's baby crawling unattended across littered floor

Young glue addict holding jar to his nose

CHAPTER 19:
MOMENT OF TRUTH

Countdown

After almost 3 ½ years in Honduras, I'm approaching the end, although hardly finished with all I'd like to accomplish. The needs just in my small corner are simply too vast. Should I consider staying on even longer? I wrestle with the possibility. I *could* keep plugging away *ad infinitum* like other expatriate humanitarians. On good days, I'm tempted to stay just a few more months, but the robber coming through my roof has shaken me. I may have already used up my nine lives. Besides, I've promised my family that I'll be leaving. A big bash is planned for Mother's 90th birthday and, after that, she definitely wants me home to stay. If she were to die while I was still in Honduras, I'd never forgive myself. So September 25, 2003, is set for my close of service. Later on, I may join up again, or give six months to PC Response, the short-term service open to former volunteers. But for now, I plan to leave, after completing a few last agenda items.

Wedding Bells

That includes attending a wedding. More than two years after Seth's departure, he and Loni are scheduled to be reunited and married at a High Mass at Choluteca's main cathedral. Loni's sisters, including the younger half-sisters born to their father's "other woman," serve as bridesmaids. Seth and his parents, divorced and living separately, arrive together. Seth's mother confides, "With our only child now getting married and the prospect of grandchildren, his father and I have reconciled."

I coach the parents on a few Spanish phrases and serve as their interpreter. Seth's best childhood friend will act as best man. The day before the wedding, Seth comes down with a virulent case of Lempira's revenge, so Loni gives him an injection to speed his recovery.

On the wedding morning, Fabio, a pink-shirted hairdresser with a blond-streaked bouffant and agile hands, arrives at the family home to arrange hairdos and apply makeup. Bridesmaids, flower girls, and the radiant bride herself undergo his creative ministrations. He buttresses tresses with abundant hairspray and inserts artificial flowers after liberal use of a ratting comb.

A whirring video camera records the traditional ceremony. Seth hands Loni several large shiny coins signifying his intent to support her and loops a knotted satin rope around her to bind them together forever. When a noisy drunk enters the cathedral, Loni's father jumps up, stopping short when the priest admonishes, "Let us forgive those who trespass against us." Left alone, the intruder stretches out on a back pew and falls asleep.

Loni thanks me for introducing her to Seth and after she is living in northern New England—with such a contrasting climate, terrain, and way of life—she sends me a letter expressing gratitude for my support and friendship, also for my efforts on behalf of her people. I'm deeply touched by her warm description of our collaboration.

Loni bravely embarks on her new life and finds work in the health field, but not yet as a physician. She, who has delivered over 500 babies and treated countless patients of all ages, is hired as a nursing home aide. Even in this humble position, her quiet competence and cheerful bedside manner shine through.

Barbie, Queen of Hearts

Denise, AKA Barbie, is a California visitor whom I meet for the first time at the Teguc airport, only weeks before leaving Honduras. "Barbie" is a nickname (no disrespect intended) acknowledging her statuesque figure, long legs, stylish clothing, and waist-length naturally blond hair. Before her arrival, we've only communicated by e-mail, so I'm surprised by Denise's stunning good looks. She's an intrepid world traveler who also happens to be totally blind. How did we connect? Simply because my website solicited items for the blind and Denise, a teacher, generously responded.

I had invited Denise because of her Spanish fluency and interest in joining the Peace Corps. Back in Washington, I'd met Sarah, a blind former volunteer who had once served in Morocco. I also knew of deaf volunteers assigned to Jamaica. Such volunteers not only provide valuable services, but act as role models for locals with disabilities. Of course, the host country must accept and formally invite a disabled volunteer, just as with any other. If Denise wanted to serve in Honduras, I was sure we could engineer it. Because of my relationship with an adult blind training center in Santa Lucía, I'd arranged a visit for her there.

Denise instantly enchanted everyone she met. Attracted by her friendly smile, Santa Lucía residents boldly approached her on the street, gazing curiously into her sky-blue eyes, caressing her pale arms, and stroking her silky blond hair. She faced them directly, conversing easily in Spanish and reaching out appropriately to embrace and kiss new acquaintances on both cheeks. Denise was eager to "see" all the sights, not just facilities for the blind. In neighboring Valle de Ángeles, she bought a *colombina*, a small autoharp hand-made by a local musician-woodcarver. The woodcarver, just returned from collecting fallen trees in the forest (never cutting them down), let Denise stroke and smell the various types of wood used to make his instruments. In Valle, she also sampled several fruit wines to take home.

Backtracking a bit, ever since my training days in Santa Lucía, I'd kept in touch with the adult blind center located there, finding its self-help philosophy compatible with that of similar U.S. facilities. Honduras also has two residential schools for blind children, one in Teguc, the other in San Pedro.

The adult center is called CAIPAC, for *Centro Artensanal e Industrial para Adultos Ciegos* (Artisan and Industrial Center for Blind Adults). The land and building were donated in a will. Its residential program, free to the blind and severely visually impaired, spans the nine-month school year, with most students returning for a second term. Students are taught cane travel, Braille, massage, music, farming, crafts, carpentry, and tasks of daily living, including cooking, cleaning, washing, and ironing. Their pottery and knit goods are sold in a little shop. Those from rural areas also must learn to use a toilet, shower, brush their teeth, and—most importantly—expand their personal horizons.

Some new residents, though physically able, have never learned to walk, dress, or feed themselves. The sighted director, Irma (not to be confused with my Valle host), makes sure they master self-care and ambulation skills, pairing up feeble newbies with more able student mentors. Students have ranged in age from 18 to 82. The 82-year-old, who'd lost his sight two years before, mastered cane travel, but refused to tackle Braille, especially since he'd never learned to read print in the first place.

Five of CAIPAC's instructors are sightless themselves, four of them center graduates. Braille teacher Timoteo, born blind, didn't start school until age 12, but went on to earn a university degree. Wilmer, blinded by childhood conjunctivitis (curable with antibiotics), teaches poultry care, neatly severing a chicken's head in one unerring chop. David, whose blindness resulted from a cat virus, sometimes uses me as a subject to demonstrate the finer points of massage. Fabio, blind carpentry instructor, shows students how to protect their fingers while operating a power saw.

Director Irma's adoptive mother, Pilar Salinas, a blind matriarch honored with a Honduran postage stamp, founded the residential school for blind children in Teguc. Pilar's example inspired Irma to establish the adult center.

Both school and adult center, in addition to teaching educational subjects and self-care skills, strive to eliminate "blindisms"— *ciegismos* in Spanish, *ciego* being the word for blind, though sightless folks prefer the term *no vidente* (non-seeing). Such mannerisms, most often found in the congenitally blind, consist of autistic-like movements—head shaking, hand flapping, and rhythmic rocking, as well as repeated touching of eyes or eye-sockets—all representing self-stimulation efforts by those lacking visual input. Peer buddies help new students break these habits.

Before Denise arrives, Irma tells me that the adult center has 17 full- and part-time employees and operates with an annual government subsidy of $45,000, supplemented by modest poultry and craft sales. Because of scarce funds, the center's phone has been disconnected and enrollment has now been cut back from 35 to 20 students. "We just can't feed any more right now," Irma sighs. As finances permit, she will drive out in her own pickup to locate new students and bring them back, often clashing with families dependent on the begging earnings of blind members.

Adult students do their own laundry and eat together in a central meeting hall. They help the cook prepare meals, attend classes until midday, and spend afternoons walking in pairs around town. They sleep in two gender-segregated dormitories, locked at night to prevent unauthorized couplings, while a watchman roams the premises.

Irma and I decide that Denise will start out visiting the adult center, then proceed to the residential school in Teguc, *Escuela Para Ciegos Pilar Salinas,* named for and directed by Irma's mother, Pilar Salinas, now almost 90. The school's 70 students, ages 4 to 20, are nearly all totally blind, since the partially sighted are rarely considered blind in Honduras. Several older graduates commute to the national university while still boarding at the school, including Leonel, blind from birth, studying criminal law, who takes exams orally. He demonstrates a rich singing voice, also considerable mechanical skill, once helping me open a recalcitrant lock.

The children's school surrounds a central patio. The two-story structure includes offices, classrooms, and dormitories, the latter divided according to age and gender, with 10 kids per room assigned to bunk beds, while an attendant sleeps in a single bed in the same room. The attendant in one girls' dorm is a young sighted widow, whose 8-year-old daughter has lived at the school since infancy. Although this seeing child attends regular classes outside, the blind school is her home and she introduces her blind dorm-mates as her sisters.

Children share common bathrooms where water for bathing and flushing toilets must be hauled in buckets from two outdoor pilas filled up only once or twice a week. These supply all the water used not only for bathing, but for cooking, mopping floors, and washing dishes, clothes, and bedding—all by hand in cold water. To brush their teeth, students must take their toothbrushes down to a pila. Girls wash their own clothes and hang them up to dry, but boys have theirs washed by female staff. Even I find it challenging to haul a bucket to a bathroom without sloshing it. Imagine a residential school operating year-round with just a bucket brigade! But no one complains; it's just the way things are.

Meals are served in a central dining room that doubles as an assembly area. After eating, kids carry their plates back to the kitchen where they often stop to pet the resident cat, Chapín, reputed to be a good mouser. A pigeon aptly named Paloma eats any crumbs spilled on the floor.

On one side of the school patio is a Catholic chapel topped with a cross where seminarians say Mass on weekends. A phone set in a patio corner has ingeniously had its dial removed to allow incoming calls, but not outgoing ones. The patio also opens onto the back door of a convenience store where students can buy snacks, with the storefront serving the passing public as *Pulpería Pilar Salinas.*

Blind Visionary

Latino women may have a reputation for submissiveness, but neither Irma nor her mother fits that mold. Irma, who can read Braille and cane-travel blindfolded, is a blunt, no-nonsense, hyperactive type. Pilar, though elderly and soft-spoken, always appears alert, dignified, and in full command, as witnessed during a staff meeting where she was giving teachers, both blind and sighted, directions and assignments.

Doña Pilar, erect, impossibly thin, with delicately bird-like movements, wears dark-tinted granny glasses and a gold cross, gold earrings, and a gold bracelet on her slender wrist. Her snow-white hair is pulled back into a bun and a dab of lipstick adorns her expressive mouth. Her regal bearing commands respect.

Orphaned as a teenager, young Pilar left Honduras to live with an older married sister in Guatemala, where she studied to become a teacher. When her eyesight began failing, an American doctor working in Guatemala diagnosed her with *iritis,* an eye inflammation. He was probably not an ophthalmologist, since Pilar said he removed her tonsils in a vain effort to eliminate her eye infection. When that didn't work, he operated first on one eye, then the other, obliterating even her partial remaining vision. Friends urged her to sue, but instead Pilar threw her energies into graduating from college, after which she began teaching at a Guatemalan school for the blind. Soon, she returned to her native country to establish a similar institution. In 1948, while still in her early 30s, she founded the residential school that bears her name.

After a sighted niece moved in with her, Pilar adopted three girls, becoming an adoption pioneer in a country where adoption laws have always been exceedingly restrictive. One of these daughters, of course, was Irma, now 50. Irma's birth mother was Honduran, her father, American. Pilar tracked down both birth parents living in the States and persuaded the father to provide child support. Later, when Irma learned her birth mother was dying of cancer, she brought the woman to Honduras, along with her teenage daughter and alcoholic husband, where she cared for her until her death. The birth mother tearfully confessed to trying to abort her pregnancy. "She admitted trying to flush me down the toilet, begging my forgiveness," Irma confides, "but I wish she'd just taken that secret to her grave."

Inspired by adoptive mother Pilar, Irma from early childhood wanted to work with the blind. She won a scholarship to study in Spain and, after returning to Honduras, established CAIPAC, the adult training center.

When Irma learned about a blind teenager being kept in bed, spoon-fed, and not yet toilet-trained, she threatened the father's civil service job unless he immediately enrolled his son at her center. She also managed to find funds to send two blind runners, one male, one female, to the Athens Para-Olympics along with their trainer.

As a widow with four children, Irma struggled to support them through college and now has only her ten-year-old daughter, Yolani, left to go. Recently, she married Alberto, CAIPAC's taciturn, gentle pottery teacher, a full decade younger and never before married. "Just between us," Irma whispers, "Younger men are better in bed."

Once, while staying at their house, I shared a room with Irma's daughter, who woke up early to play with Barbie dolls in the pitch-dark windowless room. When I asked, "Why not turn on the light?" Yolani said she didn't want to disturb me—also that her mother had taught her how to play with dolls in the dark, "just like a blind girl."

Doña Pilar and Irma are two strong—even headstrong—women who've offered countless sightless Hondurans hope, skills, and self-confidence. I feel privileged to be their friend.

St. Lucy's Emissary

When we first meet Denise at the Teguc airport, Irma and I immediately notice her wearing a medal for St. Lucy, patron of the blind, guaranteed to endear her to residents of Santa Lucía, a town named for that very saint. Denise arrives loaded down with donations, all successfully passed through customs. Included are Braille paper, Braille labelers, magnifiers, a dozen white folding canes, a Braille writer, Braille and chiming watches, slates and styluses, blank tapes, a tape recorder, and—most marvelous of all—a laptop computer programmed for Spanish mechanical speech.

Irma calls Denise "an angel from heaven." She introduces both of us everywhere as "Doctora"; I advise Denise, "Just relax, don't fight it."

At the adult center, to everyone's astonishment and delight, Denise demonstrates the use of her small personal electronic note taker, which *speaks* in both Spanish and English and also saves notes in erasable Braille dots. She teaches two of the adult center's blind instructors how to use the laptop, beginning with the standard QWERTY keyboard, with which they are unfamiliar. In conversation, Denise and center residents agree that the hardest part of blindness is not the physical challenges or sensory loss, but being devaluated as a person.

A semiprofessional dancer, Denise patiently instructs CAIPAC residents in salsa, having each take turns placing their hands on her waist and shoulders to experience the movements. She comments on the irony of having *her* teach salsa to Hondurans. Then, because we've been invited to stay overnight at the center, she and I bed down in the women's dorm. Irma warns us to keep our belongings between our adjacent beds: "Don't think just because these ladies are blind, that they are incapable of theft."

White folding canes are an imported luxury here. Adult center students, besides improvising with mop handles, also carve canes from tree limbs. Their own hand-made wooden canes display fanciful raccoon and other animal faces. One student fashions a sturdy wooden staff for Denise's hikes in the Oakland hills. Later, she has no trouble taking it back on the plane, while a tiny wrench for tuning her autoharp is confiscated by Houston's airport security.

Our next stop is a visit to the children's school in Teguc, where Denise and I are treated to a student performance featuring original guitar, piano, accordion, and recorder pieces. A teenage girl whose melodious voice almost takes our breath away sings *Yesterday* in English with such flair and emotion that she could easily become a female Jose Feliciano. Several students enact a humorous skit of their own creation, lampooning the Catholic church, their school, and even blind people. Afterward, Denise goes from child to child, passing out balloons, candy, and used clothing. Two little homesick boys, new to the school, bury their faces in their arms, refusing to respond. With soft words and gentle strokes, Denise persuades them to raise their heads and accept her gifts.

Before she leaves, I introduce Denise to the PC country director and assistant director. Both are impressed and willing to accept her as a volunteer. But because of family commitments back in California and a job there she dearly loves, Denise delays completing an application. Soon her life goes in other directions and she defers her Peace Corps plans.

Errand of Mercy

Within days of my own departure from Honduras, I travel south with Timoteo, the adult center's Braille teacher, agreeing to cover fuel costs if he'll obtain a vehicle and driver. Timoteo, who also heads up the Christian

Brotherhood's disability organization, has promised a wheelchair for my friend Bessy, a 30-year-old paraplegic woman living in Guasaule at the Nicaraguan border. According to her brother, Bessy was shot by her husband, but she gives me several competing stories: she fell out of a window, was in a car accident, was shot by a stranger. She lies in bed stark naked on a piece of soiled cardboard all day long, alone in the simmering heat, reading the Bible aloud. Her mother sells goods at the border and her teenage son lives with a sister in El Triunfo. I've given Bessy numerous urine collection bags, also several outfits that she rarely wears. Her ancient wheelchair is completely worn out after years of rolling over rough terrain. She can sit in this chair, but not go anywhere.

Hondurans often promise more than they can deliver. But Timoteo, true to his word, takes an early morning bus to a distant village to personally repossess a still functioning wheelchair whose user has grown too fat to use it. Tim has agreed to give this chair to Bessy. Right after retrieving it, his bus breaks down and he has to hitchhike to our meeting place. Despite being blind and carrying a folded wheelchair, he arrives on time. I'm amazed and touched.

After arriving in Guasaule with our car and driver, before going on to Bessy's, we stop by a dirt-floor shack, the home of Santos, an elderly gentleman with Parkinson's, to whom I give a bottle of Benadryl capsules that help reduce his shaking. Santos used to stand outdoors all day, shirtless, clutching tightly onto an overhead branch. Now he's no longer able to stand up, so his family carries him outside their one-room home on their only chair for a change of scene. But that chair has no armrests, so he often falls over onto the ground. We promise to consider the problem and to stop by again after visiting Bessy.

While our driver and Timoteo wait outside Bessy's adobe hut, I go inside to make sure she's not naked before inviting in the men, particularly the sighted driver. I also want to hide her broken wheelchair, fearing it might disqualify her from getting the newer one. I stick it into an adjoining room and help her dress. Meanwhile, curious neighbors, seeing Timoteo and the driver waiting outside with the new chair, inform them that Bessy already *has* a wheelchair. So, when I signal for them to enter, Tim demands an explanation. Sheepishly, I admit that she does already have one, but it barely functions and cannot be self-propelled. I bring it out to show them.

Putting our heads together, we decide to give Bessy's old wheelchair to Santos, as he can sit in it without falling over and be moved short distances. Bessy will get the newer chair to propel independently. But first, she has to demonstrate that she can get into and operate it, which she does after reciting the Lord's Prayer and hoisting herself up on a makeshift rope pulley installed over her bed.

Tim gives her a stern lecture: "Remember, never bathe or pee in this chair and don't use it for begging." This latter prohibition, I suspect, will be honored in the breach, since when her other wheelchair still functioned, Bessy made frequent trips to the border, tin cup in hand. But I don't mention that.

We deliver the old chair back to Santos, whose family immediately pushes him outside in it. I tell him I'll be leaving Honduras soon. When I shake his quivering hand goodbye, he begs me softly, "Please don't go." After I explain that my own elderly mother needs me, he nods in understanding.

Blind school founder Pilar Salinas honored on postage stamp

Fabio, blind carpentry teacher, instructing a student

Blind kids sitting together after classes

Doña Pilar with some of her students

Blind students' satirical play

Denise chatting with blind school students

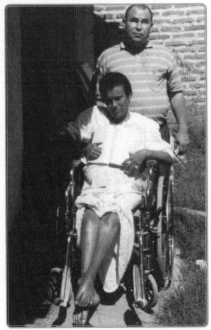

Timoteo with Bessy in new wheelchair

CHAPTER 20:
YOU CAN'T GO HOME AGAIN

Bittersweet Farewell

Now comes the hardest part, actually leaving. Joining the Corps at age 62, I never thought the experience would change me, but it has. People here have totally captivated my heart; I now feel part Honduran. Struggling to remain positive, I focus on my personal and our collective health accomplishments: infant mortality has decreased from 57 to 32 per thousand live births (compared to 6 or 7 in the U.S.), child survival is up, average family size has dropped from 5 to 3.5 children, school attendance has increased, and AIDS incidence is slowing, even as identification improves. We—I—have doubtless contributed to these results.

And while it's no secret that America's reputation has plummeted worldwide, the Peace Corps, in its own modest way, helps compensate. Nor is it just a one-way street, since we volunteers have gained as much as we've given.

Leave-taking

On my last visit to El Triunfo, I find Marina's grandson installing a window air conditioner in her bedroom. When he turns it on, she begins feeling better immediately.

I also visit Yocelyn, an 11-year-old with spina bifida, to whom I've given a water mattress to help reduce pressure sores. An old pressure sore looks almost healed after daily applications of vinegar and honey. My going-away presents to her include a cuddly bear and batteries for her favorite musical toy. She already has a wheelchair, but she 's almost too heavy for her mother to lift her into it any more. Yocelyn asks me please to adopt her, but I say her mother would miss her too much and vice versa.

Next, I reconnect with the other Irma, my first host in Valle, now working at the national lottery. She invites me to join her at her company picnic along with her two boys, now grown considerably taller. Irma, all slimmed down and stylishly dressed, confesses to being much happier working and earning a salary than staying home fretting about her wayward husband.

Later, in Teguc, en route to PC headquarters, my taxi is halted at a police barricade. I get out with my backpack, planning to trudge over there through the central cathedral square. I soon realize the reason for the barricade: an angry mob of demonstrators is pounding with cudgels on merchants' closed metal security doors. They turn out to be striking public employees protesting proposed changes to future benefits demanded by the IMF. Gang members and sympathetic anarchists have joined in for good measure. My heart pounding, I weave quickly through the crowd, trying to keep a low profile. Arriving finally at PC headquarters, I find that everyone has left early because of the disturbances.

Returning for the last time to La Esperanza, I donate my food staples, pots and pans, and dishes to the women's coop. Furniture goes to the Red Cross, with my bed destined for a paraplegic man who's been sleeping on the floor. Doña Chunga gets my hangers and all my farewell gifts, to either keep or sell. I give some toys to the family on the hill, feeling gratified when the formerly mute three-year-old calls out, *"Adios, gringa,"* in a loud, clear voice. I hope her family will continue talking to her, as her only problem was lack of attention.

Esperanza-area volunteers throw me a big farewell party at a resort still under construction. (Months later, the Iranian-American owner will be murdered.) Guitarist Richard, vowing never to return to the States, leads us in singing old favorites: "Hotel California," "West Virginia," and "Leaving on a Jet Plane."

That last song leaves my eyes moist. To bolster my resolve, I pull out a photo I always carry of my dearly departed son Andrew. His broad smile seems to say, "Good job, Mom, time now to go home."

Good-bye and Hello

The morning of my departure from Esperanza for the Teguc airport, a sudden storm arises. Carrying a suitcase of clothing and memorabilia, I wave goodbye to well wishers gathered at the bus stop under dripping black umbrellas to see me off.

"Promise to come back," they call as I climb aboard.

"I promise, *Primero Dios,* God willing." Are those tears or just rain on my face?

The following evening, flying out of Miami on to Washington, I look out the window, marveling at the stream of cars on the freeway below, lights stretching out to the distant horizon, myriad flights taking off and landing—such a massive and cavalier use of energy, maybe enough in that one city in a single day to keep a whole country like Honduras going for months. When I finally step onto *terra firma* in DC, my legs feel wobbly. I'm like Alice emerging from the rabbit hole or the children exiting the wardrobe from Narnia.

Despite the thrill of reuniting with my family, my readjustment proves more unsettling than leaving the U.S. in the first place. I can readily understand my colleague Richard's reluctance to return. Unpacking my clothes, still smoky from being dried near open fires, I'm overcome with nostalgia. And, given so many food choices, I gain 15 lbs. in as many days. There *is* life after Peace Corps, but it's not the same. I really miss Honduras.

Just before my departure, a prison fire near La Ceiba incinerated 70 people, mostly prisoners. After my return home, I learn that another fire in San Pedro has killed 102 inmates. In both cases, prison doors were kept locked to prevent escape. While Honduras has no death penalty, animosity toward gang members runs so high that these tragedies arouse little outrage. Then, the day after Christmas 2004, I hear that one of the yellow school buses I had so often ridden was hijacked by gunmen, leaving 38 passengers, including children, shot to death. A note left with the bodies warned President Maduro to stop his anti-gang crusade. These events upset me greatly. The only piece of good news is the inclusion of Honduras in debt relief for the world's poorest nations.

In Washington, I keep involved with Honduras by joining the board of a Honduran-oriented charity started by another former PCV. And I advise a Honduran environmental activist applying for political asylum after receiving death threats back home. I return to duty as a volunteer with

Amnesty International, coordinating special actions on human rights in the Caribbean.

A highlight of my Amnesty work is participation in a worldwide conference held in 2005 in Morelos, Mexico, attended by delegates from 70 countries. That same year, I receive a human rights award from the United Nations Association. In 2006, I have the rare privilege of making a humanitarian visit to southern Sudan, an even hotter, more isolated, and more challenging environment than southern Honduras.

I also join a 50+ Peace Corps recruiter to talk with folks about the rewards and opportunities for service in their golden years.

Re-entry Blues

Besides feeling homesick for Honduras, after my long absence and now at age 66, I have trouble finding suitable work; clerking at Wal-Mart holds no particular appeal. Age discrimination in hiring is illegal, but how to prove it? And most organizations serving Latinos prefer to hire the real McCoy.

The 2004 election victory of George W. Bush further depresses my spirits. I spent most of his first term in Honduras, but am now back in Washington, inside the belly of the beast. At first, Dubya's absurd gaffes seemed faintly amusing, but after so much bloodshed and disaster, they ceased being funny anymore. Following the ill-fated invasion of Iraq, apparently initially sanctioned by voters, I foresee our nation entering the twilight of empire. With so much damage already done, I only hope the situation is not totally irreversible. My bitterness is compounded when the son of family friends is killed in Iraq.

Life After Peace Corps

On the job front, I end up cobbling together several part-time occupations: freelance writing, translating, and Spanish interpretation. I've done written translation before, but interpretation is new, requiring a challenging consecutive and simultaneous test. I learn that after Mexico, the U.S. has the world's largest number of Spanish speakers, not really a big surprise.

Interpretation, unlike translation, involves contact with live human beings. I begin interpreting in Immigration Court. Anyone who's sold cocaine or robbed a convenience store certainly deserves removal. But why dredge up old offenses long after the fact? A legal resident who pled no contest to spousal abuse years before is deported after he and his wife have lived together harmoniously ever since, despite the wife's tearful protests. Another man, with ten years of paying taxes in this country, American-born children, no run-ins with the law, and a home representing sweat equity, is arrested in an immigration sweep at his workplace. Still another is caught driving without a license.

A woman awarded a work permit in 1998 after Hurricane Mitch didn't realize this allowed her to work in the U.S. legally, but not to leave. Returning after an emergency visit to her country, she is arrested at the airport pending her deportation. She neglected to read the fine print.

Still others, who fled Central America's 1980s civil wars but failed to apply promptly for asylum, are told, "You may have been raped, tortured, your parents killed before your eyes, but now it's safe to go back."

I bite my tongue whenever a judge or lawyer makes a blatant error, as my human rights work has familiarized me with immigration law. A court interpreter must strictly translate word-for-word while being recorded and not join in the conversation. Immigration court proves just too hard on my tender emotions.

So, I switch from court to hospital interpretation—which I'd almost be willing to do for free—a job bridging my two worlds. The mere presence of someone speaking their own language seems to help patients heal faster and leave the hospital sooner. An inpatient languishing for days without an interpreter often greets my arrival with tears of gratitude. I so identify with patients that I even find myself wincing at their IVs and injections. Confronting the occasional death, I struggle to keep my voice steady.

These patients represent every Spanish-speaking country, including Honduras, once even La Esperanza! Some are U.S. citizens or legal residents who've never mastered English; others are undocumented, without health insurance or even a social security number, but assisted by Catholic Charities or another nonprofit. Some are illiterate even in Spanish.

I witness a wide variety of intimate human dramas. A handsome young man, suffering from unrequited love, has slit his throat with a kitchen knife, severing windpipe, vocal cords, and esophagus. The hospital provides him with a tracheotomy and an esophageal repair, but what about his emotional needs? Bridging the language-cultural barrier with an interpreter certainly helps there.

A young father became quadriplegic after falling off a roof, shattering his American dream. On a respirator and feeding tube, he has developed pressure sores (what precipitated Christopher Reeve's death despite all his resources). He's probably not long for this world. His pregnant wife spends each day lovingly wetting his parched lips, since he's forbidden even to sip water, and combing out his wavy shoulder-length hair, which he adamantly refuses to have cut, having precious little control over anything else. He yearns to go home, but is too frail to travel. Instead of excoriating "illegals," we owe a debt of gratitude to workers risking their very lives to construct our homes and buildings.

Some Latino patients are blessed by crowds of visitors, so many they must take turns, with babies often smuggled in under coats. A male patient's friends will punch his fist in jaunty greeting, while women plant kisses on both his cheeks. Visiting pals often wear earrings, rosaries around their necks, and sunglasses facing backwards. Women in Sunday finery, dripping with perfume, bring in fragrant homemade tacos, tamales, and *pupusas*. Prayer sessions, with everyone holding hands, often take place around the bedside. Patient bulletin boards and shelves are lovingly decorated with family photos, images of the late and current popes, stuffed animals, soccer trophies, and even the familiar prints of Leonardo's Last Supper and JFK.

An older female patient's brain damage from a massive stroke sparks a bitter feud between her relatives and her American husband. He authorizes a feeding tube and tracheotomy, but balks at rescinding a do-not-resuscitate order. The husband has the legal right to decide, but while the patient has left nothing in writing, her family insists that she would have wanted her heart revived, no matter what. The husband argues that any heart stoppage would lead to further brain deterioration and if her heart should stop, that's God's will. Language problems impede communication between the English-speaking husband and his in-laws. As interpreter, I can't take sides, only help them understand each other. When Terri Schiavo's case becomes a cause célèbre, I wonder why doctors cannot do brain-wave tests to determine her level of cognition and sensation, as is done for this stroke patient.

At the other end of the lifespan, born after only 5 months gestation, is a 14-ounce preemie small enough to fit in one hand. Her mother reaches gingerly through incubator armholes to stroke the flailing legs of her tiny daughter, lying hooked up to myriad wires and tubes.

A young Honduran found wandering naked and disoriented is held temporarily in a mental health facility. He can't remember his address or phone number, so when the involuntary hospitalization period is up, he's urged to sign in voluntarily while staff continue searching for his family. Gently, I convey the concern of hospital staff, but he refuses to stay any longer. How is he planning to get home? "By walking." Where? "On the highway." I give a nurse a worried look, but she says they cannot keep him and goes to find him some clothes to wear.

I've touched so many people's lives and they've touched mine: a pregnant woman with terminal brain cancer waiting for her unborn's viability, an infant receiving a new liver, a toddler undergoing a bone marrow transplant, the parents of a child killed in a school-bus accident, a man who's lost an eye in an assault, an elderly ex-smoker with advanced lung cancer, a smiling little girl arriving for surgery wearing a princess dress, complete with sparkling wand and tiara.

Despite their habitual fatalism, Hispanic patients and families here, like those back in Honduras, place exaggerated faith in the curative powers of American medicine. Sophisticated high-tech interventions often succeed, but also occasionally fail. That's hard to accept.

It's painful, remembering the scarcity of medical resources in Honduras, to see so many items discarded after a single use: gowns, slippers, gloves, baby bottles. But I'm fascinated—after low-tech Honduran medicine—by a hospital robot scooting up and down, announcing to nurses "your delivery has arrived," then voicing a polite "thank you" before moving on.

Although my work necessarily involves the sick and injured, overall, Latinos in the U.S., despite low income and lack of health insurance, are actually healthier than the general population and have healthier babies. Strong social connections, prolonged breastfeeding, and less smoking all contribute to these favorable results.

Because our U.S. birthrate produces insufficient workers to support retirees or fill entry-level jobs, wholesale deportations would trigger economic calamity. Without Hispanic immigrants, our population would fall below replacement and who would care for children and elders, clean office buildings, cut grass, pick vegetables? Like it or not, these immigrants are integral to our social and economic fabric. Ejecting them would also be catastrophic for workers whose families, both here and abroad, depend on their earnings. Already the cost of apprehending, incarcerating, processing, and deporting the undocumented is staggering and inflicts great pain. Implementing harsher measures would cost even more and further harm our image as a free nation.

Those who decry an "invasion" from the south forget that the southwest was once Mexican territory. Indigenous people make a compelling argument that all America really belongs to them, while the rest of us are the illegal aliens. The prospect of a "Berlin Wall" along the border is further antagonizing Latin Americans already veering leftward, while globalization is blurring international boundaries in an increasingly interdependent world. Yet shrill, small-minded zealots seem bent on adding another chapter to our country's long, sordid history of ethnic mistreatment and exclusion. Their stance is un-American and certainly un-Christian.

We cannot permit open borders, but we *can* recognize longstanding "facts on the ground." I find it heartening to see hospitals providing high-quality emergency care to undocumented patients, especially to those injured on the job. The next step would be to offer amnesty to persons with several years of crime-free living and gainful employment here. While self-righteous critics label undocumented workers "law-breakers," *legal* entry is virtually impossible. (Cynics opine that immigrant labor is deliberately kept illegal to dampen wages.) Given the law of supply and demand and the mutual benefit involved, why not expand *legal* immigration to eliminate the illicit profit, fear, and danger? The old system obviously isn't working.

While not terribly remunerative, my employment proves satisfying, offering variety and flexibility, allowing me to spend time with my elderly mother. (When Mother passes away in 2006, I feel grateful for that time.)

After Honduras, not having a car, TV, or cellphone is no deprivation. When going grocery shopping, I take along my own mesh bag, just as in Honduras. And I've opted out of consumerism. My one indulgence has been acquiring a computer needed for my work.

Instead of returning to my former parish, I've joined a Catholic storefront church, *Communitas,* where the Lord's Prayer begins "Our Father and Mother…" Guitar music and hugs and kisses during the sign of peace remind me of Honduras.

A carryover Honduran habit is saying "hello" to strangers on the street. Also, quite miraculously, people from all over the world, referred only by word-of-mouth, have arrived at my doorstep to share my home. I marvel at how, in the Internet age, they've managed to find me and how we mutually enrich each other's lives, becoming part of an ever-growing international family. I feel truly blessed.

Daily Reminders

People often ask, "So, you were in the Peace Corps? How interesting! What was it like?" Well, it's taken an entire book to answer that.

My whole life, I've tried to make a social contribution, but never before felt that all my skills, energy, and commitment were fully engaged. Peace Corps service freed me to explore in so many different directions, discovering abilities I didn't even know I had. Beyond the sheer challenge and adventure, the experience revived cherished childhood memories and afforded me a profound spiritual and emotional journey. Dreams *can* come true, I discovered, though not always exactly in the way we might expect.

At Eastern Market, a local farmers' market, a young woman approaches, asking, "Aren't you Barbara from Peace Corps Honduras?" It turns out she was there too. "You know, you were legendary," she smiles, "our inspiration, our role model." I feel surprised and glad.

At home, photo collages commemorate the lives of my lost boys. They will never be forgotten, but now I see their lives and deaths more fully woven into the universal human tapestry of joy and pain. No sudden epiphanies arose from my Peace Corps service, but I've acquired more inner peace.

Neither are my Honduran friends forgotten. Among my Honduran memorabilia is a simple washcloth accompanied by a child's meticulously hand-printed note: "With much affection for my friend Barbara. I only ask her always to remember me as I remember her. May dear God keep her well wherever she may go. I love her so, Neris."

Another precious item is a flowered tablecloth bearing this hand-embroidered inscription: "For Bárbara, a memento from María de Jesús [Doña Chunga]."

Those sweet folks and many others offered me unconditional friendship, even love. I've done so very little to merit their trust and affection.

EPILOGUE:
FEBRUARY 2005

Return to Narnia

Readers can always stop now, but my own life continues, and the tie with Honduras is not so neatly severed. To quell my Honduran homesickness, I'd already been contemplating a return trip when former PCV Sandy, the medical brigade advocate, shot me an e-mail, inviting me to join her in Tegucigalpa for an upcoming surgical brigade (the first in a series of return trips). So, I departed for a three-week stay, intending simply to retrace my steps but, as always, several surprises were in store. I'm always open to improvisation, a stance that dovetails nicely with the reality of life in Honduras, where even the best-laid plans frequently go awry.

Returning was like going back through the wardrobe to Narnia, plunging again into that other world at once both familiar and strange. Leaving from frosty Washington, DC, I wore long underwear, double socks, and a wool jacket, all to be shed in Miami. I also checked through two large suitcases full of giveaway items, with my personal belongings packed into a small carry-on bag.

Our plane descended over familiar evergreen-studded mountains ringed by dirt roads, empty save for an occasional ox-cart. Then village outposts came into view and, finally, the white Christ statue overlooking the capital's disorderly labyrinth of tin-roofed hovels encircling palatial estates, no rhyme or reason to the layout of the city.

Our successful landing on the short runway prompted passengers to burst out clapping. (In 2008, five people died when a plane skidded off the runway, shorter than that in many U.S. small-town airports.) We descended the steep metal ladder onto the steamy tarmac, walking from there through double glass doors guarded by stern-faced armed soldiers wearing camouflage and broad-brimmed hats. Exiting customs, I ventured outside to scan the waiting crowd for Irma, the adult blind center's director, who had promised to pick me up. She wasn't there. I began fending off a persistent crowd of cab drivers, beggars young and old, and vendors of roasted cashews, peanuts, and bananas.

Soon I felt a familiar tickle in my throat, triggered by a combination of dust, diesel fumes, and smoke from burning trash, one of the less desirable aspects of being back in Honduras. I stood there suppressing a dry cough, just waiting. Meanwhile, I changed a few dollars into *lempiras*. Later, I would exchange more at a bank, not fully trusting the airport's freelance moneychangers. The dollar's plunge on world markets meant that since my departure, the lempira had declined less than usual against the dollar.

After two full hours, a cheery Irma finally showed up in her battered red pick-up, "You were worried? Don't I always keep my word?" Her sidekick Rony sat out behind in the open truck bed guarding my luggage while Irma, her hennaed hair flying wildly out the open window, chattered away non-stop in the driver's seat.

Since I'd be helping out with Operation Smile, a U.S.-based surgical brigade repairing cleft palates and harelips, Irma had arranged for me to stay at the residential school for blind children directed by her mother. The school named for that great lady, Pilar Salinas, was located right behind San Felipe Hospital, where the brigade would soon start receiving patients.

In the Country of the Blind

After braving a series of honking traffic jams and food sellers converging at every stop, Irma finally deposited me at the school. In the country of the blind, the one-eyed man is king, but with two good eyes, I turned out to be neither king nor queen, but, rather, clearly in the minority, feeling my way after dark through unlit rooms and identifying myself by name after bumping clumsily into others. Whenever I said my name aloud, blind students and teachers just arriving for the academic year greeted me like a long-lost friend, quizzing me on the whereabouts of Denise, the blind teacher from California who'd visited the school in 2003.

During this trip, by actually staying there off-and-on, I became even better acquainted with the school and its venerable founder (who died six months later). I first shared a room with Doña Gloria, a 75-year-old blind woman with a thick white braid running down her back. Gloria had never married, hence strictly speaking, was not eligible to be called *Doña*, an honorific reserved for once-married women. But she was included because of her age.

Gloria turned out to favor matching jewelry, bright nail polish, and color-coordinated outfits. She and her brother were both born blind. She first came to the residential school as a teenager and never left, devoting herself to initiating new students, and playing guitar duets with her late brother, who also lived on the premises. However, after his death, she never picked up a guitar again: "Music simply went out of my life."

Gloria spent holidays in her native village, but the school had been her real home for 50 years. Cheerful and articulate, Gloria expressed strong opinions about upcoming primary elections and proudly recounted her activism in her evangelical church.

Gloria snored loudly (maybe I did too). She also talked in her sleep, dreaming in sounds and touch, she told me later, since she had never seen. She tried to imagine sight, "*Mamá* thought maybe I could see when I was first born, but I don't remember."

A pesky wall clock chimed loudly every hour on the hour, day and night. And, now and then, I would awaken at night to disconcerting scratching and gnawing sounds.

After a few days of sharing Gloria's room, I was displaced by another sightless woman, Marta, and had to move to an upstairs storeroom. Marta was accompanied by a five-year-old blind girl, the two of them and the child's large doll taking over the cot I'd been occupying. Marta, likewise a former pupil, had assumed responsibility for her little companion, recently abandoned by her own family. The child, who called her guardian *Mamá*, appeared to have undergone a mild stroke and performed daily therapy exercises. Marta said the girl spent vacations with her at her rural family home, becoming the child she'd never had.

Back to School

Families soon began dropping kids off at the school with bags and bundles. When I returned after a brief absence, classes had already started. After classes, youngsters would change out of school uniforms into "civilian" clothes. Though sightless and therefore presumably not slaves to fashion, older boys had adopted the baggy-pants look favored by American teens and girls were decked out in tank-tops, tight jeans, and platform shoes.

Overprotected new students sometimes could barely walk, despite having normal limbs. Two able-bodied kids were then assigned to grab them on either side and march them regularly around the patio until their muscles strengthened. From this practice, a unique custom had arisen. Three, four, even six kids, usually of the same age and gender, fully capable of normal ambulation, linked arms and continuously circled around the patio, sometimes latching onto others in the process. Especially, when the patio was in shade, these walking chains proliferated. Kids chattered up and down the line, sang, recited poetry, laughed, and just kept on walking.

Standing on the second floor balcony one evening under bright moonlight, I was fascinated by the beautiful synchronicity of these human chains, no group ever running into another, all maintaining constant motion in a dizzying pinwheel fashion. Doña Pilar and I regarded this linking up as harmless, even salutary, but daughter Irma pronounced it an unacceptable *blindism*, forbidden at her center, the only time we disagreed on rehab philosophy.

Likewise, I never failed to marvel at how sightless boys could sprint unerringly across the patio without colliding. They often played with annoying noise-makers called "clackers," wooden balls banged constantly together. Those with transistor radios turned them up to ear-splitting volume. And the school day started early, about 4 am, when staff and students began stirring noisily in the dark. Doors slammed, pots banged, boys shouted and gave off shrill whistles. Then, at 6, a loud bell signaled breakfast time. Most youngsters soon recognized my voice and greeted me politely, but once, while I stood outside the front metal gate ringing the bell to be let in, a stream of orange juice spurted out through a narrow gap. When the gate opened, I demanded to know which giggling boy before me had sprayed me with juice. Embarrassed, 11-year-old Fabricio begged my forgiveness, saying he had mistaken me for someone else. I not only forgave him, but later gave him my travel pillow, as he had none.

At my next stop, the adult blind center in Santa Lucía, most students had not yet arrived, only a few of those I'd met before. I reconnected first with Gernán, known for his cheerful smile and empathetic ear, someone very hard to forget. With a disfiguring skin condition that Irma called *piel de pescado,* fish skin, he shed scales constantly. When he greeted me, I hesitated before shaking his rough, flaking hand. (His disease was probably "lizard skin," a black-fly-borne illness that can result in blindness.) Gernán wore long sleeves, a brimmed cap, and dark glasses to cover up, but his skin must have seemed especially repellant to other blind people connecting by touch.

Another returning student was Eva from La Esperanza, a middle-aged retired teacher with diabetic blindness. When I last saw her, she'd been complaining of feeling left out by younger women constantly listening to pop music and gossiping about potential boy friends. So she had decided to leave the center to go live with her elderly mother. Now, after her mother's death, she had returned to resume her interrupted rehabilitation.

I informed Irma about a pending artificial eye brigade. This brigade, which usually provided the prostheses to those needing just one, had once brought only blue eyes. This time, they would all be brown, though some blind people seeking two said they might actually prefer blue. Most children and adults whom Irma planned to take to the brigade were born without eyes. Even I, though pretty comfortable with disability, found empty sockets somewhat disconcerting.

Timoteo, my erstwhile wheelchair benefactor, declined the opportunity, having lived this long without false eyes. Already in his mid-thirties, with a sighted wife, three kids, and a secure teaching job, he asked, "Why bother now?"

Some of the eyeless had never seen and didn't understand the need, while others, sensitive about their appearance, were eager to be fitted with the new prostheses.

Operation Smile

My main mission was helping out with the cleft palate/harelip repair brigade known locally as *Operación Sonrisa,* taking place at San Felipe Hospital across the street from the blind school.

Before actually reporting there, I re-introduced myself to the hospital's occupational therapy (OT) department, familiar to me from my PC service. OT helps persons with disabilities, whether mental, physical, or emotional, to function in daily life. In terms of physical rehabilitation, occupational therapists focus predominantly on hands and arms, while physical therapists concentrate on legs and walking.

My larger suitcase contained a wealth of discarded hand and arm splints and other devices donated by American occupational therapists. So, after talking briefly with patients and therapists, I asked a hospital maintenance man to help me bring the donated items over from the blind school. At the hospital, I emptied out a large gunnysack as excited therapists gathered around. Someone from prosthetics, hearing the clamor, came over, demanding that the devices be placed in general inventory. Feeling proprietary, the therapists promised to share, but insisted on keeping everything in their own unit. Unwittingly, I had sparked a minor turf battle.

San Felipe had been built a century earlier, with countless confusing additions made since. Occupying a large city block, its sheer size made it easy to get lost inside. While navigating a dark corridor filled with waiting patients, I was startled to hear excited cries of "*¡Doctora Bárbara!*" coming from families from my first PC site, El Triunfo, now seeking specialist consultations. I promised to visit their town soon.

At last, I located Operation Smile and former PCV Sandy, who had originally invited me. She reported that a threatened nurses' strike, taking advantage of the brigade's presence, had been headed off by the First Lady's personal appeal.

Hundreds of parents and children were lined up for initial brigade screening. Out-of-towners usually stayed at a shelter adjacent to the hospital. As a volunteer, I'd spent many sleepless nights there myself, lying next to my patients on a plastic-covered mattress, hearing children cry out, and sharing the common bathroom, often without water. So, I was just as glad to be staying at the blind school on this round.

About 400 youngsters were scheduled for surgery during the two-week brigade, two dozen of them brought in by PCVs and left with Sandy and me. A few kids, though of talking age, were so unintelligible that they had given up trying, nor could they smile, except with their eyes. After surgery, their smiles would blossom.

Sandy and I rarely entered the operating room, although Sandy is a nurse. Instead, we closely monitored our patients and provided their food. Once between procedures, we took our patients and their families by bus on an excursion to the Santa Lucía restaurant operated by our friend Maribel. Although she was busy running for mayor, she took time out to fix them all a hearty lunch. Afterward, we led our group on a walking tour through Santa Lucía's cobblestone streets, visiting the ancient cathedral and brand new library, whose librarian was trained at the same seminar that Pedro Joaquín and I had attended four years before. The Triunfo library was still not open—more on that later.

At Maribel's, I congratulated her son and his wife, also sharing the family home, on their new baby, but asked, "Why is she wearing mittens?"

The young mother hastened to explain, "To stop her thumb sucking." I gently suggested that an infant's sucking urge is natural, instinctive really, and shouldn't be thwarted. Shyly, she thanked me for the advice, but the mittens remained.

While most of our brigade patients were children, 26-year-old Gloria's deformity was so severe that her front teeth emerged from her nostrils. Although her speech was unclear, I understood her to say, "I'm so ugly." I assured her otherwise, but because of her age, I wondered how much her appearance would actually change.

Another patient of particular concern was Tránsito, an 18-month-old, not yet walking or making intelligible vocalizations. She avoided solid food, sucking only from a special bottle. Her father reported that her siblings were normal. She was the only child I'd ever seen with a cleft palate, but no harelip. An American geneticist had told me that such a configuration more often signals developmental problems than if palate and lip are both affected, the more usual pattern.

While Sandy and I concentrated on patients brought in by PCVs, we also helped out as interpreters and advocates for others. One morning, U.S.-based Fox News filmed footage of brigade activities, so we might have appeared in some of those clips.

After surgery, Gloria, her age and the severity notwithstanding, emerged looking almost normal, losing only a couple of front teeth. Holding up a mirror, she was tearful with joy, but avoided smiling to protect her stitches. Our other patients and their parents were also pleased with the results. Fortunately, none had been rejected for lack of hemoglobin.

We then followed up on several clubfoot patients whom Sandy had assisted before my arrival. Foot surgery, especially for both feet, is a more serious and painful operation than lip/palate. We also oversaw a promising new clubfoot treatment for infants: early casting to prevent the need for later surgical correction.

PCHQ

After tending to our patients, I ventured over to PC headquarters in downtown Teguc, only to confront a terse sign posted at the guard station, "ex-volunteers not welcome, admitted by appointment only." According to the guards, this order was issued by the new country director after several former volunteers had misbehaved. The guards all knew me, but, rules were rules. So on the guard phone, I called a staff member to invite me in.

Inside, I was overwhelmed by effusive hugs and kisses from Honduran staff. I asked Carlos, the security director, to help me research newspaper articles supporting the asylum claim of my Honduran environmentalist friend back in Washington. One article included his photo and mentioned death threats made against him; others reported on the murders of colleagues protesting with him against illegal mahogany logging in their native province of Olancho. So I now could cross that item off my to-do list. (Asylum was subsequently granted and his wife and seven minor children came to the U.S.)

I also ran into a volunteer who had worked with me in La Esperanza. He was applying to medical school after helping out in the operating room during a lip/palate brigade. But few volunteers were inside the headquarters compound, having been strongly discouraged from visiting Teguc after two male volunteers (my former colleagues) had been shot in the legs by robbers late one night just half a block away.

Inside the lounge, I checked out the "free" shelf, where departing volunteers discard old medical kits and clothing. There I found a treasure trove of used clothes, rehydration salts, medications, and a dozen green hospital scrubs embossed with the name Dallas Children's Hospital. I stuffed everything into a plastic bag for future distribution.

Two program directors, one for water and sanitation, the other for health, asked me to accompany them to the training center's new location to talk with fresh recruits. I gladly agreed. Although I'd been a health volunteer, I'd also completed water projects left behind by my sitemate Seth when he left early.

Meanwhile, as an experiment, I visited a couple of pharmacies near the office and bought several prescription drugs at bargain prices. Some were of European or Dominican manufacture, but equivalent to American brands; others actually *were* U.S. brands, but even after being shipped to Honduras, they still cost less! (And they weren't fakes either, judging by their packaging and inserts.) Pharmaceutical manufacturers apparently charge whatever the local market will bear and in the U.S., that's plenty. I didn't need a doctor's prescription either, cutting out that middleman.

In the kilometer walk between PC headquarters and the brigade hospital, taxi drivers kept stopping and honking in annoyance when I refused their services. During my walk, I came upon a tiny live deer cavorting among stone saints and gnomes in front of a luxurious residence. I rubbed my eyes. What a curious creature to find in the city! Later, when I wanted to show it to Sandy, I could no longer locate the house.

Hello Trainees

Our own training had taken place in 2000 in Santa Lucía, just outside Teguc. Now the training center had moved to Siguatepeque, a more remote, lower-cost region. At the Siguat center, I responded to fresh-faced trainees asking questions and describing their personal ordeals. I tried speaking with them in Spanish, but most weren't ready for that yet.

Although I'd been less "green" than most trainees, I still could empathize with their feelings at being plunged into a totally new environment and unfamiliar language. After several trainees mentioned getting sick, I recounted the violent illness of my Flores visit—with all-night trips to the latrine and fiercely barking dogs nipping at my heels. Time and exposure, I assured them, would eventually confer greater immunity.

To my surprise and delight, the health trainer was Perth, a volunteer from my own original group. Water/san trainees now were predominantly male and health recruits mostly female, as in my own training cohort. These trainees were so enthusiastic and excited, I heartily congratulated them, and avoided thinking that not all would make it to the end, just as when toasting a bridal couple despite knowing that nearly half of marriages end in divorce.

Luis, my Esperanza officemate, was now working at the training center after our regional office had been closed due to budget cuts. He rented a room in Siguat during the week, going home on weekends. Campus recruiting centers around the U.S. were also being shut down for budgetary reasons. This, despite Bush's State-of-the-Union pledge to double the Peace Corps' size.

Reunion in *La Esperanza*

From Siguatepeque, I boarded a bus to La Esperanza, having left most of my luggage back at the blind school, bringing only cold-weather used clothing to distribute at this stop. I was prepared for the cooler elevation myself, wearing the same long underwear and jacket as when I left DC.

I stayed with Luis's family, which included his wife, baby daughter, mother-in-law, sister-in-law, maid, and a 12-year-old niece with lupus who required constant care (and later died). I hesitated to inconvenience the family, but they absolutely insisted.

Besides the home's numerous human residents, there were two mongrel bitches, both with new litters. Hondurans rarely spay or neuter pets, considering it too costly, as well as unkind and unnatural. Like most Honduran dogs, these were fed mostly on raw tortilla dough, hardly sufficient for canine nursing mothers.

I had a surprise visitor, Susan, a 50-year-old British computer programmer spending three weeks helping Save the Children construct a school in neighboring Yarmananguila. She'd paid her own way for her first trip out of England, deliberately choosing Honduras, a country she knew nothing about. Unfamiliar with Spanish, she asked my help in mastering some basic phrases.

I gave my own kids' baby clothes to Luis's daughter and donated the cold-weather clothing I'd brought to the local Red Cross, where I was asked to help out with a general medical brigade in an outlying village.

Hortensias Brigade

The village in question, Las Hortensias (The Hydrangeas), was even higher than La Esperanza, quite cool and foggy, making me glad to be warmly dressed. I was transported in a Red Cross pickup, since other vehicles rarely traveled there. En route, we passed through a cloud forest and terraced fields newly planted with cabbage, lettuce, onions, and broccoli.

This brigade, operated by International Health Service of Minneapolis, had been announced by radio and was being held in a rural schoolhouse. A steady stream of patients arrived on foot from all directions, waiting patiently for hours to be seen. For their 10-day stay, the volunteer staff had brought along sleeping tents, a solar-heated shower system, and a gasoline-powered generator for light and refrigeration.

I was assigned to assist a family physician. She knew some Spanish and struggled valiantly to communicate, but the patients' mostly indigenous dialect thwarted her best efforts. Fortunately, because I had lived in the area, I could decipher it. These thin, shy, uneducated folks brought swarms of children, many appearing frankly malnourished, in stark contrast to Luis's well-fed daughter. And while some wore their Sunday best, others were unwashed and threadbare.

The good doctor agreed to examine each family group together for efficiency, but one with 20 members had to be divided in two. Apparently, no child was left behind. Exams were performed behind a makeshift curtain under which curious kids inevitably peeked. Children were amused at having their ears examined and several asymptomatic ear infections were found that way. I made a mental note to find help for a four-year-old whose broken leg had healed badly. (On another trip, I obtained corrective surgery for her.)

By feel, the doctor discovered that several women were pregnant—to their apparent surprise. A baby due in a week was in a breech position. The doctor warned the mother: "If a skilled midwife cannot turn the infant around in time, you will need a hospital C-section." Recalling my Triunfo experience of losing a breech baby, I strongly seconded that advice.

An adjacent classroom served as a pharmacy. If medication was indicated, the doctor wrote out a prescription. Each patient also received vitamin supplements while the supply lasted and those complaining of poor vision were offered a choice of reading glasses. A woman suffering from infected upper teeth had them extracted without anesthesia by a brigade dentist, providing her with immediate relief.

Up in Smoke

Meanwhile, I'd been shocked to find that La Esperanza had lost its famous market. The entire complex had burned down in a mysterious Christmas Day fire. Getting off the bus from Siguat on that first night back, I'd lost my bearings when I couldn't locate the market. Only the white tower of the main cathedral, with its clock fixed perpetually on 10 minutes to 3, had helped me find my way.

Esperanza's market, attracting farmers and shoppers from far and wide, had been a welter of jerry-built wooden structures selling everything imaginable: live animals, food, clothing, household items, toys, and crafts.

Musicians played for handouts while colorfully dressed Lenca women offered homemade soap and candles, and barefoot boys hawked kindling. After moving there, I'd been delighted to find a wide variety of fresh fruits and vegetables.

But, alas, on December 25, 2004, the only day of the year the market was closed, a fierce blaze had burned everything down to the ground. The city had since obtained a second-hand fire truck and recruited volunteer fire fighters, but only after the fact. Now, instead of the colorful twists and turns of individual market stalls, I encountered only flat empty space and charred wood.

Right away, I located Antonio, a young man paralyzed by gunshot, still selling lottery tickets from his homemade wheelchair. "Welcome back, stranger. Where've you been?" he asked. I explained and inquired about my friend, clothes vendor Doña Chunga, but he didn't know her.

So I trekked up to Chunga's house, where I met a son just back from the States, apparently deported. He guided me to his mother's new sales location in a secluded parking lot. There, along with other displaced vendors, she was again standing up all day, as a stool I'd given her had burned up in the fire. Most goods were laid out on a table, with the rest stored in boxes underneath. The inventory was small and Chunga had to carry everything home at night, no longer able to lock up.

Doña Chunga was not surprised to see me, having dreamt about me just the night before. Standing at her side, I admired her cheerful banter with customers and vendors alike. Reluctantly, she peeled off 1,000 lempiras (about $60) for a man collecting on merchandise provided on credit before the fire. "Just paying for ashes," she lamented.

At dinner one evening, my former hiking buddy Deborah, a municipal development volunteer, reported rumors that the fire had been deliberately set to replace the market with more upscale shops. Whether to rebuild it was a contentious issue.

Deb also told me that an American friend, a retired teacher running a GED-type program, was finally thinking of throwing in the towel. A gunman had broken into the house where she lived alone, threatening to rob and rape her, only to run off after her barking dogs alerted her night watchman.

At a stop back again in Tegucigalpa, my blind friend Gloria was ecstatic. Her Liberal candidate, Mel Zelaya (who would be elected in November), had won his party's presidential primary with a get-tough message on crime and call for restoration of the death penalty. "He speaks so well,"

Gloria opined.

Zelaya's main rival, the former mayor of Teguc, would have been my own choice. He'd done a great job repairing the city's streets and was also an outspoken death-penalty opponent. Our Santa Lucía friend Maribel ended up losing her mayoral primary bid by a heartbreaking 23 votes.

Choluteca, In Search of Answers

From Teguc, I traveled south to Choluteca on an important mission: to find out why the local public hospital had amputated the fingers of 12-year-old Jorge (not the same boy whose foot tumor had been removed years before).

Let me explain. Jorge was born with the middle fingers of both hands fused together, an awkward condition that interfered with certain tasks and exposed him to ridicule. Before I left the Peace Corps, he had undergone successful surgery to separate the fingers of his dominant right hand, but the visiting surgeon had refused to operate on both hands at once.

Jorge and his father, a widower, wanted the left hand fixed as well, so after returning to Washington, I arranged for the boy to attend another surgical brigade. I couldn't accompany him myself because my mother was ill. An evangelical minister, Reverend Daniel, offered to take Jorge if I would cover expenses. I agreed, emphasizing that post-operatively, Jorge should go daily for dressing changes to the public hospital in Choluteca, where his family was now living.

Right after the brigade surgeons returned to the U.S., I called and learned that Jorge's tightly-fused finger bones had proved especially hard to separate, so he'd remained hospitalized for several days afterward. But the operation reportedly was successful.

Two weeks later, I was stunned to receive an e-mail from Daniel saying that Jorge's operated fingers had been *amputated* at the Choluteca public hospital. I re-read the message several times, hoping I'd misunderstood. The boy and his father were said to be in shock, never having been given a reason for the amputations or notified beforehand.

Anguished and distraught, I imagined everything from infection to gangrene, regretting ever having sent the boy for surgery without being there to personally follow up. Follow-up is the Achilles heel of medical brigades, since visiting physicians move quickly in and out. Among some 100 children I had previously helped obtain surgery, there had never been a bad outcome. But after this experience, I vowed never again to send a child to surgery via long distance. Better to have fused middle fingers than none at all! Young Jorge appeared to me in a dream, extending his maimed hand in silent reproach.

When Daniel failed to answer subsequent e-mails, I asked my health volunteer successor in El Triunfo to find out from the hospital exactly what had happened. She was told that Jorge's records were confidential. *Confidential*? Since when was confidentiality observed in any Honduran public hospital? I then asked Loni's medical-student sister to inquire, but she too was rebuffed.

I started wondering whether the hospital was covering up a mistake. Or had Daniel failed to convey my instructions to have the hand checked daily, or had the family failed to comply? Nagged by these questions, I resolved to go to the hospital myself with Jorge's father and ask point-blank. Then staff could hardly refuse to tell us.

Before looking for Jorge, I stopped off first at Loni's family home. No one answered my knock, so I walked over to El Regalón, their market shop, where, like Doña Chunga in La Esperanza, they worked from dawn to dusk every day except Christmas. Loni's parents, Agustín and Lula, along with their oldest daughter and her children, were on duty. Although it was only February, not the hottest month, it was still the dry season. With no sheltering cloud cover, the heat was intense.

After sipping a bag of water bearing the inscription "Partake with pleasure water from the font of salvation," I returned to the house with grandchildren Andrea and Alfredo, now 10 and 12 respectively. They were going there to meet with their master-of-ceremonies after being chosen a few months earlier to star in a local Saturday morning children's TV show. Out on the street, as we walked home together, they were greeted like celebrities. At home, Andrea, rail-thin with huge dark eyes and long honey-blond hair—a real charmer—demonstrated a few dance steps for their television host, acting almost flirtatious, making me uneasy and glad that her brother always accompanied her to the studio. The kids took the bus unescorted there every Saturday, but because the show was live, they never got to see themselves on screen.

Next, I visited Manuel, a Honduran married to an American, with whom he had three children. He'd made the colossal mistake of voluntarily presenting himself to U.S. Immigration to legalize his status. Marriage ordinarily confers residence, but since he had originally entered illegally, he was summarily deported to his native country for a two-year stay as punishment. Manuel, who had been earning $19 an hour in skilled construction, had ended up selling all his tools and bringing the family to Honduras to accompany him in his exile. His two years were now almost up and I found him caring for the kids alone, while his wife had returned to the States to hire an attorney to facilitate his return.

That evening, as the air cooled down slightly, I sat with Loni's family out in front of their house under trees that forward-thinking father Agustín had planted years before. On the radio, a disc jockey dedicated a song, *Si Yo Estuviera*, "to our American visitor, *Doña Bárbara*." What? Amused smiles were exchanged all around—those rascals had given the station my name!

A guy stopping by on a bike handed Loni's surprised father 1000 lempiras ($70) from a long-forgotten debt. Agustín mused later that the amount should really have been higher, given the lempira's plunge in value over the years. Though feeling revived by the evening air, after taking off my money belt before bed, I found the bills inside completely soaked through with sweat.

Jorge, Face-to-Face

Next morning, Reverend Daniel and I set off in a borrowed car to find Jorge's home, located on a dirt road at the city's outskirts. Jorge's father stood waiting outside. He said that he had taken his son daily to the local health center after his surgery. Actually, I'd told them to go to the *hospital,* which I considered more reliable, but hadn't realized it was too far away. A health-center nurse had reportedly washed the hand and applied fresh bandages daily, but Jorge's fingers had begun swelling and turning purple. Only after his pain became unbearable did his grandmother finally take him to the hospital, where he was put on IV antibiotics. Believing he was being taken care of, she left. She returned the following day just as her grandson came out of surgery, noticing in horror that his middle fingers were now gone.

After this grim recital, the father sent a younger child to fetch Jorge from school. Indeed, as Jorge now showed me, reluctantly pulling his left hand from his pants pocket, his two middle fingers were missing.

Taking both his hands firmly in mine, I looked at him saying, "So very sorry for your loss, but any surgery carries risks and, this time, unfortunately, the risks fell squarely on *you.* You may never become a bricklayer like your dad, but there are other jobs you can do."

Still holding onto his hands, I asked what type of career he envisioned. "A teacher," he murmured shyly. I agreed that was a job he could perform well despite his missing fingers. Although he was right-handed, I asked Jorge to use his left hand—his remaining thumb and forefinger—to pick things up, which he did, showing that hand was still somewhat functional. I explained that his father and I would go to the hospital the next morning to find out exactly what had happened, but, in any case, his fingers would never be restored.

I gave Jorge some school supplies to take back to class, then slipped his father a fairly substantial sum, just a gift of friendship, I explained, since no amount of money could compensate for his son's loss, nor was I directly responsible.

Promptly at 7 the next morning, Daniel and I met Jorge's father outside the hospital. Daniel had helped me carry over a trash bag filled with the discarded hospital scrubs, medications, and rehydration salts from the Peace Corps free shelf, intended as a peace offering. Inside, Daniel spied a nurse who had attended his religious services. When he explained our mission and introduced Jorge's father, she accepted the bag of donations and offered to look up the boy's records herself.

There we found an unsigned paragraph in English, saying that infection had spread throughout the boy's operated fingers. By the time the hospital saw him, antibiotic therapy had proved ineffective and the fingers could not be saved. So there had been no cover-up after all; the amputations sounded fully justified under the circumstances.

A hospital physician confirmed that a visiting American surgeon had amputated the fingers to save the hand. If Jorge had only come in sooner, he said, antibiotics might have arrested the infection or, at least, permitted a less drastic amputation.

I didn't want to guilt-trip Jorge's father and grandmother, despite their failure to react promptly when the fingers had become discolored and painful. But I did fault the health center nurses, who apparently merely re-bandaged the hand without examining it, the whole point of my recommending daily checkups. Most of all, I faulted myself for not anticipating these problems and not being present to resolve them. If I had been there, this never would have happened.

Pastoral Visits

With Reverend Daniel, I distributed a batch of summer clothes and several pairs of drugstore reading glasses at a home for the elderly. A thousand pairs of glasses would still have fallen short on this trip, such was the demand. I had brought different strengths, allowing folks to try them on to see which suited them best. An elderly lady named Gertrudis begged me to sit down and chat for a while, but Daniel hurried me along, wanting to take full advantage of our borrowed car.

We went next to see a three-year-old girl with normal hearing, but born with her left ear missing, her tiny remnant of a lobe now pierced with a small gold earring. I told her parents a new ear could be fashioned from a piece of rib bone and grafted skin; however, the child was still too young.

We also visited 80-year-old Juan, an emaciated soul now nearing his last days. Gathering the man's wife and son around the bedside, Daniel read aloud from Lamentations. He then sat down for a heart-to-heart talk with the son, who had recently abandoned his family to live with his "other woman" and child. I bought a watermelon from the family to take back to Loni's house and we left without resolving the son's dilemma.

Detour

San Bernardo is a village located between Cholu and Triunfo. Sandy had asked me to look in on two former clubfoot surgery patients living there. Because time was short and the temperature at least 100° F, I hired a car and driver. We bumped along on dirt roads and forded streams, finally locating both boys' homes at the end of a rough pathway where even our four-wheel drive vehicle couldn't enter.

Their surprised mothers warmly embraced and kissed me on both cheeks before sending another child with us to find the boys at school. Kelsin, age 11, who had required surgery on only one foot, was now walking barefoot on his good foot, while the smaller, operated foot was stuck into an oversized boot. Junior, 12, wore a pair of ill-fitting boots on his two operated stubs of feet. Since both had had their surgery relatively late, their operated feet were much smaller than if they had developed normally, another argument for early intervention. Still, better late than never, as both were now walking better than before.

Orthopedic shoes would have helped further, but when I reported back to Sandy, she argued against investing in operated kids *ad infinitum*, although she did send money one last time to have special shoes made locally. These families, both subsistence farmers, could hardly have afforded such shoes on their own. How long to carry kids postoperatively, given limited resources, is always a difficult question.

My driver then took me to Guasaule at the Nicaraguan border to look for Marciel, a girl with facial burn scars resulting from an overturned kerosene lamp. Because she had already been rejected by three plastic surgery brigades (and after my terrible experience with Jorge), I decided to stop sending her to any more. Her scarring made her self-conscious, but didn't interfere with talking or eating. She would just have to learn to live with her scars.

Marciel's mother wasn't on duty at the Guasaule market, where she usually stood making tortillas by hand 12 hours a day, seven days a week. Instead, the oldest of her 10 children was standing over the fire in her place, a young woman really more like a mother to Marciel than the mother herself, and the one who'd actually accompanied the girl to various unsuccessful surgical brigades. The older sister reported that Marciel was now attending school and doing well, very good news, as I had insisted that she go despite shyness regarding her appearance.

I told the sister, "No more brigades," explaining that burn scar eradication requires multiple procedures unavailable to us and that the scars would soften anyway over time. I gave her a red umbrella and other gifts for Marciel. She then asked me for a skin cream that I'd given Marciel previously and had forgotten to bring this time. Instead, I gave her a modest sum for the girl and promised to bring the cream next time, God willing (I did so in a subsequent visit.)

El Triunfo, At Last

Finally, I arrived in El Triunfo, my first Honduran home, where no PCVs were currently assigned. Because of my chance encounter with local women back at the Teguc hospital, word of my pending arrival had already spread far and wide. I barely made it to Doña Marina's front door before being mobbed by well wishers. Marina, now 89, had become quite deaf, so I shouted out my greeting.

Marina sat outside with me, frequently nodding off, but stirring in protest whenever I got up to leave. I gave her my very last pair of reading glasses, anticipating that she would now need stronger lenses. Marina showed off a new pet, a colorful, dainty, long-necked duck called a *piche* that emitted sweet, flute-like chirps, but tried to peck me on the foot. Marina also had four little piglets that she was fattening up to sell.

The current maid, 16-year-old Amanda, already on duty for several months—a real record— had cared for her own grandmother until her death. Marina evidently trusted Amanda, as she no longer locked her bedroom door.

When Marina nodded off again, I sneaked out to visit daughter Reina and her daughter Solei, now 10, who showed me a recent appendectomy scar. "Her appendix burst and I almost lost her," Reina reported, hugging the child close.

I was assigned my old room at Marina's, with the usual coterie of bats flitting about. Amanda gave me an emergency candle, also a chamber pot to use just in case. I propped open the door with a stone for fresh air, but closed it at night to keep out thieves and stray animals. But I couldn't shut out the incessant, all-too-familiar nightly back-and-forth relays of crowing roosters and barking dogs.

When I'd lived with her, Marina, advised by her grandson, was continually launching failed get-rich-quick schemes: freezing bags of ice that melted with electrical outages, melons that rotted after she refused to lower the price, and an eatery that competed unsuccessfully with long-established businesses. Now she had undertaken another venture, this time selling off portions of fresh milk that Amanda hauled daily from a neighboring farm in a large metal container. The milk, straight from the cow, was unpasteurized, so I declined a glass.

One morning, I heard Marina arguing with Ismael, an effeminate young man sporting several fake gold chains, whose high falsetto voice rose in a shrill crescendo. Marina had used a large coke bottle to pour milk into his pail, but he insisted that it didn't measure a full liter. Finally, they compromised by filling two smaller bottles.

Ismael showed me a nasty lesion on his foot, aggravated by an ill-fitting flipflop. I wrote out a referral to the local health center and gave him some cash to buy a healing pomade from the pharmacy. "God bless you, madam," he said with an exaggerated bow, offering me the little green parakeet clinging to his shoulder. I thanked him kindly but explained that the creature would never be allowed through U.S. customs.

I began making my rounds, first greeting two young Mormon missionaries, who always traveled in pairs. I called on postmistress María

Elena and looked in on several previous surgery patients, including the three lip/palate siblings. I also visited the parents of an AIDS victim and delivered a bunch of old greeting cards to Neris, my faithful little friend, who added them to the collection begun when I'd lived there. Like many girls, she carried her baby brother around everywhere.

Elderly sisters Mercedes and Mariana knocked down a couple of grapefruits for me and inquired about the health of my mother, whom they'd met during her visit four years before. At the home of Pedro Joaquín, the aspiring librarian, I dropped off a dozen Spanish-language books, adding them to the more than 1,500 books that we had collected over the years. People still came by to borrow books and Pedro always made sure they were returned. Ever the optimist, he vowed that as soon as the current mayor, a reputed illiterate, left office, the library would definitely be up and running because of growing community support.

People consulted me about various medical problems, again calling me *Doctora Bárbara*, although my remedies were almost gone by then. One woman begged me to arrange a liver transplant for her son, quite beyond my modest capabilities.

I had left El Triunfo for La Esperanza in September 2002, so more than two years had elapsed since I'd actually lived there. Yet people surrounded me as if I were a rock star, complimenting me on how pale and fat I had become. (Thanks a lot, folks!) Children, mere toddlers when I'd left, greeted me excitedly; passing cyclists shouted out my name; and everywhere I heard cries of "¡Doña Bárbara!" or sometimes just the affectionate diminutive "Barbarita." People coaxed me into their homes to drink coffee, juice, soda, anything: "Surely you wouldn't just walk right by." Because of the heat, it was good to stop now and then. Once I was amused to find myself chatting with a woman wearing one of my old outfits.

"There's never been another volunteer like you," folks insisted, "Please come back." Their praise was flattering, but really quite exaggerated and undeserved. I felt like I was under siege and understood how real rock stars might want to escape such persistent attention.

Time did not permit hitchhiking out to see two faithful health promoters, so I prevailed upon an old friend to drive me there, Reverend Jaime, director of Corcride, the evangelical development organization that I'd worked with during my volunteer service. He had just lost a mayoral primary bid, perhaps because of the scandal of his earlier affair. The Canadian cooperative sustaining his organization was now diverting its grain to Iraq, forcing the lay-off of his entire staff. Furthermore, one of his sons had left his wife and baby behind saying he was going to Guatemala, only to call weeks later from the U.S. after a harrowing border crossing. "I warned him not to go," Jaime muttered, "but he wouldn't listen." So the reverend was not a happy man, but he agreed to take me out to the villages if I would spring for diesel fuel.

Our first stop was Matapalos where Lea—midwife, local health promoter, mother of 11, and grandmother of countless more—stood outside bathing a grandson before school, pouring water over his naked body. She dropped her bucket with a startled cry and ran toward me, wrapping me in a wet embrace. All around, poinsettias bloomed and birds chirped sweetly. The elevation was higher than El Triunfo and marginally cooler. Lea's family proudly showed off a new acquisition, a black-and-white TV with a giant antenna hooked up to a car battery tuned to nearby Nicaraguan stations.

Although Matapalos still lacked electricity, it now had water, thanks to a water project I'd helped townspeople to fund and construct. Water collected in hillside cement tanks during the rainy season was used in dry weather to irrigate corn, fill up tilapia fishponds, and supply individual homes. Lea took me on a hike to demonstrate that the system was still in working order. Along the way, we stopped by two iron crosses marking the graves of *los viejitos* (the old ones), that is, her parents. I gave her a few items of used clothing and medical supplies, nearly my last.

Next stop was Río Grande #1 where I looked for my friend Blanca, a widow with 10 children, likewise a midwife and health promoter. She wasn't home, reportedly having biked to El Triunfo to visit her brother.

I left my very last donated clothing and medications with her kids, then Jaime dropped me off at the brother's, where I found Blanca sipping Coca-Cola out of a plastic bag. She burst into surprised laughter when she saw me, exclaiming, "So it's really you!" A son working as a Triunfo security guard, she explained, had come home the night before, insisting that Doña Bárbara was back in town. But Blanca had argued that was impossible because I'd left Honduras long ago. Now she saw that he was right after all.

With maternal pride, Blanca updated me on the saga of her 29-year-old son's rise to the rank of second lieutenant in the Honduran army, one of the chosen few sent to Iraq, where he'd directed troops doing inspection and surveillance. He was never in combat, thank goodness, but she was greatly relieved when Honduras pulled out of Iraq and he came home.

Both Blanca and Lea insisted that they still provided routine medical advice and medications, but apparently not as regularly as when I had been mentoring and encouraging them.

On my last afternoon in El Triunfo, feeling exhausted and sweaty, I bathed and washed my hair with a bucket of cooling water; also washed my last remaining outfit, having already given everything else away. I sat outside in my nightgown while my clothes were drying, listening to birds twittering overhead and watching juicy crimson cashew fruits with dangling nuts—really exterior seeds—plop languidly to the ground. It was not yet mango season, so my old admirer, Mango Man, did not appear bearing fruity gifts.

Out of Gas

On that last afternoon, when my clothes were dry, I'd planned to trudge down the road to the home of Yasmín, the girl with spina bifida for whom I'd once provided a water mattress. Her family surely must have heard I was in town and would feel hurt if I didn't stop by. But I'd run smack out of energy in the debilitating heat, so this item on my to-do list remained undone. I sat there shamefully inert, almost paralyzed, my body rooted to the spot. I'd finally been overcome by compassion fatigue, or perhaps just plain fatigue, after three tumultuous weeks in Honduras.

As Marina sat dozing, her son Roger, his signature toothpick clenched between his teeth, came striding in, bare-chested, perspiring, his belly hanging out over tight jeans. "*Mamá*, how about 300 lempiras [$20]?" he teased. Suddenly alert, she opened her eyes and reached out her hand.

Then daughter Reina appeared and Roger told her somewhat self-righteously, "*Ya días* [it's been days now] since I've spoken to Gabriela; this time she went too far." I gave Reina a puzzled look. "His 'other woman,'" she whispered.

Roger, who had recently begun selling sesame seeds, poured some roasted seeds into my hand, warning me of their aphrodisiac properties. "If so," I asked, "Dare I eat them?"

Persistent matchmaker Roger then launched into his usual spiel about the joys of marriage and his determination to find me a husband. I reminded him of the sorry candidates he'd introduced to me before and said, "No thanks." Finally it was dark and definitely too late to go see Yasmín. (That was the last time I would see Marina, who died in 2007. But I did visit Yasmín that year.)

Comfort Food

One more stop, this time, *way* off the beaten track to Nueva Armenia, where I'd once spent five weeks of health training. As usual, just getting there was half the battle. Heading north from Choluteca, I asked the bus driver to please stop at the Armenia turn-off near Sabanagrande. Despite my frequent reminders to both driver and faretaker (the latter making out with a female passenger in the rear seat), the bus overshot the mark and I had to walk back about a kilometer to join a group of other hitchhikers. Daylight was fading fast when a pickup finally stopped and we all piled into the back, holding on for dear life as it bounced precariously along.

Dismounting in Armenia, I walked straight into Lilian's kitchen, where she stood stirring a pot of *catamales,* fragrant concoctions of beef and pork mixed with rice, potatoes, onions, and spices, all wrapped up in corn meal and a flavorful banana leaf (a *tamal* is just plain corn meal cooked in a banana leaf). After giving me a welcoming hug, Lilian opened one of the steaming envelopes for me to sample. She'd made 200 catamales to sell at a weekend festival commemorating the town's 158th anniversary. Live music emanated from the nearby municipal hall where townspeople had gathered to celebrate.

If Lilian was surprised to see me, she didn't show it. I'd tried to call her beforehand, as their phone can receive incoming calls, but the whole town's phone system was down.

Lilian sadly reported that their pet fish Nemo had mysteriously vanished. She speculated that he might have leaped out of a basin while she was cleaning out the pila and been devoured by the chickens.

Apprehensively, I asked about Doña Julita, her 95-year-old neighbor, who'd been hospitalized with a broken hip before my departure. Lilian said that Julita's bones had been found too delicate for a pin, but her hip had healed anyway, leaving her with a pronounced limp, but still ambulatory with a walker. Then Lilian was called out to a patient's home on an emergency, even though it was Saturday. Inspired by her dedication and example, both her children had decided to study medicine.

After Lilian left, I went next door to visit Julita, who, likewise, seemed unsurprised to see me. She was still living in the modest wood-frame house where she was born, constructed by her parents over a century before. Like Lilian's place, it had an outdoor latrine and shower stall that Julita reached only laboriously, using her walker. She told me about her long hospitalization in Teguc after fracturing her hip. To her dismay, 8,000 lempiras ($500) hidden away for her funeral expenses had been stolen in her absence.

I asked Julita about her pet chicken, now nowhere to be seen. "Oh, Pollita stopped laying eggs and kept falling over, so I ate her." What! Ate her coffee-drinking companion? "Yes, she was kind of tough." My goodness!

On the Bus

To tote giveaway items, I'd sometimes hired a car. But as my load lightened, I'd gone back to riding familiar yellow school buses.

An ancient, wheezing bus left Nueva Armenia at 4 am with standing room only and extra passengers mounted on the roof. I could barely breathe, squeezed inside against a mass of other bodies. Then, on a precipitous mountain pass, the bus suddenly lurched to a halt. The engine had died. Driver and faretaker rolled up their sleeves and went to work.

Now, at least, we could get out and stretch our legs. We were stuck in a bleak no-man's-land about halfway between Armenia and the paved road at Sabanagrande, 25 km. in either direction, too far to walk. A couple of bike-riders, who had been hitching onto the bus's back fender (breathing in fumes), were also stuck, the terrain being too steep for them to easily cycle out on their own. We all could only wait and hope. Two hours later, the driver gave a triumphant whoop and we rushed back inside, as the bus began lurching up and down the mountain once again. I prayed the brakes would hold despite their terrible screeching. At Sabanagrande, I stood out on the highway to flag down another bus into Tegucigalpa, about an hour and a half away.

This second bus made a rest stop after just 10 km. There, we passengers encountered only one breathtakingly smelly toilet, flushed with a paint can dipped into a nearby pila. "*Échele agua, no seas tan cochino* (Pour in some water, don't be so piggish)," a woman rebuked a young man just leaving the stall.

Avoiding those particular facilities, I turned instead to the crowded snack bar with its array of sugary homemade buns, pork rinds, chips, sodas, and sweetened chocolate, strawberry, and banana-flavored milk, never just plain milk. I chose chocolate as the least objectionable.

On the outskirts of Teguc, familiar graphic signs began popping up: a real tire indicating a tire repair shop, a dented radiator for radiator repair, a shoe for a shoemaker, and depictions of eye glasses, false teeth, and medicine bottles respectively.

The Circle Unbroken

I reconfirmed my return flight as required. But on departure day, fog and drizzle began rolling in, quite unusual during the dry season. The Teguc airport always makes landing difficult, but this made it impossible. The single daily American Airlines flight kept circling—the same plane scheduled to take us back to Miami. I waited alone forlornly in the airport, afraid of missing my connecting flight.

A break in the clouds allowed the arriving plane to finally land. We outgoing passengers scrambled quickly aboard and it took off. (Departure is easier than landing.) Dashing frantically between gates in Miami, I barely made my connection to Washington. José, a Mexican grad student living at my house, met me at the airport. We rode home together on the subway, so wonderfully fast and convenient.

During my entire trip, I never once got sick. Of course, I drank only bottled water, never touched raw vegetables, and avoided street food altogether. I'd also left my malaria prophylactic behind to prevent having weird dreams, reasoning that in the dry season, mosquitoes are fewer.

Back in the States, back from the magic of Narnia, I underwent the whole re-entry transition again, adjusting to the excessive production and waste of everything, tight time pressures, and dizzying array of choices, although my re-adaptation went faster this time. Within days, I began dreaming again in English. It also helped that my PC training group held a reunion of local members soon after my return.

Yet, I still consider it rather arrogant, just because of an accident of birth, that we feel entitled to turn on hot and cold running water at will, enjoy an uninterrupted flow of electricity, regulate indoor temperature with the flip of a switch, and drink water straight from the tap. Not to mention having reliable and affordable transportation always at the ready. We shouldn't be hogging earth's resources and starting wars to provide these amenities exclusively for ourselves.

Sifting back through memories of my trip, one thing stands out. Whenever I showed up unannounced, Hondurans welcomed me with open arms. If home is where they have to take you in, I'm certainly at home in Honduras.

Blind girls forming walking chain

Blind boy with noisy "clackers"

*Gloria, age 26,
before surgery*

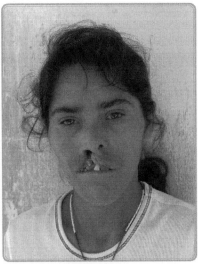

*Gloria with
her father
three hours
after surgery*

Chunga and Chunguita in makeshift market stall after the fire

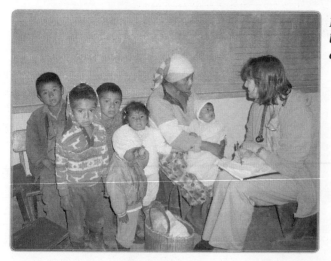

Hortensias brigade doctor examining family

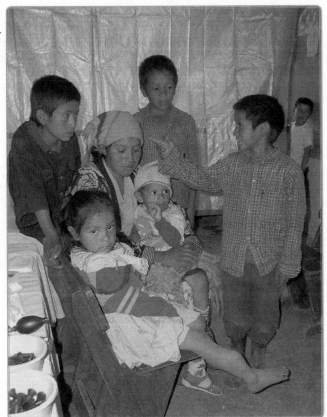

Four-year-old Sandra showing untreated leg

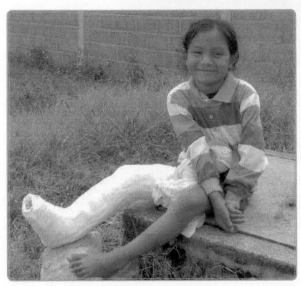

Sandra with cast after surgery

Author with Sandra and Arcenia before surgery

Arcenia with parents after surgery

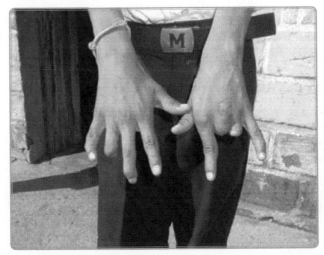

*Jorge showing
missing fingers*

*Village health
promoter Lea
bathing grandson
before school*

ABOUT THE AUTHOR

Barbara E. Joe, MA, a native of Boston, Mass., is a writer, Spanish interpreter, and translator living on Capitol Hill in Washington, DC.

Readers are invited to sign onto her blog, post comments and questions, and get updates on her periodic return visits to Honduras: **http://honduraspeacecorps.blogspot.com**

Con mucho Amor
y cariño de Neris
Para mi amiga
Doña Barbara Solo
Le Pido que me Recuerde
Siempre como yo La
Voy a Recordar siempre
Que Diosito La cuide
Donde quiere que

valla
La quiero mucho

Neris